WHERE TO
NORFOLK AN[...]

BY JOHN W[ILSON]

JARROLD
PUBLISHING

For John (Jinx) Davey of Bungay, Suffolk, who
first showed me where to fish in East Anglia.

ISBN 0-7117-0833-9

Fifth edition
© Jarrold Publishing 1995
Jarrold Publishing, Norwich
Printed in Great Britain. 5/95

The Author

After careers in hairdressing, the merchant navy and printing, angling fanatic John Wilson achieved many a fisherman's dream when in 1971 he opened his own tackle shop in Norwich.

John has caught sailfish in Mexico, sharks in Fiji, and most species in between in over fifty countries. However, the author's first love are the fish of East Anglia where his specimen-hunting exploits regularly make angling news. His impressive list of specimen fish includes dace 1 lb 1 oz, grayling 2 lb 5 oz, roach 2 lb 14½ oz, rudd 2 lb 15 oz, chub 6 lb 7 oz, tench 8 lb 0 oz, bream 13 lb 12 oz, barbel 12 lb 12 oz, zander 11 lb 3 oz, grass carp 15 lb 1 oz, pike 30 lb 13 oz, mirror carp 33 lb 1 oz, sea trout 9 lb 4 oz, brown trout 9 lb 2 oz, rainbow trout 11 lb 4 oz, bass 11 lb 4 oz, pollack 15 lb 9 oz, cod 26 lb 3 oz, tope 40 lb 6 oz and conger eel 76 lb.

When he isn't fishing or in his tackle shop, John – a full-time angler in every way – writes on a freelance basis for angling journals and films for television, provided, of course, his wife, Jo, and assortment of family pets permit.

Working on the basis 'if you can't beat them', John has scuba-dived many of the local waters and considers the knowledge gained invaluable in his quest for ever-better specimens. Always abreast of current developments, John is ready with a word of advice for the visiting angler who comes to his shop, which – like many a tackle business – has become a centre for the exchange of angling information.

During the past decade John's face has become familiar to millions as presenter and co-producer of the highly acclaimed *Go Fishing* for Anglia and Meridian Television, which is also shown nationwide on Channel 4 and regularly attracts an audience of between two and three million viewers. *Go Fishing* is the most successful and longest-running series of television angling programmes, which has resulted in over forty of John's half-hour shows being made into videos, featuring species and techniques both in the UK and abroad. John is currently working on specialist technique videos for the home market.

Contents

The Author	3
Introduction	7
Norfolk Rivers	9
Suffolk Rivers	42
History of the Broads Enigma	54
How to Fish the Broadland Waterways	61
Boat Hire and Slipways within Tidal Broadland	67
The Broads	68
Map: The Broads (north-west)	*70*
Map: The Broads (north-east)	*73*
Map: Little and Great Ormesby, Rollesby, Lily and Filby broads	*75*
Map: Rockland Broad	*79*
Stillwaters	82
Day Ticket	*83*
Map: Alton Water Reservoir	*84*
Members Only	113
Caravanners Only	127
Campers and Touring Caravanners	127
Match Fishing Only	128
Syndicate Waters	128
Hotel Accommodation	129
Holiday Cottages	130
Farmhouse Holiday Accommodation	130
Trout Fishing	
Day Ticket (Rivers – Fly Only)	130
Map: Trout Fishing on the River Wensum	*130*
Day Ticket (Stillwaters)	131
Syndicate Waters	136
Salmon and Trout Association Waters – Open Membership	136
Rivers	136
Stillwaters	137
Sea Fishing	137
Sea Baits	146
The Tides	*148*
Local Specimen Fish	*149*
Index	*159*

Introduction

The purpose of this book is exactly the same now, in this completely revised and updated fifth edition, as it was in the first, way back in 1973. That is to help the angler in his choice of venues from the vast amount of water in Norfolk and Suffolk. Whether he prefers game, coarse or sea fishing in East Anglia, and whether he is local or just visiting the area, I sincerely hope that the following pages will help his fishing.

There is such an array of available fishing in East Anglia that much of it is little known, especially by the coarse angler, who often tends only to think in terms of the Norfolk Broads and their accompanying tidal rivers. However, quite apart from the clean flowing upper reaches of the big rivers, several interesting mini-rivers and many streams, there is so much sport to be found in the unlimited acres comprised of ponds, gravel and sand-pits, lakes and meres.

Naturally, as time passes, the cost of both day and season tickets is bound to increase and no doubt numerous venues within the following pages will either cease to be available as fisheries or change hands and revert to being strictly private. So I ask the reader's indulgence in this and hope that perhaps he might even inform me of any important changes as they occur.

To those who have already freely given information and assisted with the preparation of this book, I should like to express my gratitude. These, unfortunately, are too numerous to name, but my particular thanks go to George Alderson, Chris Newell, Len Head, Neville and Marge Bailey, Dave Batten, Brian Finbow, John Nunn and the late Bill Cooper of Norwich. I should also like to thank Paul Kerry for his invaluable help with the sea section and to thank my typist, Jan Carver.

Tight Lines!

John Wilson
Great Witchingham 1995

NORFOLK RIVERS

The River Ant

The Ant is unique as the only Broadland river which actually feeds a broad. It enters at the northern end of Barton Broad, where one may follow the course upstream by boat to Honing Lock, and floods in and out at the southern end, giving the broad colour and an ever-changing circulation of fish.

The Ant's watercourse is actually born in the village of Antingham in the ponds of the same name and, from here, flows in a south-easterly direction through Swafield and on to the market town of North Walsham. The fishing in these upper reaches has greatly deteriorated over the years, and almost everywhere one finds cases of silting and dilapidation at the mills and around the bridges and locks. From North Walsham, where the river is canalised, the Ant meanders down to Ebridge Mill. It is perhaps difficult for the visitor to accept that such large vessels as Norfolk wherries did sail up the Ant here, when one considers the present state of silting and the fact that a wherry, when fully laden, must have drawn 3 feet of water, for the average depth here nowadays is about the same and, in many parts, even less.

Two miles downstream from Ebridge Mill is Briggate Mill and then a one-mile stretch leading to Honing Common, which can offer good roach fishing. There are also tench, bream, eels, pike, perch and ruffe. From Honing Lock to Tonnage Bridge at Dilham one finds the same species, with bream and roach predominating. It should be noted that motor cruisers cannot pass beyond Tonnage Bridge. Fishing here can be rewarding during the winter months but sessions in summer time should be kept to late evening or early morning as the boat traffic may prove frustrating even this far upriver.

About half a mile downriver from Tonnage Bridge, Dilham Cut joins the main stream from the southern bank. There is good fishing all the way up this navigable channel to Tylers at the top end, where navigation ceases at the road bridge carrying the Honing to Dilham road. Species to be found here are plenty of medium-sized bream to 3½lb fair roach and some pike.

A little further downstream from the Ant's junction with Dilham Cut, Wayford Bridge spans the river, carrying the A149 to Stalham, an excellent winter spot. Boats can be hired here from Urwin's Day Boats (Tel: 01692 582071). Pike fishing is excellent from here down to Barton Broad. A mile downstream from Wayford Bridge, Stalham Dyke enters from the left bank. This leads up to the boatyards at Stalham, where one may hire boats with or without motors and launches from Stalham Yacht Services (Tel: 01692 580288). These must be booked well in advance and are available all year round.

Fishing can prove rewarding from the boatyards, especially at the tail end of the season, and the boatyard of R. Richardson issues day permits to fish from its property. There is also a certain amount of free fishing from the public staithe.

Halfway along Stalham Dyke, a short dyke leads in from the staithe at nearby Sutton, where the fishing is entirely free from the roadside. But one requires a boat to fish the dyke itself as the banks are privately owned. Access to the north bank of the Ant between Wayford Bridge and Stalham, along which one finds lovely Hunsett Mill, is via Chapel Field Farm, off the A149, a little west of Stalham. This entire area offers excellent coarse fishing for bream, roach with some perch, tench, plenty of eels and often (among lots of jacks) a really good pike. As with much of the Ant, sport improves from October onwards, or at dusk and dawn during the summer.

9

Following on from the confluence of Stalham Dyke with the mainstream, there is just half a mile of reed-fringed river before the Ant enters Barton Broad (see The Broads). After furrowing down the length of Barton, the Ant emerges from its southern end as a river of changed character. The average depth has increased to around 6 feet with a good colour, over a silty bottom. The flow is often strong at times from here on, as the Ant passes through the famous Irstead Shoals. There is superb bream fishing from the bank along the public staithe at Irstead, particularly at night when the boats are dormant. Bream here run to over 5 lb and roach average between 4 and 8 oz. Best tactics when night fishing is ledgering flake or maggots and using a quiver-tip if bites prove delicate. Daytime sport improves from late October with mixed catches of sizeable roach and bream falling to anglers who trot or lay-on maggots anywhere along the three-and-a-half-mile course from Irstead through How Hill, Johnson Street and finally to Ludham Bridge.

Fishing is free on the left bank when walking upstream from Ludham Bridge, with access for one and a half miles until a dyke stops progress.

The entire area of Ludham Bridge becomes a hive of activity during the summer and, as with much of the Ant, only night and early morning sessions are really worthwhile.

Small roach and bream, together with many eels, can nearly always be pulled out, but this is little consolation for the serious angler. The fishing improves only when the boats tie up for the winter, which nowadays is characteristic of the tidal rivers in Norfolk and Suffolk. However, for those wishing to boat-fish, dinghies, with or without motors and day launches are for hire at reasonable rates from Ludham Bridge Services (Tel: 01692 630486). Bait and tackle are available, and the manager, Robert Paul, will give additional information and is only too pleased to advise anglers (Tel: 01692 630322).

Leaving Ludham Bridge and the wide water, the Ant courses on its last half mile before joining forces with the Bure at Ant Mouth, just above St Benet's Abbey. The swims at this junction offer some of the

St Benet's Abbey, River Bure – excellent roach and bream fishing

best tidal river fishing in Norfolk for quality roach, hybrids and bream, particularly during the autumn. Best tactics are to ledger on the bomb with a quiver-tip and baiting with maggots or breadflake or trotting through with maggots or casters.

Day tickets to fish the Ant's junction with the Bure are available from Thrower's Stores (Tel: 01692 678248) and from the bungalow at the top of St Benet's Lane.

The Babingley River

This miniature, narrow river rises just nine miles inland from the Wash. It appears to obtain most of its water from the ponds in the grounds of Flitcham Abbey and makes its way due west through Flitcham and on to Babingley, where the A149 crosses its path just two miles south of Sandringham Park.

The Babingley offers rather difficult coarse fishing for dace, some trout, pike, roach and, rather strangely for such a limited water, bream up to the 4 lb mark. Upstream of the A149 road bridge, fishing is private but, below, the King's Lynn Angling Association controls over two miles of fishing. The secretary is M. Grief, 67 Peckover Way, South Wootton, King's Lynn PE30 3UE (Tel: 01553 671545).

The river here is not over-fished, which stands to reason really for the fishing is frustrating because of ridiculously clear water running between high banks that bear little vegetation. One needs to crawl about a little in order to present a bait without scaring the ultra-shy fish.

The Babingley ends at the Wash, where it spills its water through the marshes and into the North Sea.

The Blackwater Stream

Rising in the villages of East Bilney and Gressenhall from an amalgamation of brooks, the Blackwater winds its way north-easterly for just three miles before joining the River Wensum at Worthing. It is a delightful mini-river holding some jumbo-sized dace, roach and brown trout. Access throughout is limited and privately controlled, although there are one or two spots where the polite, enquiring angler will find sport.

Just before it joins the Wensum at Worthing, there is a super but short stretch available on a day ticket. These cost £2 and are available from Mr Eve of Tannery House, Worthing (Tel: 01362 668202) and includes fishing in an adjacent 1-acre lake (see Tannery Lake under Still Waters). The river fishery starts at Worthing road bridge, running upstream on the southern bank for about 200 yards and includes a lovely little deep pool plus some slow, wider water above the Mill, holding good roach, dace, perch and a few trout. Below the road bridge on both banks the fishing is controlled by the Dereham and District Angling Club.

The River Bure

If one studies an Ordnance Survey map of north-east Norfolk and, in particular, the area of Broadland, it will become apparent that the major river is the Bure. With its tributaries, the Ant and Thurne, together with the vast complex of broads and dykes that they collectively feed, the Bure is indeed a mighty waterway. But this river is also two-faced because its deep, tidal, broad connecting reaches bear little resemblance whatsoever to the peaceful and comparatively tiny upper reaches which start high up in mid North Norfolk, near Melton Constable.

The Bure is predominantly a highly reserved trout fishery in these narrow, streamy upper reaches as it flows through the miniature, highly picturesque mills of Corpusty and Itteringham in an easterly direction. Nearly all the fishing is private but the individual can do no harm by asking permission, especially if he possesses a fly rod and shows interest (see also Bure Valley Trout Lakes under Trout Fishing – Day Ticket (Stillwaters)).

The first actual accessible part of the

river is immediately downstream of Ingworth Bridge, which carries the old A140 from Norwich to Cromer (see Salmon and Trout Association Waters). The Bure here is a most enchanting and challenging venue, being an almost miniature replica of the famous Itchen and holds numbers of really large dace in addition to brown trout.

From Ingworth, the Bure courses south-easterly towards Aylsham where, just above and below the town, the banks are privately controlled. However, there is a stretch worth exploring for big dace in the area where the Aylsham bypass crosses the river. Local farmers are usually sympathetic to the serious angler if permission is asked first.

The river-bed is constantly changing character with a depth variation of between 2 and 8 feet. The deepish runs between weedbeds generally hold the better-sized fish but the water is absolutely crystal clear in the summer, which makes fishing painfully difficult. A stealthy approach is always advisable even when rain colours the stream.

The upper Bure is probably the most difficult to fish of all Norfolk's rivers. Per acre of water this river has extremely limited fish stocks, although individual fish are often of specimen size. Two miles down from Aylsham the Bure flows beneath the tiny humpbacked road bridge at Burgh and divides around the old mill. There is little access above this area, but below the mill on the northern bank – stretching all the way down to Oxnead road bridge – the fishing is owned by T. Colchester (Tel: 01603 279274) who gives anglers free access, provided they telephone beforehand.

From Oxnead Mill to Buxton Mill, a syndicate of the Norfolk Anglers' Conservation Association (NACA) has the fishing rights along the right-hand (southern) bank, looking downstream. Anglers wishing to join the syndicate should contact John Nunn (Tel: 01493 393249). The NACA fishery also extends above Oxnead Mill to the first bend upstream of Brampton Bridge.

The Bure in these winding two miles starts narrow but widens and deepens as it nears Buxton. It is very much a specialist's water, holding small shoals of bream in the 4 to 8 lb range and roach between 1 and 3 lb. There is also a prolific stock of large roach-rudd hybrids, many going well over 2 lb. These probably originated some years ago, when the Bure above Oxnead was stocked with lake rudd. There are also pike, including the odd good fish, plus odd dace, trout and chub.

Below the mill at Buxton, chub really start to feature with numerous fish over 3 lb plus the odd specimen to 5 lb along with some quality roach, dace and odd big bream. There are some good dace and chub runs immediately above and below the old railway bridge where the NACA fishery starts again (around the mill fishing is private), extending downstream for half a mile on the downstream (southern) bank.

Immediately below Mayton Bridge is an excellent dace run, and one or two large brown trout inhabit this stretch. The river now twists and turns between banks lined with beds of tall reeds for a distance of two miles down to Horstead road bridge. There is a lovely overgrown wooded part with free access along the southern bank via a footpath behind Horstead church on the B1354. Here there are numerous chub, some quality roach and odd good bream and pike. Access to the opposite (northern) bank starts at Horstead road bridge, where fishing is free from the public footpath all the way upriver to the first dyke. The wide, double S-bend 400 yards above the bridge is known as Bream Corner, where bream to 8 lb have been caught in past seasons. The shoals are numerically nowhere near so strong today but the chance of taking just one or two slabs to 7 lb plus is still there. Fishing into darkness with ledgered breadflake takes some beauties and occasionally produces a whopping great roach. A few specimens to 2½ lb still exist here, along with some good dace and large roach/rudd hybrids. Locate a double-figure pike, of which there are several in this stretch, and its feed will not be far away.

Four hundred yards below the road bridge which carries the B1150 from Norwich lies Horstead Mill, the boundary line between the Bure's upper and tidal reaches. The pool is deep, 15 feet in places and much of the bottom is strewn with large boulders and discarded rubbish. This terrain provides shelter to the many huge eels but makes any attempt to extract a sizeable specimen almost impossible on standard equipment. There are some whopping roach at the tail end of the flush, together with odd large perch, chub and brown trout. Dace and gudgeon are numerous in all the fast, shallow water, and between the cabbage patches live some pike. Several are well into double figures, and the chances of a specimen over 20 lb are excellent.

At certain times throughout the summer, shoals of sizeable bream enter the pool from downriver. These bronze beauties run to a good size and, in the mid-1960s, a local angler, the late George Woods amassed an incredible 140 lb of fish to 4 lb. Such numbers don't exist nowadays, however, but individual fish are much larger. Access to anglers is from the roadside adjacent to the pool's south bank, and fishing is free.

The Bure divides below the pool around a long island for about 400 yards and then meets again to pursue its course towards Coltishall Common, a popular holiday spot and an excellent winter fishery when the summer boats have been put away. However, small 'bream flats' and roach are taken here during the summer, even when things are in full swing, but for better sport and quality fish one concentrates on either early morning or evening sessions. Fishing dinghies can be hired on the common during the summer months only.

Fishing from the towpath on the common is free. The fishing in these now tidal reaches is far easier than in the upper reaches, due mainly, I think, to the permanently coloured waters. Another plus factor is that actual shoals of most species, except dace, are so much larger. One may fish the same swim all day and accumulate a bag which many consider an impossible task upriver.

From Coltishall to Belaugh and on to Wroxham there is four miles of fishing, which is largely inaccessible from the banks, due mainly to surrounding marshland and private controls. However, one may navigate upriver from Belaugh or even put a small dinghy in from Coltishall Common and Horstead Mill and enjoy sport with good concentrations of roach plus a few bream and numerous pike which are to be found in this reach. In the village of Belaugh there are two public staithes. One is adjacent to the house on the left of the boatyard, and to the right is the mooring staithe where one can park the car.

The river then meanders slowly down towards Wroxham through beautifully wooded marshes.

Belaugh Broad, the small, badly silted broad on the northern bank one and a half miles upstream of Wroxham is private, although it is reputed to contain numbers of tench, bream and even carp.

A mile upstream from Wroxham there is around 500 yards of free fishing on the south bank along Caens Meadow, adjacent to the school. Access is from the Norwich–Wroxham road, turning down by the Castle public house. Cars must be left at the top of the lane.

At Wroxham, the Bure is the busiest spot in Broadland, especially during summer, when the serious angler leaves well alone. However, small 'bream flats' and young roach are caught among the hustle and bustle. River craft, large and tiny, plough down the river with parties of tourists attracted to the local sights. Boats hibernate from November onwards, however, and until the season ends Wroxham becomes a mecca for anglers. It offers easily accessible fishing from comfortable bankside swims where good roach, bream, perch, ruffe and even odd tench are taken most of the winter through. If the mainstream does not pay dividends, then there are usually some concentrations of medium-sized fish to be found in the now deserted boatyards. Favourite tactics are light float-fishing with casters or maggots or ledgering in the river's central channel with maggots or worms, with light cereal groundbait for added attraction. Boats may be hired through the Wroxham Angling Club (Tel: Bob Westgate on 01603 401062) and from Summercraft of Brimbelow Road (Tel: 01603 782809). The pike fishing here is really excellent, with hordes of fish in the 4 to 12 lb range and fish over 20 lb are taken regularly throughout the winter. The river record was taken in 1980 quite close to Wroxham Bridge by Roger Westgate and weighed 32 lb 13 oz. Bridge Broad (west), also known as Little Bridge Broad, is worth a try (see The Broads), particularly during the winter for pike. Its entrance is half a mile upstream of Wroxham via the southern bank.

Travelling immediately downriver from Wroxham, one passes numerous dykes and quay headings which offer good roach and bream fishing, especially during winter. Numbers of decent-sized pike lurk around the entrances to these boat dykes. The angler should note that nearly all the banks here are privately owned, so use of a boat is the only means of fishing the most productive swims. In recent years, trotting the stream with casters and maggots has produced some cracking bags of quality roach up to and sometimes over the 1½ lb mark plus the odd nice perch. There is over half a mile of the Bure harbouring these dykes and cuts, with interesting swims all the way along as it channels through picturesque woodlands.

From the southern bank, two navigable dykes lead to Wroxham Broad (see The Broads) a mile below Wroxham Bridge, while on the opposite bank lies the first of five dykes which feed Hoveton Great Broad. This is the largest of the Bure-fed broads but, being a nature reserve and private, it is out of bounds to anglers.

The Bure bends slowly between Wroxham and Hoveton broads for almost two miles before the first of two entrances to Salhouse Broad is visible (see The Broads). The fishing during winter time is both uninterrupted and rewarding but is best forgotton during the summer daylight hours. The course winds downstream with Hoveton Marshes on the northern bank and Woodbastwick Marshes on the southern. As the the Bure skirts Decoy Broad (see The Broads), it bends sharply and continues down towards the village of Horning. On the northern bank lies the entrance to Little Hoveton Broad (private) while on the southern is Woodbastwick Staithe and the second of two entrances to Decoy Broad.

The river is quite wide and often has a strong pull. Summer boat traffic at its peak has to be seen to be believed, with little serious fishing until darkness, when the river-craft cease. Then from dusk until dawn the Bure opens its arms to keen anglers and offers large nets of sizeable bream in the 2 to 4 lb range. Breadflake or paste are the baits to tempt the larger bream, with maggots running a close second.

Much of the waterside in this area is private marshland with little public access. However, from Woodbastwick Staithe on the southern bank downstream, Norwich and District Angling Association controls about one mile of excellent fishing for members only. Access is the same as for Decoy Broad and there are no day tickets (see The Broads).

As the Bure channels down towards Horning, it bends acutely by the Yacht Club House, close to the Swan public house. Here the Bure is quite deep and, although the whole scene is chaos in summer, from October onwards fishing is first class, with quality roach and the odd big hybrid predominating, as well as some bream to over 4 lb.

Naturally, with such a larder of feed in this area, many sizeable pike move in for the pickings. Fish of over 20 lb are taken every season with countless other fish weighing high into double figures. Mostly, the better fish succumb to large livebaits trotted close to the bottom and to ledgered deadbaits. There is excellent sport to be found in the numerous boat dykes and yards, particularly during severe weather – but permission should always be obtained first.

Running parallel with the Horning village reach along the north bank is Horning Lower Street, which leaves the B1354 from Wroxham and leads to the Horning Ferry public house. Here, there is limited bank fishing as far as the first boat dyke downstream.

Exactly opposite Horning Ferry on the Woodbastwick (southern) bank, there is half a mile of excellent free fishing controlled by the river authority. This extends both upstream and downstream of the access road which leads direct from Woodbastwick village. Because this length is popular with local anglers, anyone intending to fish should arrive early. Travelling still further downstream, the Bure bends slowly for two miles through lonely, thickly wooded marshland, until it reaches Ant Mouth. There is little or no access along this stretch because of the soggy nature of the banks. However, one may tie up a boat to a firm piece of bank to fish. Boat-fishing is often better during the winter for one is able to float-fish and hold out in the fast current. Anglers' dinghies can be launched from the slipway adjacent to the Swan public house (see Boat Hire and Slipways within Tidal Broadland).

Halfway between Horning and Ant Mouth, situated on the southern bank, lies Ranwworth Dyke, which leaves the main flow to feed Ranworth Inner Broad, where boats may be hired (see The Broads). The dyke can fish quite well at times but is obviously prone to heavy boat traffic in summer, except in the early morning and late evening.

Where the River Ant joins its water with the Bure, one mile below Ranworth Dyke, there are more easily accessible bankside spots. Here width is considerable with both depth and, according to the tides, a strong flow to match. The stretch from Ant Mouth downriver to St Benet's Abbey is considered one of the most productive spots in Broadland rivers, especially during summer and autumn. Sport is particularly keen during the early hours, though it can often last for much of the daytime if one can beat the ever-increasing number of pleasure boats. Trotting maggots or casters close to the bottom produces good mixed catches of roach, plus the odd big hybrid and bream that can run to 5 lb plus.

To concentrate on the bream, ledgering is best using flake, paste, maggots or red-worms, rolled down on the bomb or stationary in conjunction with a block end swim-feeder.

The northern bank from Ant Mouth by St Benet's Abbey down to Thurne Mouth is controlled by the Norwich and District Angling Association. Day tickets are on sale to non-members from Thrower's Stores in the village of Ludham or from the bungalow at the top of St Benet's Lane. Practically opposite the remains of the abbey, some of which lie encrusted with tackle at the bottom of the Bure, Fleet Dyke leaves the southern bank to feed South Walsham Broads (see The Broads). This is a wonderful stretch to trot from a boat during the autumn and boats may be hired (the closest spot) with or without motors from Ludham Bridge Services (Tel: 01692 630486).

The river authority controls fishing on the entire south bank of the Bure, starting

15

from and including Fleet Dyke, stretching downriver past Thurne Mouth and beyond Upton Dyke. This fishery includes both banks of Upton Dyke and offers highly attractive fishing. Access points are from South Walsham boatyard, Upton, and Acle where the A1064 spans the Bure. Fishing is of a similar nature along this entire stretch, with most anglers content to beat the fast flow by ledgering and using plenty of groundbait. As in the whole of the lower Bure, bream and roach predominate.

Below Acle Bridge, where fast tides are common and the water is deep, there are good shoals of quality roach, and bream to 6 lb.

At the Bridge Inn, anglers may use the car park out of the holiday season, provided they ask first. Around three-quarters of a mile downstream, off the northern bank, the Muck Fleet Dyke joins the Bure. This tiny drain is weedy and unfishable during the summer but from autumn onwards it provides good sport with small roach. Season permits are available from N. Jarmey of the George Prior Angling Club (Tel: 01493 780531).

Below the Muck Fleet Dyke's junction the Bure roars on past Stokesby, and roach and bream can often be taken but – like the other tidal rivers such as the Yare and Waveney as they in turn near the sea – salt tides are the factor governing whether sport is worthwhile or not, especially in winter.

The very last point of access as far as viable summer fishing is concerned is the Stracey Arms public house, which can be seen dividing the River Bure from the Yarmouth A47 in the middle of the Acle Straight, a fast six-mile length of road bordered by shrub willows and marshland leading into Great Yarmouth. This crosses the Bure a little upstream from Breydon Water, before it makes its way to Gorleston Harbour and out into the North Sea.

The River Burn

This tiny, shallow trout stream rises near South Creake and completes just six miles before it flows beneath the A149 North Norfolk coast road and into the estuary at the top end of Overy Staithe, via Burnham Overy Mill. It holds stocks of brown trout, and the fishing is mostly private.

The River Chet

The River Chet rises in the village of Poringland, near Norwich, and for the following eight miles that it takes to reach Loddon is of little interest as a fishery, although there are a few trout, dace, roach and pike present. It is for the most part narrow, shallow and quite overgrown. In Loddon, however, it quickly changes into a tidal channel with a wide marina and staithe. This has been enlarged in recent years, and during the summer months the entire area is a hive of activity and most popular with the boating fraternity. However, during the winter months, particularly in spells of high water when floods spoil sport throughout the area, roach, bream and large hybrids pack into the marina, so sport is excellent.

From Loddon until the Chet joins the Yare via its southern bank at Hardley Cross, there is three miles of river which offers somewhat patchy fishing.

There is a terrific circulation of fish from the Yare into the Chet, especially on the flood tide, so for the very best results one should become acquainted with the tides. Generally, the best results are obtained in winter when the pleasure boats are tied up. During this season good bags of sizeable roach along with some bream can be expected. Trotting or dragging bottom is favoured near Loddon, with the ledger paying dividends in the deeper, faster water lower down close to the Yare, where there is accessible bank-fishing from the south bank via the B1140 road leading to Reedham Ferry.

The River Delph

Although born at Earith, where the Great Ouse divides its waters, the Norfolk boundaries of the Delph start just above Welney Bridge, carrying the A1101 Outwell to Littleport road. The Delph here is between 40 and 60 yards wide with a depth of between 10 and 14 feet, and the banks – like all fenland drains – are very open. It fishes well in summer for roach, rudd, bream and even the occasional carp into double figures, with specimen zander and pike for those wishing to specialise. Peter Redman, secretary of the Welney Club, caught a 20½ lb carp from the Delph in February 1989. It is prone to autumn flooding by the farmed washes and thus is a rather temperamental river to fish. It even becomes unfishable during the winter due to an excess of water, but when in trim and on form zander to 14 lb and pike over 25 lb can be taken.

Fishing is controlled by Welney Angling Club, and Day Tickets cost £2 from Welney Post Office Stores (Tel: 01354 610201). This covers around three miles of the Delph from Welney Bridge to Welmore Lake Sluice, where it empties into the Hundred Foot. Access is from the bridge at Welney or at Salter's Lock End, near Downham Market. Anglers should note there is a wildfowl reserve between the Delph and the Hundred Foot Drain, of about one mile in length and out of bounds to fishing.

The River Glaven

See Trout Fishing – Syndicate Waters.

The Great Ouse

The southern boundary of Norfolk crosses the Great Ouse at Ten Mile Bank where the Little Ouse runs in. The Ouse is wide and deep here with raised banks and contains tremendous bream shoals with fish from 1 to 4 lb and large stocks of roach. There are, of course, hordes of eels, some perch, dace, good tench, which are not regularly caught, and plenty of pike and zander.

Ledgering tactics usually pay good dividends when seeking the bream,

The Great Ouse at the junction with the Little Ouse at Brandon Creek

which at times will accept any baits, though flake and worms often account for the better-quality fish when presented over groundbait. This should be mixed stiffly for throwing, or loosely when used in swim-feeders, when maggots can be laced in if using them on the hook. Roach often fall to the ledger too with some specimens up to the 1¾ lb mark, and there are some much larger. Winter fishing generally offers the best prospects.

However, float anglers generally account for the largest bags of roach, with wheat, punched bread, maggots, casters and hemp all proving effective at times.

When the water is on the clear side, a deadly method of presentation is to loose-feed with hempseed and to fish a single caster, with a grain of hemp or an elderberry on the hook. Trotting proves effective, but when the water is 'dead', lay-on for the quality fish, though bites may prove spasmodic.

Fishing along the Ouse here is controlled by the London Anglers' Association (LAA) on both banks from Littleport High Bridge, downstream to Low Farm on the west bank and Modney Drove on the east bank – some fourteen miles of bank, where day tickets are available at £2 from the bailiff who calls round. From these two points downstream to Denver Sluice, where the Ouse pours its water into the sea-going tidal channel, there is six and a half miles of river on both banks controlled by the King's Lynn Angling Association. Day tickets cost £2 from all local tackle shops.

Anyone may join the King's Lynn AA, which has an open membership with club cards costing £15 (£7 senior citizens and £3.50 juniors) from all local tackle shops or from the secretary, M. Grief, 67 Peckover Way, South Wootton, King's Lynn PE30 3UE (Tel: 01553 671545). The club controls a wealth of local fishing in both rivers and lakes.

The Great Ouse Cut Off Channel

This tremendous length of water stretches due south from the sluices at Denver, where it is separated from the Relief Channel and travels nearly thirty miles to Mildenhall. It seems, in fact, almost a

The Great Ouse at Denver, a favourite roach, bream , pike and zander spot

replica of the Relief Channel and holds an identical stock of fish, though it is nowhere near so wide and impersonal. The banks are rarely more than 50 yards, apart with a depth varying between 8 and 10 feet.

There are good shoals of quality roach spread throughout the Cut Off with numerous specimens topping 1½ lb and isolated shoals of bream between 3 and 6 lb. The Cut Off contains a strong head of zander in all size ranges from schoolies of 1½ to 3 lb up to huge double-figure fish. Many specialists expect a 20-pounder to come from this prolific fishery one day.

Pike fishing is also good, with numerous fish in the 6 to 12 lb range – and whoppers of 20 lb or more.

In recent years both the Cut Off and the Relief Channel have suffered badly from run-off, where the water is purged from the system at an alarming rate. This certainly upsets the fish, and consequently sport is often very patchy. Nevertheless, when on form, some marvellous catches of quality roach are taken.

Day tickets cost £2 and are available close to Hilgay Bridge from The Stores (Tel: 01366 387926), open six days a week, except Tuesdays. Local tackle dealers also sell day tickets and club cards of the King's Lynn Angling Association, who control the Cut Off Channel. Although thirty miles in length, fishing access is limited to an eight-mile section along both banks from the sluice at Denver to Wissington Bridge.

The Great Ouse Relief Channel

This channel, which is up to 100 yards wide, does exactly what its name implies and relieves the Great Ouse of its excessive water, which is stored in the Channel to run parallel with the Great Ouse for eleven miles before it reaches King's Lynn, where there are exit sluices. It really is a formidable single sheet of water, covering nearly 400 acres. Depth varies between 10 and 15 feet through the middle, with a constantly good depth one-rod length out, just over the drop off. The banks are, of course, extremely steep, being 15 feet above water level in some sections, to accommodate any sudden massive injection of floodwater. There are usually enough spots, however, particularly where beds of reeds line the margins, to provide a flat platform just above water level.

The history of this enigmatic water has been well documented over the years since the introduction of zander in the early 1960s. Many, including Anglian Water, have blamed zander for the fluctuating levels of sport during the last three decades and particularly for the present low level of fishing potential. If this were true and the zander had eaten everything in sight, including those massive shoals of 5 and 6 lb bream that used to be around (and this, of course, is ludicrous), we should all be catching very thin zander with ridiculous ease. Whereas, the fact, today as I write in 1995, is that both zander and pike are spread just as thinly throughout the eleven miles as the roach and bream.

Prior to the long and heavy flooding of the 1976–7 winter, I regularly made the journey from Norwich to enjoy the sport provided by the pike and zander in the Channel. Downham to Stow was my favourite length, and – funnily enough – it is probably still the best bet for contacting roach and bream in the Channel. But in the early to mid 1970s, while walking to a favourite zander hot spot, I regularly kicked myself for not taking along the other rods. Huge shoals of specimen bream could be seen topping through the middle section as dawn broke. The shoals were hundreds of yards long. There were roach everywhere too, with enormous shoals of quality fish. Naturally, there were predators to match, and it was a healthy balance suiting both the pleasure and specialist angler alike. Then, quite suddenly in 1977 it was all gone, and much of the stocks had in fact gone – straight through the sluice gates into the tidal Ouse and out into the Wash. Lug-diggers were finding heaps of dead zander, roach and bream on Terrington Marshes, and local trawlers were netting the corpses of coarse fish.

The Channel once held the record for zander with a monster of 17¼ lb, caught by Dave Litton from St Germans in 1977, and though limited in numbers, a jumbo-sized zander is still on the cards from this mysterious fishery, as are specimen roach, bream and pike on the right day. In their pursuit, however, one must endure endless numbers of blank days.

It appears that prolonged run-offs during the winter (now unfortunately a regular policy with our river authorities) have done more harm, particularly to fry which cannot tolerate the force of continual heavy flow, than zander ever will. But then the Relief Channel was not designed for somewhere to fish but to get rid of flood water off the land. So, in truth, we anglers have little say.

However, during the past decade there have been massive injections of quality bream and roach into the Channel from Grafham Reservoir, with the result that in the summer and autumn of 1984 some good yet isolated catches were made close to the bridges at Downham and Stow. So what of the future? Well, we shall simply have to wait and see.

Fishing along the entirety of the Relief Channel is controlled by the King's Lynn Angling Association, who issue day tickets at £2 through local tackle dealers. Contact Rose's Tackle Shop in Downham Market (Tel: 01366 382938 or The Tackle Box in King's Lynn (Tel: 01553 761293).

The Hundred Foot
(New Bedford) Drain

This tidal channel originates at Earith with surplus water from the Great Ouse and flows for over twenty-five miles through Welney, Denver and King's Lynn, gathering drainage water pumped off the land from numerous dykes and channels, finally dumping it all into the Wash.

From its Norfolk boundary just upriver from Welney, where it runs parallel with the River Delph and the Old Bedford, fishing is entirely free and the width about 30 yards, although it widens considerably as it flows seawards through Denver. Depth fluctuates between 4 and 12 feet, depending on the state of the tide, and naturally the current is extremely fast at times, necessitating heavy leads. The water is always thickly coloured and, although there are numbers of roach, bream, eels, pike, zander and numerous flounders, sport is anything but consistent.

With such excellent fishing available close by on the River Delph and the Old Bedford, few anglers bother with the patchy rewards offered by this tidal drain.

The odd good bag of bream is taken, however, and as far downstream as Denver, where it really rockets through and looks more like the estuary it really is than a fenland drain.

The Little Ouse

The source of the Little Ouse starts where the Waveney also begins its life, at Redgrave Common, just six miles due west of Diss. It flows west throughout its lengthy forty miles and is, in fact, the county boundary between Norfolk and Suffolk almost all the way.

The Little Ouse passing through Garboldisham Common, just three miles downstream from Redgrave, navigates the villages of Riddlesworth, Rushford and on to Euston where a stream called Black Bourne enters from the Suffolk bank. There is a little fishing in the Bourne itself up to Ixworth (ten miles), where the A143 Bury St Edmunds road spans its course. The angling in these narrow, shallow upper reaches to beyond Euston is nearly all private but, as the river reaches

Barnham, the Thetford and Breckland Angling Club controls about one mile of excellent fishing on the Suffolk bank for big dace, roach and odd chub over 4 lb. This beat starts at the common and is available on day tickets. These cost £2 from the Rod and Line Tackle Shop in Thetford (Tel: 01842 764825). This part of the river was ravaged by pollution early in 1989 but it has since been restocked.

From Barnham, the river runs for three miles until it enters Thetford, where it joins forces with the River Thet. But the Ouse retains its title and leaves Thetford to hide for seven miles within the huge expanse of Thetford Warren, the largest pine forest in East Anglia.

In Thetford itself along the haling (towpath) path, where the river winds within the town boundaries, there is free fishing along the southern bank down as far as the Staunch. The river runs clear and fast, with excessive weed during the summer, and it also generally fishes better from October onwards, with long-trotted maggots or casters producing the best results.

From the bypass bridge carrying the A11 for about one and a quarter miles on the northern bank downstream to the sewer works there is free fishing. Dace of a large average size, between 6 and 10 oz, are to be found in this town reach together with one or two good roach. A popular spot is by the Staunch (sluice) where the water deepens considerably.

As the Little Ouse winds through beautiful Thetford Warren, it reaches Santon Downham, where – from the road bridge going downstream for around one and a half miles on the southern bank, past the camp site and almost to Brandon – there is a super length controlled jointly by the Thetford and Breckland club and the Bury St Edmunds Angling Association. Again, as throughout this lovely river, big dace predominate, with roach, chub and pike also present. Numbers of fish are not large, but individual size is usually well above average. Seven hundred grayling were introduced here in 1986.

Going upstream from Santon Downham road bridge along the northern bank, fishing is free up to the second staunch. A barbel is not unlikely in this part of the river, having been introduced as a joint effort between the National Rivers Authority (NRA) and the Bury club.

The very best sport starts from September onwards, when the summer weed starts to ease and the normally gin-clear water colours a little. Favourite baits are casters, maggots and redworms which, if long-trotted on light float tackle, will soon sort out the kind of dace for which this river is so justly famous.

The English record dace of 1 lb 4½ oz was caught in the Little Ouse by J.L. Gasson in 1960. The average size is so high that the late Bill Clarke regularly took pound-plus dace. The roach are taken to 1½ lb with odd 2 lb-plus fish, while the chub exceed 5 lb though they are quite isolated in many parts of the Little Ouse, with one or two real monsters still uncaught. There are more big dace in the river at Brandon, where the local club has a mile of the Little Ouse. Membership costs £7 (no day tickets) from the secretary, P. Cooper of 16 High Street, Feltwell, Thetford (Tel: 01842 828448).

From Brandon, the river bends for six miles down to Lakenheath Holt (with little access along the way) and then flows beneath Wilton Bridge once it has crossed the Cut Off Channel. From Wilton Bridge downstream for a distance of four miles on the Norfolk bank to Redmyre, fishing is controlled by Bury St Edmunds Angling Association. There are no day tickets but anyone may join the club. Yearly membership costs £17 for adults and £8.50 for juniors, available from Tackle Up in Bury St Edmunds (Tel: 01284 755022).

The Little Ouse changes somewhat in the Wilton Bridge area, where depth increases to around 6 feet, but the water, although often slightly coloured, can just as easily begin clear. The current is much slower than in the upper reaches. The predominant species are fine roach up to the 2 lb mark, with bream averaging about the same, although specimens in excess of 5 lb are sometimes taken. There are also dace, of course, perch, chub and pike, which can prove a nuisance in the warmer months, including fish to 20 lb plus. Favourite local tactics are to lay-on with flake or maggots during the early mornings or late evenings in conjunction with just a little groundbait, if quality fish are sought. This works well during the summer, but light float-fishing, casters and maggots are preferred winter tactics.

Three miles downstream from Wilton Bridge, Stallode Wash (a tiny drain) enters from the south bank at Botany Bay. From here down to where this wonderful river loses its identity by entering the Great Ouse at Brandon Creek by the Ship Inn public house, a huge network of dykes criss-crosses its path. The fishing in these last four miles is similar in that the pace is slow and species are roach, dace, bream, perch and pike, but much of the fishing on both banks is privately owned by local farmers, with little access.

The Middle Level Drain

This super fishery starts its life at the junction of Popham's Eau and the Sixteen Foot by the bridge at Three Holes, which carries the A1101 Outwell to Littleport road. It averages around 50 yards wide and between 10 and 16 feet deep throughout the middle, with deep water close in over dense beds of reed. The water is usually pleasantly coloured with next to little flow, unless it is being run off, and it fishes consistently well throughout its eleven miles, particularly during the summer and autumn, before emptying into the tidal Ouse at King's Lynn.

There is a good stock of roach of all sizes, including some over the pound, with shoals of bream up to 4 lb. Pike fishing is excellent from October onwards, and among a horde of lesser fish there are some good doubles plus a sprinkling of enormous fish approaching the 30 lb mark. At the time of writing the Middle Level probably offers the best zander fishing in England. It contains shoals of schoolies in the 1 to 2½ lb range in addition to chunky specimens from 6 lb upwards to 18 lb. There is, of course, no reason why zander much larger should not exist, and they probably do.

If there is one thing wrong with this drain it is that there is a lot of it, and the bigger fish cannot be everywhere. The best way of latching on to these bigger zander is to ledger deadbaits at night.

September and early October is the best time, when eels are less active. During daylight a paternostered livebait takes a lot of beating, and sport can suddenly switch on whenever it starts to run off.

Fishing on the Middle Level is controlled from Three Holes Bridge to the aqueduct at Outwell by the Wisbech Angling Club, and day tickets are available from Welney Post Office Stores (Tel: 01354 610201) for £2. From Outwell to Wiggenhall St Germans is controlled by the King's Lynn Angling Association with £2 day tickets available from Rose's Tackle Shop in Downham Market (Tel: 01366 382938) or from the Tackle Box in King's Lynn (Tel: 01553 761293).

The River Nar

The little River Nar rises just west of Litcham village and flows through the lake (private) at nearby Lexham Hall. It is a narrow, shallow river in these upper reaches as it winds its way through the villages of Castle Acre and West Acre, covering some ten miles before it runs alongside the huge lake at Narford Hall (private). Most of the fishing in these upper reaches is privately owned and really excellent trout fishing.

As the Nar progresses steadily downstream, it unfortunately suffers badly from water abstraction, which is a sad state of affairs because this wonderful little river once produced numbers of roach in excess of 2 lb and really huge dace. Nowadays, quantity is limited throughout much of the river although quality is still high, particularly with dace. In Narborough, the Nar divides around Narborough Trout Fisheries (see Trout Fishing – Day Ticket (Stillwaters)), passing through a beautiful old mill and beneath the old King's Lynn to Norwich road. Below the bridge, stretching for two miles downstream to the waterworks at Marham, is an excellent stretch holding trout and controlled by the Salmon and Trout Association (see Trout Fishing). From Wormegay High Road Bridge all the way downriver to the Pennstock tidal sluice in King's Lynn (a distance of around seven miles) is all King's Lynn Angling Club water with day tickets costing £2 from local tackle dealers. Telephone the Tackle Box in King's Lynn on 01553 761293 or Rose's Tackle Shop in Downham Market (Tel: 01366 382938). Access is then from bridges carrying the A1101 and A1122 roads and from several minor roads and tracks between Outwell and Wiggenhall St Germans.

Access points are also from road bridges as the Nar winds down through Wormegay and on to Setchey and vary from bank to bank, following the public footpaths. There are isolated groups of large bream up to 8 lb in this part of the river, with some really large pike, plus lots of small roach and chub from below Wormegay Bridge down to the Pennstock sluices, which is only a couple of hundred yards from the A47 King's Lynn ring road. Water floods into the tidal pool through an enormous teapot-like lid, and during the spring good numbers of smallish sea trout use it to make their way upriver. There are some large pike over 20 lb in this area both above the sluice and in the tidal pool itself, but the banks here are dangerously slippery. A monster bream of 13½ lb was found in the throes of dying in this pool several years ago and now rests mounted in a case in the King's Lynn Museum.

A mile below the pool the Nar spews its water into the tidal Ouse. All the fishing in these tidal reaches is free.

The Old Bedford River

Although originating from the Great Ouse at Earith in Cambridgeshire, this narrow drain commences where it crosses the Norfolk boundary south of Welney. Here, the River Delph and the Hundred Foot (both drains) run side by side below its southern bank and like the Old Bedford eventually shed their water into the Wash.

The Old Bedford varies between 4 and 8 feet deep and contains some good roach and rudd plus tench, bream, perch, pike and the odd zander. It is an excellent summer fishery for quality roach and bream, being attractively covered in dense patches of lilies, while during the winter it may turn up a really big pike among numerous fish into double figures.

The first three miles down from Welney Bridge are controlled by the Welney Angling Club. The following three miles down to the sluice at Salters Lode are controlled by the Spratts Angling Club. Day tickets for all this water are available from Welney Post Office Stores (Tel: 01354 610201). Access is from the A1101, crossing the bridges at Welney, and from a farm track at Nordelph and from the northern bank going down to Salters Lode sluice.

The Pulver Drain

This narrow channel is just two miles long and empties into the Great Ouse Relief Channel, opposite Wiggenhall St Peter. Depth varies between 4 and 6 feet, and during the summer weed can prove rather troublesome, but some bream and tench to 3 lb are there for the catching. Sport from autumn onwards is perhaps best when water from the drain is regularly pumped into the Relief Channel, trotting then produces some quality roach, and for the pike enthusiast there are some good doubles. A stealthy approach is often rewarded on this drain.

Season permits for the Downham Angling Club, which controls the fishing, are available from Rose's Tackle Shop in Downham Market (Tel: 01366 382938). Access to the fishery is then from the road running parallel to the Relief Channel, between Watlington and St Germans.

The River Stiffkey

This charming little river rises near Fulmondestone in mid North Norfolk and takes sixteen miles to reach the sea at Blakeney Harbour. Throughout its length it is not much more than a stream but does contain numbers of brown trout. It spasmodically suffers from pollution in the upper reaches and fishing above Great Snoring should not be considered.

Travelling downstream through East Barsham, Walsingham, Wighton and on to Stiffkey, much of the fishing is available to the polite angler, who will find local landowners generally obliging when asked permission. The trout average on the smallish side, with any fish exceeding the pound a specimen.

The River Tas

This charming and intimate mini-river rises two miles east of New Buckenham, near Carlton Fen, gathering strength from countless brooks and streams as it meanders on its course through some twenty miles of Norfolk's quietest countryside until it joins forces with the Yare at Norwich.

From its source and for the initial eight miles, the Tas is but a stream until it reaches the mill at Tasburgh, where rivulets from Hempnall and Wreningham join up with the mainstream, adding width and depth. These side streams are worth exploring for dace and the odd trout. So too is the entire river above Tasburgh, but large numbers of fish should not be expected. One must, of course, always obtain permission to fish from the respective landowners who, if approached politely, will generally oblige, and this rule applies to much of the fishing along this little river for there is little day ticket or club water. Where, however, the fishing is obviously private and reserved for trout only, the angler must show respect.

From Tasburgh Mill, the Tas gradually improves in depth and width until it reaches the mill at Newton Flotman, where the main A140 Ipswich road passes over the river close by. Between these two points most of the river is inaccessible, except for a length which runs beside Taswood Lakes in Flordon. Telephone 01508 470919 for information about these excellent carp waters (see Stillwaters). The river here runs fairly shallow with odd deep holes containing some good dace and a few roach.

From Newton Flotman Mill, the Tas meanders down to Shotesham. There is no access around the mill but below on the eastern bank there is around 400 yards of 'streamy' water where 'thoughtful' anglers are allowed to fish along Smock Mill Common. Access is from the Saxlingham road opposite Duffields Mill, and fishing is from behind the houses down to the wood, which is the boundary line.

At Shotesham Park, the stream splits into two channels and links up again just upstream of the ford, where a deep pool holds some cracking roach, dace, trout and one or two pike. Fishing in the pool is free. From the ford downstream the water level is obviously low, and this is due, so it seems, to the removal of the old water mill. However, there are shoals of dace about, and for the fly-fisherman this type of water is indeed an irresistible challenge. The river deepens again as it flows down to Swainsthorpe, with some glides and undercut banks at many of the bends, which harbour specimen roach in addition to numerous dace and several trout. Unfortunately, there is no public access here.

Downstream from Swainsthorpe is the mill at Stoke Holy Cross, which was converted into a restaurant (highly recommended) several years ago. The mill pool and within the mill grounds is strictly private, but the owner, Mr Rio, does issue the occasional day ticket to the serious fisherman. Telephone the Old Mill on 01508 493337.

Upstream of the mill for a distance of about half a mile on the eastern bank, fishing is allowed. In this slow stretch depth averages around 5 feet, and there are some good-sized shoals of quality roach topping the pound.

Going still further down this pretty little river, the Norwich to London railway line can be seen high on the hills above the western bank and it does in fact run parallel with the Tas all the way into Norwich. There are some nice dace and the odd good roach along this stretch, and from here on downstream chub start to become evident.

At Caister St Edmunds, just a mile off the A140 Ipswich road, the Tas flows beneath an old bridge next to a farm. Here, once again, polite anglers who ask first are usually granted permission, and this covers a good mile of the river above the bridge and a long way downstream into Old Lakenham. At a spot known as Six Arches, where the railway line spans the adjacent River Yare, there is an interesting oblong-shaped piece of water belonging to the farm at Caistor, which is in fact an old 'dead' piece of the Yare. It holds a few tench and one or two large carp in addition to roach etc.

The largest roach from the river was taken by local angler Bill Coleman in 1972. It weighed 2 lb 10 oz. Actual shoals of roach are never huge, though, and one generally sees upwards of a dozen to thirty fish of varying sizes in a glide which they occupy all year through. It is possible to creep up on such a shoal with the aid of polarised sunglasses, and to cast a freelined bait, such as a lump of breadflake or a lobworm etc., in their direction and a little upstream of the largest fish. If they are unaware of your presence, then they may well accept it. However, if they do, the moment one gets hooked or is lost, the rest become agitated and exceedingly difficult to tempt. This, of course, is due to the crystal-clear water of the Tas, where even during the winter, unless there has been an appreciable rainfall, most species behave cautiously, so one must long-trot a long way to encourage bites.

It has been my experience that high water after several days of hard rain is the ideal time to fish this river, especially when the water is fining down and is coloured but not dirty. It is on such occasions that an actual bag of fish is possible, and the largest of the dace start to show themselves. The best dace thought to come from the Tas was taken way back in 1943 by C. Comer and weighed 1 lb 3½ oz, but few are taken over the pound these days. A good average would be around 8 oz, with odd fish exceeding 12 oz. I would, however, rate the Tas in sixth position behind the rivers Wensum, Bure, Thet, Little Ouse and Tud as a big dace water.

Below the road bridges at Old Lakenham which span the River Yare, the railway line and the River Tas, there is just a few hundred yards of the Tas left before it loses its identity and merges with the Yare. There are some sizeable roach, dace and chub in this area, which is well worth exploring during the summer months, when the water is gin-clear, to see the lie of the land with winter trotting in mind.

The River Thet

The Thet starts around Attleborough where many tiny brooks join together. However, it is not until one reaches Shropham Fen that something tangible from an angling outlook can be seen.

Immediately below the road bridge in Shropham there is a short 300-yard stretch owned by the adjacent carrot factory, where permission is usually given.

The river runs fast and quite shallow here and unfortunately has over the past few years suffered from several mild bouts of pollution. This has minimised the chances of latching on to the really large chub for which this part of the upper Thet was once renowned. However, there are still a few chub about, plus some perch, dace and numerous pike. Travelling downstream, the river flows between large pits on either side (see Stillwaters for Snetterton and Shropham Pits) and runs through Snetterton, of motor-racing fame. It then flows beneath the road bridge carrying the A11 at Larling, where one must ask local farmers for permission. Again chub and dace are predominant, with odd roach to the pound.

Because the river is so shallow and weedy and in summer runs gin-clear, fishing is invariably more fruitful in winter. However, the overgrown banksides do offer cover for the specimen-hunter seeking chub when they can be seen in the summer months hiding beneath weed rafts and under low-hanging branches.

Two miles below Larling road bridge, the river flows beneath the B1111 in East Harling and then twists down to Bridgham, skirting Harling Conifer Forest along its southern bank. There are some good dace, roach and chub along this reach for the angler who likes the roaming style of fishing, because shoals are not large – although individual specimens are. Access is limited, although there are local farmers sympathetic to the polite angler.

Fishing on the northern bank, starting a mile above the roundabout on the A1066 Diss–Thetford road, is controlled by the Thetford and Breckland Angling Club. Day permits cost £2 from the Rod and Line Tackle Shop in Thetford (Tel: 01842 764825). Here there are a few good chub to 4 lb plus, with roach, rudd, pike and specimen dace up to a pound. Again, winter long-trotting sorts out the better fish, particularly after a good flood when the river is fining down but still holds some colour. As the river enters Thetford, it tumbles over a weir and flows beneath Nuns Bridge, adjacent to the neighbouring Little Ouse, with which it amalgamates some 600 yards further on, but the Thet loses its name in the process.

Nearly all the fishing rights in these last few miles of the Thet are private, though one is quite at liberty to ask permission from local landowners, who can only say no.

The River Thurne

Although this tidal river is Norfolk's shortest, with an overall length of just five miles. It is nevertheless of paramount importance both as a connecting vein to several famous broads and a really first rate fishery in its own right. Moreover, the river authority controls such an enormous amount of the Thurne's bank space that there are indeed very few parts where the angler cannot find comfortable free fishing in a truly Broadland setting.

The Thurne starts as a river in the village of West Somerton with a network of feeding dykes and streams adding their water in the area of nearby Martham Broad (sometimes called Somerton Broad), which is private (see The Broads). The Thurne actually runs through the middle of this shallow water and then winds slowly downstream between thick reedbeds towards Martham Ferry. This length is perhaps the most pleasant, quietest part of the Thurne and, compared to other tidal rivers in Norfolk, it is quite sluggish. The fishing is thus comparatively relaxed, nearly all float-fishing in a depth of around 4 to 5 feet of water, which at the Somerton end only is incredibly weedy and crystal clear.

However, the tidal influences can still dictate how the river will fish and, at certain times, quite without apparent reason, it just seems to switch off. Summer boat traffic can also prove a menace in the Thurne's limited width, so only early or late sessions are recommended during the warmer months.

Half a mile below Martham Broad, there is a double S-bend at Dungeons Corner (a good pike and bream spot), below which the river often becomes heavily coloured due to a drainage discharge. Anywhere along this part of the Thurne can throw up a massive pike, like the 37½-pounder taken by A. Cottrell in the summer of 1982 and the 42 lb 2 oz former record caught by Derrick Amies in 1986. These monsters in all probability do most of their feeding in Martham Broad but wander into the river whenever there are sufficient concentrations of roach and bream close by. One usually needs to wade through numerous jacks, however, before a big one turns up. There are some good shoals of quality bream and roach all the way along the river down to Martham Ferry and, during the summer, night fishing is recommended for the bream.

For mixed catches, mild spells during the winter can produce some really good bags on trotted maggots or casters. The National Rivers Authority controls most of the Thurne, and the entire reach on both banks from Martham Broad to the ferry swing-bridge is open to free fishing, with access from Martham Ferry only.

Four hundred yards below Martham Swing-bridge Ferry, Candle Dyke, which is the link between Hickling, Heigham Sound and Horsey Mere, enters from the northern bank (see The Broads). This wide junction often fishes well in the late autumn as the bream shoals leave Hickling and the Sounds on their downriver migration through Candle Dyke into the Thurne. Fishing is entirely free in this section save that from the privately owned chalets and bungalows which front the Thurne's southern bank immediately down from the ferry. Boats may be hired at Martham Ferry to fish Hickling Broad etc., from Martham Ferry Boatyard (Tel: 01493 740303).

Situated close to the ferry on the opposite side of the dyke are Martham Pits, which are excellent alternative venues, particularly in the summer (see Stillwaters – Day Ticket). From Candle Dyke's junction downstream, the flow increases somewhat with the extra push of the water from Hickling, and one finds a greater depth, though only 6 inches of water drop between tides.

Preferred and well-proved winter tactics for this length of the Thurne are to trot down casters or maggots, along, or just off the bottom and to loose-feed with the same. It is in fact wonderful stick-float-fishing.

Occasionally, one needs to offer a static bait, and ledgering is widely used along the Thurne here. Quiver-tipping is much favoured and can prove a deadly efficient method of hitting those delicate bream bites which occur in very cold temperatures. At such times a tiny red worm will often render more positive bites as opposed to bread or maggots.

A mile further downriver, one reaches Potter Heigham, where the A149 from Stalham to Great Yarmouth spans the now slightly wider Thurne. Access is from the bridge, with free fishing on both banks both upstream and downstream, except for a few areas where private businesses and chalets front the water's edge.

As far as summer angling is concerned, the entire area around Potter Heigham is, at best, very poor, although fish are about if one night fishes certain locations. In any event, winter fishing or, at the earliest, from October onwards is a far better bet, with roach and bream predominating. Boats can be hired at Potter Heigham from Phoenix Fleet Boatyard (Tel: 01692 670460).

Between the old and new bridges is a popular winter spot where the roach and hybrids pack in tight. A distance both above and below the bridges of 100 yards also offers potential, and the odd pike over 20 lb is not unlikely.

A mile and a half below Potter Heigham, with accessible, free fishing on both banks along most of the way, Womack Water leads off from the mainstream on the northern bank (see The Broads). Here, one may fish on both banks of Womack Dyke and the river and also from a strip opposite on the Thurne's southern bank, access to this part being from Thurne village. Returning to the north bank and a little way downriver from the authority's holding around Womack Dyke, the Norwich and District Angling Association controls a slice of the bank known as Cold Harbour, with day tickets available from Thrower's Stores at Ludham (Tel: 01692 678248). In these last two miles, as the Thurne nears the River Bure, it widens, and tidal currents are more pronounced, with ledger taking over from the float. One also requires a substantial amount of groundbait to hold fish in the swim, with worms, paste, flake and maggots all proving effective. Quiver-tips prove successful indicators here.

From Thurne, there is just half a mile of this river remaining before it enters the Bure at Thurne Mouth, an area well worth fishing for quality roach and large hybrids to 2 lb. Although rarely fished for pike, some large fish do inhabit this reach of the lower Thurne, and anyone taking on the strong tides could be pleasantly surprised.

The River Tiffey

This tiny river rises in Wymondham at the confluence of several streams. It flows down to Kimberley Park and into the 30-acre lake, which is now badly silted and worthless as a fishery, although years back, before water abstraction became a problem, it held a fine head of fish and was very deep.

From the lake, the Tiffey makes a four-mile journey until it feeds the Yare at Barford. There are dace, roach, rudd, perch and pike to be found en route, along with an increasing population of chub. Permission to fish is sometimes given by local farmers.

The River Tud

This enchanting river starts life a little south of East Dereham by obtaining water from three separate sources and rambles in an easterly direction through sleepy farmland for some fourteen miles until it reaches the suburbs of Norwich.

Unfortunately, it never really gains in stature in all its length and, where it passes through the villages of North Tuddenham, Hockering, Honingham, Easton and Costessey and finally Hellesdon Mill, merging with the Wensum below the pool, one is able to wade across at almost any point. However, its shallowness and lack of width makes no difference to the stamp of fish it produces. For the Tud's water is crystal-clear, fast-flowing and has lush weedbeds full of aquatic life, including crayfish, lampreys, bullheads, freshwater shrimps and stoneloach. While all are superb natural baits, anglers should remember that to use crayfish for bait is now illegal.

Species to be found in the Tud, some of which can be taken with the above baits, are dace, roach, chub, trout, perch and a few grayling. Dace and trout are the predominating species, especially in the upper reaches. Tud dace are most prolific and renowned for their high average size, being beautifully coloured and proportioned. I have spent countless hours in pursuit of them and taken many fish from 14 oz to 1 lb 1 oz. Most of these have been taken on long-trotted maggots in winter, when the water has some colour to it. However, these larger dace can sometimes be tempted during the summer months by the fly-fisherman, especially at the early part of the season, before the weed becomes too thick. Slow-sinking nymphs work well, especially the black beetle and mayfly variations. A tiny, dark, dry fly fished at dusk will also take its fair share of big dace.

The largest dace recorded was caught by Andy Davidson in January 1972 and weighed 1 lb 2½ oz. Andy had another of an ounce less on the very same day.

Unfortunately, the river has suffered rather badly during the past two decades from odd bursts of pollution caused by careless farmers, and in places the stocks of dace and trout are still rebuilding.

Although much of the fishing is privately owned, there are still accessible spots where the polite enquiring angler will find landowners sympathetic.

Well Creek

This narrow and steeply banked drain runs adjacent to the A1122 road for seven miles from Outwell to Salters Lode, near Downham Market, where its water empties into the tidal Great Ouse.

There is free fishing all the way wherever the banks are accessible – which is almost throughout – and, because the water is always well coloured, sport is excellent for roach, bream, zander, pike, and some fine tench topping 4 lb. Occasionally, there is even a small run of sea trout. Depth varies between 4 and 6 feet, and the banks are heavily lined with reeds and sedges.

The River Wensum

This, the loveliest of Norfolk's rivers, begins its life above the village of Raynham, where several small streams amalgamate and flow through the lake at Raynham Park. The Wensum is then joined by the tiny River Tat along Tatterford Common as it trundles downstream to Shereford and on to the market town of Fakenham. The Wensum is a highly attractive little river flowing clean and fast through lush countryside, holding dace of a high average size. Dace over 8 oz are common, and specimens from 12 oz upwards are taken each winter when the weed has gone and the river is pleasantly coloured. There is also a sprinkling of quality roach, pike and brown trout, plus the occasional grayling. Although much of these high upper reaches are privately controlled by fly-fishing syndicates, the Fakenham Anglian Club controls around two miles of the southern bank, starting from the first bridge upstream of the mill (see the map of the river under Trout Fishing (Rivers – Fly Only). To join the Fakenham Angling Club, anglers must live within a ten-mile radius of the town. Apply to Dave's Tackle Shop, Norwich Street, Fakenham (Tel: 01328 862543), who also issue day tickets costing £3 for a two-fish 'limit' to non-members.

Below the mill, there are two miles of free fishing along Fakenham Common, stretching down to the old railway line – all good fly water during the summer and super long-trotting during the winter for dace especially. Travelling downstream, much of the fishing is in private hands as the river slowly increases in both depth and width.

Between Guist and Bintree, the fishing is unfortunately now all inaccessible to anglers, and again immediately below Bintree Mill fishing is private, except for a delightful fly-only beat immediately downstream of Bintree Mill, controlled by the Salmon and Trout Association (see Trout Fishing), who have an open membership. Contact the membership secretary, P. Pledger (Tel: 01362 820677).

Winding through Bintree Hills, the Wensum reaches North Elmham and flows beneath the B1145 towards Billingford Common. Much of the river in these high upper reaches is under private control with little access, except for an extremely interesting three-quarters-of-a-mile stretch that includes two mill pools and a bypass channel at Elmham Mill. The mill has, in fact, been divided into self-catering apartments, let to anglers on a

The River Wensum immediately above Costessey Mill holds big roach and chub

holiday basis for a day or two or for longer periods, who then have full access to the river, which is renowned for its prolific stock of chub, bream and the occasional specimen roach. Telephone Mr or Mrs Shearing on 01362 668928, who also, during the winter months only, issue a limited number of day tickets to the serious angler.

Starting 200 yards below the B1145 bridge spanning the river Wensum at Elmham, at the junction of the tiny River Blackwater, there is a lovely, twisting, streamy half-mile of the southern bank controlled by the Dereham and District Angling Club. This shallow fishery holds some good dace, roach, barbel, chub and odd trout and runs behind Worthing gravel pits, also controlled by Dereham and District Angling Club (see Stillwaters – Members Only).

To join the club, which covers additional local fishing on the Wensum and pits, contact the membership secretary, D. Appleby, 6 Rump Close, Swanton Morley (Tel: 01362 637591). The tackle dealers in Dereham, such as Churchill's (Tel: 01362 696926) or Myhill's (Tel: 01362 692975), also sell Dereham and District club cards, which cost £10 yearly. There are no day tickets.

Half a mile downstream from Worthing, Swanton Morley Fisheries hold the fishing rights on part of the southern bank and also on the adjacent gravel workings, with day permits available (see Stillwaters) at £5 from the bailiff who calls round. Season permits are also available, costing £30 from Churchill's in Dereham. Here there are really good specimen chub, huge dace and roach in the Wensum, with some sizeable trout and pike spread along the shallow runs, glides and in the deep holes on the bends. Excellent trotting in winter.

At Swanton Morley, the Wensum divides and flows over two attractive sluice pools: one large and called locally 'The Falls', where the B1147 road passes over its tail-end, and a smaller one, situated further upstream, which runs alongside and beneath the same road. Really large dace are numerous, together with an occasional good roach or brown trout, but

30

only the small pool and the narrow stretch of side stream running beside the road are publicly accessible. Two hundred yards below these road bridges, the Wensum links up again and flows down to Elsing Mill. Much of the land between these two points runs through Castle Farm, where fishing is available to Dereham Angling Club members only. This one-and-a-half-mile stretch of the river runs slowly and it is quite deep in parts, holding limited numbers of roach, bream, pike, perch, chub and dace, but all grow to specimen size. At Elsing Mill, all immediate parts of the river and for a distance downstream of over a mile are strictly private. There is then a short, quarter-mile, narrow piece, controlled by the Dereham Angling Club with access on the southern bank via Lyng Pit (see Stillwaters).

The last mile of the northern bank between Elsing and Lyng Mill is controlled on a syndicate basis (Sparham Hall Reach) by the Norfolk Anglers' Conservation Association. Contact Tim Ellis, 41 Kabin Road, Costessey, Norwich. Members of NACA can obtain day tickets costing £3 from syndicate members to fish the above section and a superb one-and-a-half-mile length called 'Sayers Meadow Reach', starting at and including the two mill pools at Lyng Bridge, going downstream towards Lenwade. It provides prolific fishing for dace, roach, chub and barbel, which were introduced by NACA following their habitat improvement programme. It was in this vicinity that my good friend, Jimmy Sapey, took on fly one of the largest brown trout to come from the Wensum. It weighed 7 lb 15 oz and fell to a large wet fly in July 1971. Anglers wishing to join NACA should first contact Malcolm Hitchens, Woodside House, 5 The Meadows, Aylsham NR11 6HP. (Tel: 01263 732752). Only then can they apply for the Association's syndicate waters on the Wensum.

As the Wensum flows further downstream towards Lenwade, there is access to the northern bank at Lenwade Common via Common Lane in Lenwade directly from the A1067 Fakenham to Norwich road. Day tickets cost £3 from the bailiff who calls round, and in addition to three-quarters of a mile of the Wensum this includes excellent stillwater fishing in the Common Lakes (see Stillwaters – Day Ticket).

In Lenwade Mill pool, a brown trout weighing 9 lb 12 oz was taken in 1964 by the mill's owner and is, to date, the heaviest Wensum trout to be grassed, although double-figure fish are known to exist. Unfortunately, the river around Lenwade is now mostly under trout syndicates and private control. There is, however, a short, 600-yard, fast, streamy piece of the Wensum containing chub, bream, roach and barbel immediately below Lenwade Road Bridge on the northern bank available on a £5 day ticket from the Bridge public house (Tel: 01603 872248), which includes fishing on a 5-acre lake (see Stillwaters – Day Ticket).

The River Wensum holds a prolific head of chub – like these beauties caught by the author's brother, David Wilson

From Lenwade, the Wensum winds its way for four miles to Ringland Road Bridge with little access save for a one-and-a-half-mile syndicate stretch at the farm of Mr and Mrs Oram. For details about their beat, which holds numbers of chub, dace and pike plus a few roach and trout and includes fun-fishing in a single-acre, irregularly shaped lake beside the river for roach, tench and carp (Tel: 01603 867317). There are no day tickets.

Upstream of Ringland Road Bridge on the southern bank, it is common land for the first two meadows, with access down a track in the village close to the post office. For a short 200-yard stretch on the northern bank, above the bridge, and on both banks for about 100 yards below, the fishing is open to all. Here the Wensum runs clear and shallow between huge flowing weedbeds over a gravel bottom, where roach, dace, trout, chub, huge gudgeon and grayling are caught on trotted baits or with fly tackle. In fact, the Wensum at this point is an excellent training ground for fly-fishermen because it always contains a fair head of brown trout. One of the best ever caught here rests in a glass case in the public bar of the Swan, adjacent to the bridge. It weighed exactly 6 lb and was caught by the late Cyril Bullard in 1957, not on a fly but a minnow.

Half a mile below the bridge the Wensum starts to slow in pace and deepens as it flows through beautiful Ringland Hills towards Taverham, where most of the fishing is privately owned. However, there is a good length containing pike, roach and dace available on the northern bank, controlled by Leisure Sports, together with seven pits.

Day tickets cost £3 and must be purchased in advance from John's Tackle Den (Tel: 01603 614114) or Tom Boultons (Tel: 01603 426834) both in Norwich (see Ringland Lakes in Stillwaters – Day Ticket).

A short length (around 80 yards) of the southern bank is open to public fishing where it runs alongside Ringland Road, and then everything is inaccessible down to Taverham, except for a superb stretch of around three-quarters of a mile immediately upstream of Taverham Mill on the southern bank, which includes the mill pools and downstream on the same bank to Taverham Road Bridge. This is all syndicate water and part of the Taverham Mills Fishery (see Stillwaters – Day Ticket), owned by Anglian Water. Only a limited amount of yearly tickets are issued for this fabulous piece of river which contains big roach, numbers of chub, pike, dace, barbel into double figures and even a few carp. (Telephone Taverham Mills Fishery Lodge on 01603 861014 for details).

Below Taverham Road Bridge, the river winds for two miles down to Costessey Mill with three access points. The first stretch is a lovely, twisting, three-quarter mile piece full of quality 3 to 4 lb chub, plus the odd good roach, dace and pike, controlled by the Norwich and District Angling Association. This lies behind Costessey Pits on the southern bank and forms part of the Wensum Fisheries complex, including four well-stocked lakes (see Stillwaters – Members Only). For entrance to the club, which has much fishing in local pits, broads and rivers, contact local tackle dealers or the secretary, C. Wigg, 3 Coppice Avenue, Norwich (Tel: 01603 423625).

Continuing on from the NDAA stretch, on the same (southern) bank with access via West End in Old Costessey, is a half-mile yearly syndicate beat, controlled by Mrs Mann (Tel: 01603 743877 for details).

The third and final access to fishing between Taverham and Costessey is a short length (one meadow only) of the northern bank, immediately upstream of Costessey Mill. This is available only to NDAA members, and anyone may join through local tackle dealers.

At Costessey Mill, three separate sluice

pools all hold fish, which include dace, roach, perch, chub, barbel, pike, eels and the odd bream and brown trout. Some of the fishing (around the big pool only) is free from the roadside, and during the winter months, when the river is high and coloured, good numbers of chub over 3 lb pack into the big deep pool along with odd big roach and barbel. From here on downstream for the next mile or so is where most of the Wensum's barbel live. The river authority first stocked the river below Costessey Mill in 1971 with over 150 barbel, although a couple of dozen were introduced several years before. These fish are now well established, albeit still in this particular reach, due to the fast water over gravel which suits them well, and they seem to reproduce no more than is sufficient to keep up their numbers. Hence the reason for their maintaining such a high average size, between 6 and 8 lb. There is also a sprinkling of double-figure fish to 13 lb. Most of these are 'well known' individual fish which are recognisable to those who fish the Wensum regularly. I have records and many photos of one particular fish being caught nearly twenty times, and on each occasion it has blessed its captor with a 'double-figure barbel'. So the entire river is far from being one big barbel swim, as much of the angling press would suggest.

Perhaps they will spread eventually throughout the upper reaches, perhaps not. Either way, they offer superlative sport for the specialist, together with chub of a high average size. Throughout these last four miles of the Wensum, until it reaches Norwich, there is a splendid head of chub in the 3 to 4½ lb range, with specimens topping 5 lb, plus a limited number of mirror carp running into double figures, which escaped during floods a few years ago from the NRA fish farm at Hellesdon Mill. Roach are nowhere near so thick on the ground as they once used to be but whoppers over the 2 lb mark are still there for the taking in the deeper, slower swims, along with occasional bream in the 4 to 6 lb range.

The next accessible fishing is a lovely half-mile winding stretch, and completely free fishing on the northern bank, known as Drayton Green Lanes, with access through a steep spinney from the Low Road linking Drayton to Hellesdon. The Wensum is a most secluded spot here, where great willows overhang the water as it narrows into a double S-bend before flowing down to Hellesdon. In this part of the river almost anything can happen, as it did for me during an unbelievable evening session in October 1984. I experienced just four bites on breadflake after dark while laying-on with a betalight float in a five-foot-deep swim. The first produced a mirror carp of 10½ lb. The second a barbel of 12¾ lb. The third a roach of 2 lb 7 oz, followed by a chub of 4 lb 6 oz – and all in an hour's fishing. That's what the Wensum is capable of producing when it feels like it, and for optimum results it is worth trying to catch the river just when it is starting to fine down after a flood. There is no better time for latching on to a whopping great roach, chub or barbel.

At Hellesdon Mill, one finds most species, including roach, dace, big perch, pike, some very good trout, chub and eels. A brown trout of 6¼ lb was taken from the pool in 1971 by local angler, D. Hewitt, on a minnow.

To scuba-dive this famous pool is quite educational for – although the surface current is fierce where it pours over the sluice – down below things are much quieter. Huge shoals of gudgeon move hungrily over all the gravel bars with chub lingering within pouncing distance. The perch and trout hang below the sluice within the undercut gorged out by years of running water, while hordes of eels hide among the accumulation of rubbish, including bottles, bedsteads, tree roots and bicycle frames. The angler bent on catching any large fish here might bear these facts in mind.

Above the mill on the south bank is the National River Authority's fish farm, the first publicly-owned fish farm in Great Britain. The tiny River Tud enters the tail end of Hellesdon Pool, and there is a good swim at this confluence, close to the Tud's south bank where the water deepens somewhat. However, from here down to the road bridge the Wensum is quite shallow, with a gravely bottom where dace are the predominating species together with roach and chub. From the road bridge downstream the river deepens, especially on the bends, and offers good sport. An occasional tench or carp is not unlikely in this vicinity as the river, now all free fishing (coming within the boundaries of Norwich), flows down to the Gate House public house, where it passes under the Norwich Ringroad.

Some 400 yards below the bridge the river skirts the waterworks, holding numerous pike and some cracking roach, perch and tench as it deepens on the many bends. There are also good numbers of bream to 7 lb here, plus a strong head of carp to over 20 lb.

As the Wensum enters the City of Norwich, it passes beneath Mile Cross road bridge and then becomes quite wide, mostly shallow and extremely weedy in summer before it flows under Dolphin Bridge. However, below the bridge is a deep length where good roach and sizeable pike are taken. There are also elusive bream in excess of 7 lb and still more carp.

A quarter of a mile below Dolphin Bridge, the Wensum runs alongside the large inner ringroad roundabout and flows down to the City Mills, being the last of the upper reaches. After extensive dredging in 1983, this last mile has been producing excellent bags of roach up to 1½ lb in recent seasons, along with sizeable chub and carp into double figures.

At New Mills Yard, the Wensum is tidal, with quite a drop in level between tides, but the pool is generally quite clear and exceptionally weedy in summer.

There is no accessible bank-fishing as town houses and factories sit along the waterfront for the following half mile. However, anyone may boat-fish, as they are able to do on any tidal channel in Norfolk and Suffolk. In fact, boat-fishing is the best way of getting results from these tidal reaches. There are none for hire, but anglers may launch their own dinghies from the public slipway at Friars Quay halfway between St George's Street Bridge and Fye Bridge.

New Mills tidal pool is deep and holds a fair head of quality roach and many pike into double figures, especially in winter. There are also some perch, plenty of medium-sized dace, and often in residence is a huge shoal of bream running from 2 lb to over 5 lb. These move upriver from the lower reaches, attracted by the well-oxygenated water of the sluice. Stuart Moir caught a massive mirror carp from the pool in 1985, weighing 31 lb exactly.

Also present in the Wensum along this stretch are some huge brown trout. They have been taken up to 6 lb but could possibly reach the double figure mark. In any event, if the brown trout don't, there are many sea trout which migrate up the Wensum each year and these most certainly do. I have seen several fish up to at least 14 lb in this area as early as Easter and as late as September. However, catching them is far from easy for – although one may occasionally snap at a small plug or livebait – they are generally shy and difficult to tempt. The last creature that inhabits this length of river I would not usually associate with tidal waters. It is the crayfish. So at any rate at least the Wensum must be fairly clean in Norwich.

As the Wensum passes through the City of Norwich, it widens and flows down to Fye Bridge where limited free fishing for some cracking roach and bream exists at the three sets of steps. There is excellent stick-float fishing here. Further on, the river bends around an

The River Wensum, Norwich – excellent roach fishing during the winter

ancient Norman watch tower called Cow Tower, where there is a deep bend with really good roach fishing. Maggots or casters for quantity and breadflake for quality is a good point to remember. The Wensum flows quite straight now as it runs adjacent to Riverside Road and approaches the Yacht Station, just up from Foundry Bridge, which is a mere stone's throw from Norwich Railway Station. Fishing is free from all the accessible bank space here and, although boats may prove troublesome in summer, the whole length fills up chock-a-block with roach in the winter. Below Foundry Bridge, the Wensum increases its width to accommodate sea-going coasters which bring wood and steel to Norwich, so the angler will always find a good average depth under his rod tip. The water has a good tinge of colour too and often a strong pull to it, particularly on the ebb tide. This stretch is popular with angling matches and is a known caster water with quality roach and bream showing up from October onwards along with numerous pike, including specimens over 20 lb.

A hundred yards below Carrow Bridge, bank access ceases, and there is just another half-mile of the Wensum before it joins forces with the Yare. This last section can fish particularly well during the winter for pike, roach and bream – but angling is by boat only.

The River Wissey

From its source near Shipdham, the little River Wissey travels but a few miles before it becomes a trout stream. It navigates between the villages of Bradenham, North and South Pickenham, Hilborough, Ickleburgh, Mundford and then on to Northwold, growing in stature and nearly all the way a private trout reserve. There are large chub and other coarse fish present, however. In fact, the Wissey has the distinction of producing the largest chub ever taken from a Norfolk water on rod and line, a fish of 8¼ lb taken near Stoke Ferry in 1960 by M.J. Roberts. More over, most of the chub introduced into other rivers such as the Waveney etc. were obtained by the river authority from the Wissey.

From Hilborough to Northwold the river passes through deeply wooded countryside and flows through lovely Didington Park, where it runs alongside the lake (private). In this area the river holds really monstrous brown trout, possibly into double figures, with 2 to 4 lb fish in good numbers. There are also numbers of rainbow trout introduced by the respective owners.

The Wissey is an ever-changing little river, with narrow, shallow, sandy parts, deep holes, especially at the bends where most of the fish lurk and is full of weed in summer. It can change from a narrow stream to a fairly wide channel in the course of a few yards, and all the time the water is crystal clear. The fishing is consequently most difficult.

From Northwold, the river winds down to Foulden, through Borough Fen and on to Whitington. This four-mile stretch contains a prolific head of quality chub, some bream and isolated shoals of roach, including specimens approaching 2 lb. Unfortunately, it is all in private hands, although the polite enquiring angler will find sympathetic farmers provided permission is asked first. From Whitington to Stoke Ferry, where the river passes beneath the A134, the course has widened a little and the depth is greater. The first half-mile upstream and downstream of the bridge along the southern bank is controlled by the King's Lynn Angling Association with day tickets costing £2 from local tackle dealers. On the opposite (northern) bank, fishing is controlled by the Whitington Angling Club upstream for around half a mile to Sampson's Hole.

The Wissey offers really good mixed fishing here, with dace, roach, perch, tench, good bream and some thumping great chub. There are also some extra large pike and even the occasional sea trout. Travelling further downstream, the Wissey passes beneath the Cut Off Channel via some sluices.

In the mainstream of the lower Wissey, boats may prove troublesome during the summer so early fishing sessions invariably produce better results, especially for bream. Some good bags are taken, together with the odd large roach to bread baits hard on the bottom. Bread takes some beating in the warmer months, with maggots, caster or worms as alternatives. But from October, when the weed disappears and the water has a little more push to it, right through until the season ends, maggots or casters reign supreme for good bags of quality roach. Fish over the 2 lb-mark are not uncommon in this section as the river meanders down through the famous Wissey Pools to Wissington road bridge. The stretch above the road bridge, starting from the stile and including one pool on the southern bank, is controlled by the LAA. Day permits are available from the bailiff, who calls, with access from the car park at Five Mile Home Farm on the southern bank. Immediately upstream of the bridge, the choicest northern bank (including the island) is controlled by the British Sugar Corporation's social club, with season tickets from the secretary. This entire area of the Wissey Pools provides fabulous fishing in depths varying between 6 and 20 feet for specimen roach, bream into double figures, big tench and numerous pike into double figures with a good sprinkling over 20 lb. There is also a good head of quality zander between 6 lb and 10 lb and the odd large brown trout. In fact, Norfolk's largest brownie was caught here in 1949 by G. Mays and tipped the scales at 12 lb 14 oz. Others from around the 8 lb-mark and running into double figures have also been taken.

Immediately downstream from the road bridge to the disused railway bridge is strictly private. The Wissey then winds down through Hilgay Fen and beneath the A10. The King's Lynn Angling Club controls these last two miles of the Wissey (on both banks) before it joins the Great Ouse just one and a half miles upstream from Denver Sluice. Day permits cost £2 and are available from The Stores at Hilgay Bridge (Tel: 01366 387926) or local tackle dealers. This stretch of the river offers marvellous sport with roach of an exceptionally high stamp, including specimens over 2 lb-plus bream and chub, with pike very much in evidence at the Ouse confluence. Winter fishing is particularly productive.

The River Yare
One of the most underrated and under-fished of all Norfolk's rivers is the Yare, which rises close to the village of Shipdham, just one mile from the source of another famous river, the Wissey. But unlike the Wissey which flows west, the Yare, which in its infant stage is but a brook, winds east for twenty miles towards Norwich. For several miles it is fed by other brooks and so by the time it passes beneath the B1135 road to East Dereham it has materialised into a delightful little river holding some good dace, among other coarse fish.

The Yare is fed below the road bridge by a stream from nearby Thuxton and flows downstream on a narrow course through spinneys and hedgerows to the villages of Barnham Broom, Barford and on to Marlingford. Nearly all of the Yare in this region is privately controlled by local landowners. However, there are a few spots where permission to fish is often granted to polite anglers who ask first.

There is access to around one mile of this lovely little river, starting immediately below the Barnham Broom Golf Course on the southern bank on a £3 day ticket which must be obtained prior to fishing from Mr Glazier of Meadow Farm in Colton (Tel: 01603 759258).

From Marlingford Mill, the river snakes downstream to Bawburgh, Much of the fishing is controlled by Marlingford Estates with yearly permits available from the assistant keeper at Mill Cottage adjacent to Marlingford Mill. These cost £12. Special holiday-makers day tickets cost £2.

This is a lovely reach, wooded in parts, with deep holes on the many bends and long straights which provide excellent mixed catches on the float during the winter months. There are some cracking dace, roach and chub to 5 lb plus the occasional large perch and numerous pike. There is about one and a half miles of bank accessible each side of the river, except where cottages front the water. It stretches from Marlingford Mill pool to the small pumping station half a mile upstream of Bawburgh.

In Bawburgh Mill pool (private), depth exceeds 16 feet but quickly tails off to where one is able to wade across through just 12 inches of water. A sad thought and proof of the extent to which silting due to water abstraction is slowly strangling Norfolk rivers, is that at this very point large barges once passed, taking coal to the mill and returning with flour. Colossal eels live within the decaying woodwork of the loading pylons alongside the mill, with odd perch and many ruffe present. There are also dace of an exceptionally high average size, along with roach, chub, the occasional barbel and smallish pike. Fishing is free from beside the road for a short distance both above and below Bawburgh road bridge, and some good bags of quality roach are caught here during the winter, when there is colour in the river.

Travelling on downstream towards Norwich, the Yare is spanned by the A47 southern bypass before bending between large gravel pits on either side and contains small numbers of specimen chub, roach and dace. The only access here is along a 500-yard beat bordering the most westerly of these large gravel pits. This is a members-only water of the Yarmouth, Norfolk County Angling Association, who issue £16 season permits through Tom Boulton's tackle shop in Norwich (Tel: 01603 426834) (see Stillwaters Members Only – Bawburgh Pit) and includes excellent gravel pit sport, with pike in addition to the short stretch of river.

Future access to this massive gravel pit complex and three miles of the River Yare on the northern bank between Bawburgh and Earlham is uncertain, due to a water recreation centre planned for the adjacent Bowthorpe estate. There are proposals for diverting the course of the river, around the pits, with facilities for yachting, windsurfing and wildlife sanctuaries in addition to using the pits for angling, and at the time of writing in 1995 I am not sure how access to the river itself will be affected. There is little doubt, however, that there will be fishing on this part of the river, as Norwich City Council own the last one and a half miles along the northern bank, with free fishing at present to within 500 yards of Earlham Bridge. Access to this stretch is through the housing estate in West Earlham. The narrow dyke coming in at the first bend, when walking upstream, affords good sport with roach when the Yare is hopelessly in flood. Below Earlham road bridge where the B1108 Watton road spans the Yare, fishing is free from the northern bank through Earlham Park for a distance of around two miles, all the way to Cringleford, the boundary being where the A11 crosses the river. High up on the hill sits the University of East Anglia, which has its own University Broad (see Stillwaters – Members Only) offering excellent sport adjacent to the river. One may either walk downstream or upstream from the road bridges, or gain access from Bluebell Road, which runs parallel to the river along the northern bank.

This entire stretch is excellent fishing for dace, roach, some specimen chub, plus the odd bream and pike. Depth varies between 2 and 5 feet along the straights, going down to 10 feet on at least a couple of the numerous acute bends. During the summer, weed growth can be rather heavy, and it is usually a case of presenting baits like breadflake in the holes, preferably at dawn or dusk, to tempt the better-quality roach which run to over 2 lb. After the first frosts, however, and especially when the Yare holds some colour, mixed catches – with roach to over the pound predominating – are taken, trotting casters, maggots or punched bread. At weekends this is a popular club venue.

At Cringleford the river divides into two large pools. The mill pool is private but the picturesque sluice pool may be approached from the north bank only. It contains some large roach, some dace, perch, chub and perhaps a large trout or two. Only part of the one and a half miles of river from Cringleford Bridge to the next mill downsteam, which is Keswick, can be classed as free fishing, with access via Church Lane, which starts at the traffic lights on the old A11 road. One hundred yards below the old bridge, the Yare divides around a long, narrow island, where access is somewhat limited, but where it converges again there are some super swims. This section is rather silted up in parts but, because of this irregularity, there are deep, undercut bank swims holding many perch, roach, good-sized pike and just the occasional really large chub. These swims are in the vicinity of the railway line which bisects the river some 400 yards upstream of Keswick Mill. Below Keswick Mill pool (private), the Yare winds its way down to Harford Bridge, offering one or two good swims on the way, containing roach to 1½ lb, a small shoal of bream to 7 lb and the odd good chub.

Anglers may walk upstream on the southern bank from Harford Bridge, which carries the main A140 Ipswich road. Below the bridge, the Yare skirts Harford dump.

The Yare is now on its last two miles of non-tidal river before it is joined by the River Tas, and they both flow into the pool at Trowse Mill. Access is limited above the mill, especially as it winds through Old Lakenham, but the angler who politely asks permission will inevitably find good fishing, and within the Yare here there are some cracking roach. A really big chub to 5 lb is not unlikely, along with very occasional perch, bream and numerous pike.

A short, secluded, syndicate stretch is available here (Tel: 01603 712510).

The Yare can be seen from the new A146 road, which links to the A47 southern bypass some three-quarters of a mile upstream of Trowse Mill, and in these final stages of the upper Yare some big roach, chub and carp to over 20 lb are to be found.

Trowse Mill pool, although gin-clear in summer and rather weedy, is nevertheless tidal, and from here on the Yare quickly changes its character from a quiet stream to a full-bodied Broadland river. One may, of course, row up stream into the pool to fish, but the banks are privately owned. There are some quality roach in the pool together with numerous dace, a prolific stock of chub, plus the odd huge brown trout, several barbel and the odd carp. I have enjoyed the company of the pool's inhabitants on many occasions while scuba-diving and can only assume that the barbel arrived in the pool by coming down the Wensum from Costessey where they were stocked by the river authority in 1971. Other visitors to the pool include migratory sea trout at varying times throughout the summer and an ever-present horde of flounders, which at times pinch a single maggot all too readily. A really big pike is not unlikely towards the latter part of the season, but throughout most of the year there are few pike of any size from the pool downstream to the road bridge. A massive carp of 31 lb 6 oz was taken by Mark Pye from the river here in 1992.

Another piece of the Yare passes beneath the old A146 road, 200 yards away, and joins in with the flow from Trowse Mill pool close by Trowse church, 300 yards downstream from the road bridge. This weedy channel is in fact the old bed of the River Tas, which no longer feeds it and was once a flowing sluice stream before water abstraction stopped its flow from above Trowse Mill. Now, its level rises and falls with the tidal influences of the Yare.

On the south bank, starting from the church, Norwich and District Angling Association controls the fish-ing for about 300 yards. Anyone may join the association through local tackle dealers, or through the secretary, Cyril Wigg of 3 Coppice Avenue, Norwich (Tel: 01603 423625). There is then just a further 150 yards of the Yare before it merges with the Wensum. But the Yare, which at this stage is a narrow channel compared to the Wensum, quite unfairly becomes the major river. This last intimate length of the Yare can afford good roach fishing with the chance of an odd specimen and produces numbers of pike during winter, with a fair sprinkling of doubles. There are also dace, perch, eels and odd shoals of bream, plus a head of carp in the 15 to 30 lb range.

Half a mile downriver from the junction of the Wensum and Yare, the New Cut separates from the old course which flows along by Thorpe Green, creating a huge island (private). On the north bank, it can be seen running parallel with the old Yarmouth Road and offers excellent fishing in winter, when the pleasure-cruisers are tied up. Roach are the main species, but bream appear frequently in many swims, together with some jumbo-sized hybrids. There is around half a mile of bank space at Thorpe Green with a varying depth of 5 to 7 feet. Anglers may launch their own dinghies from a public slipway, immediately to the left of the Santa Lucia Hotel. Boat-fishing is by far the best way of exploring around the island at Thorpe, as much of the bank is inaccessible, and – in addition to roach, bream, pike and tench – numbers of mirror carp running to over 20 lb have been taken in this part of the Yare in recent years. From the end of the island downstream on the north bank to as far as one can walk is free fishing, with access via Thunder Lane traffic lights and footbridge from Thorpe Road.

Following downstream past May Gurney's yard with access via Griffin Lane, there is then an excellent half-mile length controlled by the Wymondham Angling Club, which incorporates the famous bream hot spot opposite Postwick (sewer) Outfall. Club membership includes the pits at Shropham (see Stillwaters). The club's secretary is T. Binks (Tel: 01603 405341).

Boats to fish this area can be hired at £8 per day from Griffin Marine, who also sell tackle and bait (Tel: 01603 33253). Their slipway can be used for £4 by those with their own craft.

Starting back again on the southern bank, there is a lovely length accessible from Whitlingham Lane, close to Trowse road bridge. Public access commences at the wide bend where a dyke joins the main river, a favourite pike location with local anglers. There are one or two fish over 20 lb here, along with a terrific head of pike between 6 and 12 lb, and no wonder, for shoals of quality bream live close by and the concentrations of roach are enormous.

Winter trotting produces some bumper nets of roach and hybrids all along Whitlingham Lane (a popular summer picnic spot), where the river runs parallel to the road. Public access then stops at the sewerage works. There is a wonderful panoramic view of the River Yare valley from the A47 southern bypass where it spans the River at Whitlingham, just above Postwick Sewerage Works. The famous Postwick outfall swim can, in fact, be seen from this long bridge if looking to the right when travelling towards Great Yarmouth.

The next easily accessible free fishing is at Bramerton, on the south bank, known locally as Woods End, and lovingly named after the public house which stands next to the water. Anglers wishing to park only should ask permission from the landlord (Tel: 01508 538296) who is usually sympathetic to anglers. There is no fishing directly in front of the pub without prior permission. Fishing here is quite comfortable, and bags of roach and dace are not difficult to come by, with the flood tide usually providing better sport. Recent years have shown that fishing casters close to the bottom takes some beating, though maggots still produce fish when trotting with the stream. However, the ledger invariably contacts a better class of fish, including bream which run from 1 to 4 lb. Fishing after dark in a baited swim is the best way of taking a real bag of bream along this reach. Fishing is free from the public footpath which stretches from the Woods End public house downriver for a short distance. A little further downstream, in the vicinity of Surlingham church, the highest match weight ever for the River Yare was made by Denis Pratt in 1993 during the Yare Champion-ships with a staggering 150 lb of bream that included specimens to 8 lb. Further downstream on the northern – opposite – bank lies the village of Brundall. Access from here to Surlingham Broad is just across the river, where the broad is fed from the Yare via the south bank (see The Broads).

Fishing in Brundall can be good around the boat dyke areas and in Brundall Dyke itself. Early-morning sessions during the summer can produce quality roach and some average-sized bream, but fishing from October onwards can be particularly rewarding. A big pike is not out of the question, especially if roach are numerous at a particular sport, which they often are. However, one often needs to move around a bit to locate them. Tackle and bait may be obtained from Brundall Angling and Yare Boatique (Tel: 01603 715289) situated on the riverside. Angling dinghies are available at £8 per day from Fencraft at Riverside Estate, Brundall (Tel: 01603 715011). To use Fencraft's slipway costs £5. Travelling still further downstream, the Yare cuts through Strumpshaw Marshes, where there is little access to the waterside. However, on the next slow bend a dyke leading to Rockland Broad (the shorter of two dykes that feed Rockland) marks the start of access on the southern bank side, where fishing is free and controlled by the river authority. There are nearly three miles of fabulous fishing on this bank, down to just beyond Langley Green, with access via the Beauchamp Arms roadway, which is off the Rockland St Mary road from Norwich. The NRA also has a half-mile piece of the north bank with access via Buckenham Carrs (private) and a tiny section downriver at Cantley.

As throughout much of the tidal Yare, roach are of a high average size in these reaches. One seldom takes fish under 6 oz and yet, rather strangely, few are caught over the 1½ lb mark but monster roach do exist, and just a sprinkling of 2 lb fish are recorded each year. Bream are localised and found in numbers mostly where the river bends slowly, where if the angler is lucky there might be just a few yards of slow water close to the bank, provided the tide is flowing the right way, of course.

The Yare in these wide, deep tidal reaches is indeed a formidable river, and the person used to light float-fishing such venues as canals and ponds will need to rethink his tackle arrangements.

The combination of strong currents and deep water, from 12 to as much as 20 feet, necessitates plenty of lead on the line. Float-fishing close to the bank is often possible, but the bait should be kept well down. When the tide is at its strongest, even ledger-weights of an ounce or more may bounce along the bottom, but this can be remedied somewhat by restricting casting distance and actually casting downstream rather than straight out. This will lessen the angle of drag on the line and keep the bait on the bottom. In any event, a certain amount of juggling with end tackle is necessary as the flow increases from slack water to the top of the tide. Bite indicators are generally of little value when the tide is really pulling, except a fast tapered quiver-tip, which is ideal for tackling the Yare.

Mostly, though, bites are positive and unmistakable if a fish is pulling from downstream. However, if a fish takes the bait upstream, it merely dislodges the ledger-weight and the rod eases back until the weight catches again. Many anglers ignore these bites, thinking that the ledger-weight is merely repositioning itself, so to be certain, hit anything questionable, once the weight has reached a holding position.

As far as baits are concerned, I prefer breadflake, maggots and worm, in that order, because I hate catching tiny eels, of which the Yare in places is chock-a-block, but meaty baits do prove effective, especially for bream. In any event, and whatever bait one uses, some stiff groundbait will be needed to keep the fish in the swim. It should be used in quantity and thrown well upstream to allow for the time it takes to reach the bottom. I often prefer to use a block end feeder if using maggots, to make doubly certain that my bait ends up close to groundbait; or bait with flake for the quality fish. Play a sizeable fish very carefully in this tidal water and try not to hurry it towards the net. Many a huge bream has been lost in this way, so if a slab-sized beauty will not play ball and comes upstream against the flow, go downstream and net it when on the surface.

Opposite Cantley, on the sound bank side, lie Langley Marshes with a neighbouring dyke that runs almost to the road and adjacent public house. Sport can be good in the dyke for roach, bream and occasionally a tench or goodish pike, especially where it enters the Yare.

Slowly bending downstream, one reaches Hardley Cross, where the River

Chet joins the Yare, but half a mile upstream from this confluence lies Hardley Dyke, which might be worth exploring. It lies on the south bank, with access from Hardley Street. Further downriver, one reaches Reedham Ferry, the only operative ferry across the river (there is a slipway controlled by Reedham Ferry Inn, Tel: 01493 700429, where for a charge of £3 anglers may launch their own craft) and then the deep New Cut joining the Yare and Waveney which flow two miles apart at this point but gradually run together to Breydon Water. Here, they enter this huge brackish broad which is four miles long and one mile wide and which enters Great Yarmouth, with the River Bure flowing in from the north, finally to spew its waters into the North Sea at Gorleston.

Fishing on these last ten miles of the tidal Yare, from Cantley downstream, is from October onwards solely dependent on salt tides and whether or not the sugar-beet factory at Cantley is working. Many local anglers leave this area well alone because of this factory, as its waste pipe, which flows into the Yare, turns the water orange and ruins sport.

SUFFOLK RIVERS

The River Alde
Although close on forty miles long, this little river offers limited potential. It starts with feeder streams in the Dennington area, which amalgamate in Bruisyard. At this stage a tiny river, it then flows south-easterly through Rendham and close by Great Glemham. It holds some shoals of dace and even the odd trout in this area, which is mostly under private control with no public access as it trundles down to the bridge at Stratford St Andrew. From here onwards, there are odd shoals of roach in addition to dace, but fish density is still quite low. In fact, the most productive length is the last one and a half miles of its course from Langham Bridge down to the tidal sluices just upstream from Snape road bridge, carrying the B1069 road.

The northern bank, starting from the railway bridge above Langham Bridge and going down to the Holland Sluice, just up from Snape Bridge, is owned by Mr Turner of Burnt House Farm, adjacent to Langham Bridge. Polite anglers are usually allowed access to this two-mile beat, provided they ask first.

The flow is fairly slow (unless the sluice is in operation, when the water really rockets along) with a depth of around 2 to 3 feet, plus the odd hole going to 6 feet. These are ideal conditions for stick-float fishing, in fact, and there are some good dace and roach present – winter fishing usually producing more consistent results.

Below the bridge at Snape Maltings, the Alde – now tidal – grows steadily into a wide estuary and meanders for over twenty miles through lonely marshes until it swaps its name to the Ore and flows out into the North Sea, five miles south of Orfordness (see Sea Fishing).

Additional information plus fresh-water and sea baits may be obtained from Brian Finbow at Saxmundham Angling Centre (Tel: 01728 603443).

The River Black Bourn
This interesting little river starts its life a little south of Ixworth with an amalgam of streams. It flows beneath the A143 in Ixworth and in a northerly direction through Bardwell and on to Honington. Depth varies between 4 and 6 feet, and the flow is quite gentle, allowing a prolific weed growth throughout. Naturally, winter fishing is much favoured, and there are some good-quality roach to be had on

the float along with dace and some excellent chub to over 4 lb. Between Ixworth and Honington access is extremely limited, but on the western bank, from Honington downstream thorough Little Fakenham to Euston Weir, a distance of about four miles is controlled by the Bury St Edmunds Angling Association. Day tickets are not issued, but the club has open membership and boasts a strong junior membership. Yearly membership costs £17 from N.J. Bruton (Tel: 01284 766074) and entitles members to fish in two large, well-stocked lakes in addition to the Black Bourn. Below Euston Hall, there is little access for the remaining mile of the Black Bourn before it ends its life by feeding the Little Ouse.

The River Blyth

This little river is born from streams which rise to the west of Halesworth, near Linstead Parva and Wissett. They flow easterly and pass beneath the A144 Halesworth to Bungay road under the railway bridge and on to Holton. From here on downstream, there are numbers of roach, with some topping the pound, plus dace and the very occasional trout. There is a public footpath running with the northern bank, starting a little way upstream from Mells road bridge, stretching most of the three miles down to Blythburgh bridge, carrying the A12 road from Ipswich. There are some attractive bends below Mells bridge, with the occasional deep hole, and winter fishing has the edge as the river has a prolific summer weed growth.

At Blythburgh, the river opens into a wide estuary which flows through Tinkers and Reydon marshes and empties into the North Sea at Southwold. There is excellent mullet fishing throughout these tidal reaches, with eels, flounders and odd bass.

The River Deben

The River Deben is of two distinct parts. It has nearly twenty miles of non-tidal upper reaches before it runs to Woodbridge and enters the estuary, whereupon there is a further six miles of wide river until it pours its water into the North Sea a little north of Felixstowe. The course actually begins life in the village of Debenham as a tiny stream but is of little value as a fishery until it reaches the village of Cretingham where, unfortunately, accessible fishing is rather limited, despite there being the odd group of good roach present.

Throughout these upper reaches, the river passes between picturesque villages and is very narrow, weedy and continually bending. The water is mostly shallow with a sluggish stream. Consequently, laying-on with fine tackle and using such baits as breadflake, maggots or worms, is generally favoured. Species to be expected are predominantly roach and perch in the 4 to 6 oz class, with some dace, eels and numbers of small pike.

The first piece of accessible fishing in these upper reaches starts at Glevering Bridge, where over two miles of the northern bank are controlled by the Woodbridge and District Angling Club which has an open membership. Club cards are available from Saxmundham Angling Centre as are £3 day tickets for this section.

The Woodbridge water stretches down to where the Wickham Market A12 bypass bridge crosses the river and offers varied fishing all the way in depths ranging from 4 to 12 feet. In addition to a head of roach, rudd, bream and tench, there are also some carp which leak into the Deben from a nearby reservoir. Being slow, the flow is very much to their liking, and during the summer months they offer excellent alternative sport.

Immediately below the A12 bypass bridge, half a mile along the eastern bank is controlled by the Framlingham and District Angling Club. Club cards are available at £12 yearly from Saxmundham Angling Centre; telephone Brian Finbow on 01728 603443. Here the flow is also sluggish, and in addition to some good quality roach to well over the pound there are numbers of bream to 4 lb, plus perch and some pike. There is good winter trotting here.

A mile below Wickham Market, the Deben flows into a circular lake called Loudham Decoy and out of the lake's southern end, where it is spanned by the Ipswich to Saxmundham railway before it meanders down to Ufford. There is unfortunately little public access, although the fishing is quite good in these last couple of miles before the Deben pours into the deep weir pool at the Iron Bridge in Melton and becomes tidal with the fishing free.

Flowing beneath Wilford Bridge and on to Woodbridge, where it widens considerably into the estuary, the Deben is now on its last six miles. Fishing is most varied and – although species have changed to mullet, bass, sea trout, flounders and eels – many anglers use their freshwater gear to good effect. All worm baits work well in this estuary, which finally pumps into the North Sea as the boundary between Bawdsey and Felixstowe (see Sea Fishing).

The River Dove

The River Dove is of little consequence as a fishery until it reaches the town of Eye, but from here on there are five miles of interesting fishing, suited in particular to the roaming type of angler, until it joins the Waveney one mile north of Hoxne, with quality dace and roach predominating. Generally, the flow is quite sluggish, and during the summer months weed growth can be prolific. Some of the fishing is free to those who show politeness by asking permission from local farmers, and for a short stretch immediately down from Oakley bridge to where the Dove joins the Waveney fishing is controlled by the Diss Angling Club. This last section of the Dove can produce some good bags of roach, particularly during the winter whenever the river runs coloured, and to fish it anyone may join the Diss Angling Club which also has four miles of the Waveney, plus a large mere in the middle of Diss (see Stillwaters – Members Only). Club membership costs £14 annually from Myhill's Tackle in Diss (Tel: 01379 642465) or from Waveney Angling in Harleston (Tel: 01379 854886).

The River Gipping

The River Gipping rises due east of Stowmarket as a result of two streams merging, and flows in a narrow and winding course, passing beneath the Norwich to London railway line on its way to Stowmarket. Here it is joined by the Rattlesden River, and the Gipping becomes a slightly larger course, holding predominantly roach, plus some dace and pike. Along the west bank in Stowmarket for a distance of 400 yards at Greens Meadow, the fishing is controlled by the Gipping Valley Angling Club. Club membership costs £12 from Bosmere Tackle, Needham Market (Tel: 01449 721808).

Starting half a mile below Stowmarket on the east bank, there is over two miles of free fishing from the towpath all the way down to just below Hawksmill. As the Gipping flows down through Needham Market and on to Baylham, it passes several excellent stillwaters, namely Needham Lake, Bosmere Lake, Alderson Lake, Causeway Lake and Barham Pits (see Stillwaters – Members Only). In Needham Market, a short stretch of the river, running beside Needham Lake, is also controlled by the Gipping Valley Angling Club, holding quality roach, dace, chub, perch and pike. Those desiring maximum access to the River Gipping should note that an enormous length, over ten miles in fact, is controlled by the Gipping Angling Preservation Society, which – under the guidance of its general manager, George Alderson – has transformed much of the river from its pollution-problem days of the 1950s and 1960s into what is now the most prolific running-water fishery in the whole of East Anglia. Massive stocking programmes were carried out between 1953 and 1973, which included most species of freshwater fish, among them tench and carp. Anyone may join the society by applying to George Alderson, 19 Clover Close, Chantry Estate, Ipswich (Tel: 01473 602828). Yearly subscriptions, which also cover extensive lake and pit fishing, cost adults £33, with reduced rates for senior citizens and juniors. For adults and students there is also an extra, first-year joining fee of £10.

Going downstream from Baylham, the river is still mostly shallow, with odd deep holes holding large quantities of roach and chub. It consistently produces good bags of chub to the 4 lb mark and roach over the pound, with stick-float fishing during the autumn to winter months offering the best prospects. Due to a prolific weed growth, summer fishing is not easy. The Gipping meanders onwards towards Ipswich, passing beneath the B1113 road in Great Blackenham and then beneath the Norwich to London railway line. On the east bank at Station Road in Claydon, a few hundred yards are controlled by the Gipping Valley Angling Club, but nearly everywhere else is in the control of the Gipping Angling Preservation Society. Below where the A1100 crosses the river down to Bramford is not so prolific as the upper reaches, but the stretch at Sproughton road bridge, starting along the eastern bank and following the footpath for two miles down to the first railway bridge, is also controlled by the Gipping Angling Preservation Society and is excellent fishing. Day permits are available for this stretch from all local tackle dealers. Winter roaching on the float is fabulous.

From the railway bridge below Sproughton, the river widens considerably, with depths between 10 and 15 feet, and here is a super one-and-a-half-mile length controlled by the Ipswich Borough Council.

The Gipping has now entered Ipswich and transformed into more of a slow-moving canal than a river, holding a good head of roach and bream plus some tench and even the odd carp. Fishing along this reach is allowed only from the purposely constructed angling platforms, and day permits or season permits are available from all local tackle shops in Ipswich.

This stretch is managed for the council by the Gipping Angling Preservation Society, which has regularly stocked this part of the river, as throughout. The stretch ends at Yarmouth Road bridge, below which sport slowly peters out as the river becomes tidal at West End Sluice and feeds the Orwell estuary. There is still some saltwater sport to be had, however, from the power-station downstream, with flounders, eels, mullet and school bass. A huge, thick-lipped, grey mullet was caught from the Orwell mouth in 1994 by Andy Gallagher, weighing 8 lb 3¼ oz. It accepted free lined breadflake.

The River Hundred

Were it in Lincolnshire, this little river would be called a drain, and that is exactly what it looks like, being narrow, shallow and a sluggish channel throughout most of its length. Its life starts with an enormous network of drainage dykes, ditches and streams a few miles south of Beccles, to meander easterly towards Kessingland, where it is spanned by the A12 Lowestoft to Southwold road. Much of this lower part of the river, which holds numbers of good quality roach to the pound, some rudd, tench, the occasional specimen bream and pike, is unfortunately inaccessible and controlled by local clubs. After passing through lonely marshes for another two miles, it finishes its short life by spilling out onto the beach via a pumping station.

45

The River Lark

The River Lark rises from a source of numerous streams, several miles due south of Bury St Edmunds, and flows in a north-westerly direction through Bury, Hengrave and Lackford, where the West Stow Country Park lies adjacent to the northern bank (see Stillwaters – Members Only). The course then follows the A1101 Mildenhall road through Icklingham and on to Barton Mills, where it flows beneath the A11 Norwich to London road. Fishing in the high upper reaches is predominantly for trout and dace, although limited numbers of roach and pike also exist. Much is in the hands of trout syndicates with little public access. However, the Lark Angling and Preservation Society, for a £100-a-year fee covering a two-fish-per-visit limit, allows access to a fly-only section all the way from Lackford to Barton Mills. This covers nearly four miles of trout fishing for brownies, which are regularly stocked. This is open to members of the Lark Angling and Preservation Society only, but anyone may join the club, and the membership fee is £10 yearly. The secretary is E. West, 8 Arrowhead Drive, Lakenheath (Tel: 01842 861369).

At the Gasworks Pool in Mildenhall, the Lark divides and passes through double lock gates and changes pace to a more sedate river, so typical of fenland roach and bream rivers. The Mildenhall Club then controls the cricket field section, followed again by the Lark Angling and Preservation Society almost halfway to the Jude's Ferry pub, where the West Roe road spans the river. Below this point, the Mildenhall and Lark clubs swap sides all the way across the fen at West Roe.

I used to love fishing this part of the Lark many years ago when in my late teens, and the long drive from North London, where I then lived, always seemed well worthwhile, with quality roach showing in good bags during the winter months. Unfortunately, pollution struck the Lark throughout this region several years ago and now it is only just on the mend, with some reasonable roach being caught once again, plus dace, chub, perch and bream. Weekly permits at a cost of £3 cover all the bank controlled by the Lark Angling and Preservation Society.

At Isleham Lock, the Isleham Angling Club issues day tickets from Isleham Post Office (Tel: 01638 780256), and fishing includes the side stream loop from the footbridge and immediately downstream from the lock on the western bank, for a distance of around two miles. This length was dredged in 1984 after suffering the pollution of several years before. The roach, however, are showing again, and they run to over the pound, in addition to bream up to the 4 lb mark, plus the odd tench and pike. It is all float-fishing in a slow flow with depths varying between 4 and 6 feet, and sport can be patchy. Below the Isleham Angling Club holding, there is then a private piece, after which the Lark flows down to Lark Grange, where it leaves Suffolk and enters Cambridgeshire to eventually feed the Great Ouse, just south of Littleport.

The River Minsmere

The Minsmere is a tiny but comparatively lengthy river, which in its upper reaches is known as the Yox. It flows down through Sibton Park with its adjacent lake (private) and holds most species of coarse fish. Access to the river is rather limited, and anglers should always ask the permission of local farmers and landowners prior to fishing.

The river finally ends as a maze of dykes and lakes within the nature reserve at Minsmere (private) and enters the sea through the New Cut via a sluice. From the bridge at Eastbridge going towards the sea along the southern bank of the New Cut is a stretch worth a try for roach, rudd and bream, although it is prone to odd salt influences.

The Rattlesden River

This little river joins the River Gipping in Stowmarket, having come just six miles from its birthplace in Rattlesden. It holds predominantly roach and dace, being quite narrow in most parts and, apart from the odd hole, rather shallow. It is a most suitable venue for the young angler.

Apart from asking local farmers for permission, the only public access is a short, 300-yard section along the south bank at Combs Ford in Stowmarket, where control is in the hands of the Gipping Valley Angling Club. Anyone may join for just £12 from Bosmere Tackle, 57 High Street, Needham Market (Tel: 01449 721808). This card entitles members to fish other parts of the Gipping and a lake controlled by the Gipping Valley Club.

The River Stour

For most of its course, the beautiful Stour, so wonderfully portrayed by Constable in his paintings, is actually the county boundary between Suffolk and Essex.

The Stour flows on a lengthy trail from its source in Cambridgeshire, through the villages of Wixoe, Clare, Cavendish and on to Glemsford, where the River Glem enters at the northern bank. All along these reaches, the Suffolk Stour breeds specimen dace, with roach predominating. The Long Melford and District Angling Association controls a two-mile length of the river at Clare, with day tickets costing £3.50. These must be obtained in advance from the secretary, N. Mealham, 6 Springfield Terrace, East Street, Sudbury (Tel: 01787 377139). Club membership costs £23.

Beginning one mile above the old railway station at Glemsford – just off the A1092 road – and continuing downstream to a point 200 yards below Rodbridge, between Long Melford and Sudbury, is nearly all double-bank fishing controlled by the Long Melford and District Angling Association, which also has a 6-acre pit known as Starfield. At Glemsford, the Stour skirts three lakes controlled by the London Anglers' Association (LAA), which also has two short stretches of the river at Clare and Cavendish. The river here is clean-flowing, fairly weedy and predominantly a roach and dace water. Following the stream down from Glemsford, the Stour flows through Long Melford and then to Sudbury, where the Sudbury and District Angling Association controls over eight miles of the fishing. All sections except the Island and Priory pieces are available on day tickets at £2 from bailiffs on the river. The club also controls a one-and-a-half-mile piece at Great Cornard, called Wright's Meadow. Additional information can be obtained from the Sudbury and District Angling Association, whose secretary is T. Fairless (Tel: 01787 312536) or from the local tackle shop, The Tackle Box of Acton Square (Tel: 01787 312118).

Within the town limits of Sudbury, the Stour offers excellent stick-float fishing in a gentle flow for dace, some quality roach to well over the pound, maybe even over 2 lb, some tench (six-pounders have been caught) and for bream up to 9 lb. Winter trotting when the river holds colour is particularly rewarding, and almost anything can turn up in mild conditions. A massive 29 lb 6 oz pike was caught by G. Baxter from the Stour here in 1980. In recent years, perch of all sizes have once again started to appear in numbers throughout the middle reaches of the Stour with specimens to 2½ lb.

Downstream from Sudbury, the LAA controls much of the first six miles towards Bures. Day tickets are not issued but anyone may join through their own clubs or as an associate member. The yearly subscription costs £25 and covers a wealth of fishing not only in Suffolk but all over southern England. Apply to the London Anglers' Association (Tel: 0181-520 7477). Their membership represents excellent value for money.

I have fished most of this section from Middleton, down through Henny, Pitmore Lock (now private) and Lamarsh to Bures itself but many years ago when the roach shoals were very much stronger than they are today. Chub, however, have spread and are now fairly common around the 2½ lb-mark, with odd fish to over 6 lb and have something to do with the demise of the roach. Chub are now to be found throughout much of the middle river from Brundon above Sudbury to as far down as Wormingford and provide good sport, along with the occasional barbel. These were introduced several years back by my old mate Len Head, in conjunction with the NRA, and are fairing well. Future sport with barbel is certainly an exciting prospect for the river. Sport with roach, including a few whoppers, is still to be enjoyed along the famous Rookery stretch in Bures, where the water is exceptionally deep in parts.

I can well remember on one cold day in February, at the age of fifteen, taking nearly 200 roach at one sitting from the Stour here, together with several dace and only a dozen or so fish measured less than 8 inches. The best went to 1½ lb. While catches of this size are now generally out of the question because the shoals are nowhere near so numerically strong, quality seems not to have suffered – and in the mill pool at Bures there is a large resident shoal of specimen bream up to 8 lb. Bream of up to this size have always lived in the Stour, and during the early 1970s there was an injection of enormous bream from Abberton Reservoir. Many of these fish weighed over 10 lb, and one such fish weighing 12 lb 14 oz was caught by Gerry Harper from Great Cornard in 1971 and actually held the British record for several years. Nowadays these giant fish are conspicuous by their absence, and we can only assume that the Abberton bream have all passed on.

A little way downriver from Bures Mill there is an extensive lake (also LAA) where tench over 8 lb have been taken in past years. Although nowadays such fish are rare, the lake holds a good head of quality tench plus carp to 20 lb.

It was in this part of the Stour that the old English record perch was caught (before it was deleted from the list by the present fish committee), weighing just a shade under 6 lb. Before the national perch disease of the late 1960s, a big perch was always a possibility from the river at almost any point, and in recent years two-pounders have been showing again throughout the river. Two miles downstream from Bures, the river passes beneath the bridge at Wormingford where it is rather narrow and nicely streamy, holding good dace and chub along with the roach. The northern bank down to just above the weir (private) at Wissington is controlled by the Colchester Angling Preservation Society, which also has several more miles (varying from bank to bank) of the river, stretching over ten miles down to Dedham. The Colchester club does not issue day tickets, but anyone may join by contacting the secretary, M. Turner, 29 Lodge Road, Braintree (Tel: 01376 323520). Season permits cost £30 and cover a wealth of local fishing, including the famous Layer Pits and several other stillwaters in Essex, including a new, 20-acre lake at Pedmarsh on the Essex-Suffolk border (see under Stillwaters – Members Only). Between Wormingford and Dedham, the Stour flows through Nayland and then down to Stratford St Mary. Zander have slowly filtered into the Stour but are in such small groups that as yet they have not disrupted the indigenous stocks. If anything, the roach fishing actually improves in these lower, wider reaches below Stratford, where depth averages around 6 feet and the flow is gentle. There are also a few more bream present, one or two good pike plus carp to 30 lb. Canoes pose a problem along this part of the river, especially at weekends.

From below Dedham Mill pool, starting one mile downstream on the northern bank, there is a one-and-a-half-mile beat controlled by the Gipping Angling Preservation Society. No day tickets are issued but anyone may join by contacting George Alderson, 19 Clover Close, Chantry Estate, Ipswich (Tel: 01473 602828).

The stretch on the opposite bank, all the way down to Flatford Mill, is controlled by the Elm Park Club, with day permits available from the bailiff on the bank.

Flatford Mill was once the end of the upper Stour before it became tidal and passed into the estuary down to Harwich harbour and into the North Sea. However, when the dam was constructed across the estuary at Cattawade, near Manningtree, with the fish-pass for the odd sea trout wishing to swim upstream, it provided extra fishing between Flatford and Cattawade. This is controlled for a one-and-a-half-mile reach along the south bank by the Lawford Angling Club, which issues day permits from its bailiff on the bank. Immediately below the sluice at Cattawade, where the A137 passes over the Stour, the river immediately spreads into a mile-wide estuary for ten miles to Harwich and the sea, providing some first-class sport with mullet.

The River Wang

Although the streams which feed its infancy travel for many miles before finally amalgamating between the villages of Uggeshall and Wangford, the River Wang then flows for just another two miles between the A12 bridge at Wangford and the A1095 bridge at Reydon Marshes before becoming tidal and joining the Blyth estuary to pump out into the North Sea at Southwold.

Between Wangford and Reydon, the Wang meanders along, lined by dense beds of rushes and reeds, and holds roach up to the pound. The Wang has suffered catastrophically from pollution during the past decade and – although restocked by the NRA – even if the fishing was

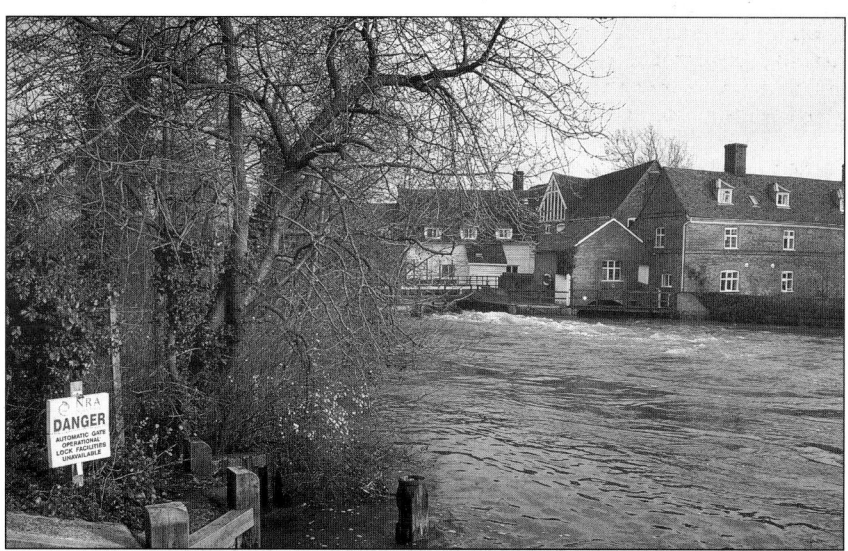

Flatford Mill is the last mill on the Suffolk Stour before it becomes tidal

worth attention, the once 'club-controlled' stretches are now all privately controlled with no access to anglers.

The River Waveney

The Waveney originates from the fen on Redgrave Common as the county boundary between Norfolk and Suffolk. It flows easterly through Roydon and on to Diss, but it is hardly worth consideration in these initial six miles, although numbers of dace and roach exist.

Just beyond Diss, the river is fed by two streams and flows on for one mile to Scole. In this area and in particular from Scole downstream, the fishing is good, predominantly for roach to over the pound, tench and pike. The stretch from Billingford Bridge downstream on the Suffolk bank is controlled by the Diss Angling Club. Anyone may join through local tackle dealer Myhill's of Diss (Tel: 01379 642465). Season permits cost £14 which includes the local Diss Mere (see Stillwaters – Members Only).

The club's stretch goes through Hoxne, where the tiny River Dove joins the Waveney, down to Brockdish, a distance of about four miles. The Waveney begins to mature and becomes more varied in character, with the odd deep hole to 10 feet on the bends between long, weedy glides. Tench are also to be found here, sometimes topping 4 lb, together with some quality roach, dace, pike and the odd good chub. Chub do, in fact, start showing up in numbers from Brockdish going downstream. In 1994, Gordon Pierce took one of the best ever match weights for the upper reaches of the Waveney with 106 lb of bream to 7 lb 2 oz from Brockdish.

In the Needham area, most of the river is inaccessible but, going down to Weybread at Lucks Mill, the local Harleston, Wortwell and District Angling Club controls around 1,000 yards of the Suffolk bank above the mill and also below on both banks down to Shotford Bridge. This is all a lovely part of the river, holding roach, dace, chub, pike and even the odd carp. Day tickets are not issued but anyone may join the club for the cost of a £12 yearly fee from the local tackle shop, Waveney Angling, in Harleston (Tel: 01379 854886).

It is all Harleston water again on both banks below Shotford for the two miles down to Mendham with Weybread Pits (fabulous carp etc.), running parallel to the Suffolk bank (see Stillwaters). The river varies its course dramatically almost every few yards with chub lurking beneath the overgrown swims where bushes shade the narrow twisting parts. Along the open, more even-paced glides, there are roach, real beauties up to 2 lb or more, and hordes of dace, together with a fair head of perch and pike. A good bream or tench is not unlikely either, though never in numbers. When the Waveney runs clear and weedy during the summer, freelining baits before the sun hits the water will take the chub and better-sized roach, but bags are not taken until the river colours and the weed dies. This is the time to sit well upstream of any easy-paced run and to feed in loose maggots or casters, followed by light float tackle with the bait just off or trundling along the bottom. Punched bread works well also.

As the Waveney winds downstream through picturesque farmland, it passes through a beautifully restored mill at Mendham (private fishing) and on to Wortwell, where it separates into several dykes, holding good chub, apart from some excellent dace and a few roach. The source then channels just south of Waveney Valley Lakes (see Stillwaters – Day Ticket) and makes its way on to Homersfield where fishing is free between the old and new bridges. It next winds through sleepy farmlands in the control of the Harleston club for a distance of over one and a half miles and provides excellent roach and chub fishing with large tench to be found in the holes. The Bungay

Cherry Tree Angling Club has two stretches here. Anyone may join the club, which controls a wealth of local fishing, Contact the secretary, Ian Gosling, 37 St Mary's Terrace, Bungay (Tel: 01986 892982). Membership costs £20 for seniors, £10 senior citizens and £6 juniors.

The river passes the Otter Trust and meanders down to Earsham, where it divides around a long island and flows through a weir sluice and a mill pool. Way back in the early 1960s, a goliath chub of 9½ lb was found alive one morning in the mill's eel trap and returned to the river. It was probably one of the original stock fish obtained from the River Wissey by the water authority for introduction into the Waveney but was unfortunately not seen again. This is a most interesting area to explore both summer and winter for quality roach, dace, chub, pike and even bream throughout the network of dykes starting below the mill. These meander across Earsham Common towards Bungay with much of the banks being free or easily accessible to the polite angler who asks first.

At the end of the Earsham Common, three narrow channels flow beneath the old A143 road. The Cherry Tree Club has control of these streamy runs which hold some quality dace, roach and some good chub. The Waveney then flows beneath the bypass and does a three-and-a-half-mile circuit around Bungay Common. There are plenty of good fish along this common and, if one starts at the Golf Club House and follows the flow from the Suffolk bank, many chub swims are to be found. Day tickets to fish the common are available from the caravan park on the Common (Tel: 01986 892338). Freelined flake, cheese, worms and slugs are killing chub baits here, which should hide a large single hook tied direct to nothing less than a 5 lb line.

These chub run to better than 6 lb with many in the 3 to 4 lb-class and have in recent years taken over from roach as the main attraction. In fact, one sees few roach on the common these days unless a long walk to the far end is made where the river deepens. Shoals are not large but individual fish are. Tench are to be expected here also, together with large bream in holes deepening to 10 feet or more. In the summer of 1992, Malcolm Runacres smashed the five-hour match record for the Waveney with 162 lb of bream, including specimens to 8 lb when pegged behind Earsham Pits halfway round Bungay Common. Pike fishing is also good along the Common, particularly for the wandering enthusiast who fishes artificial lures or wobbles deadbaits. Numerous double-figure pike are found, too, with odd fish over 20 lb. At the end of the Common, the Waveney flows beneath the bypass and then under Bungay's narrow Town Bridge. Immediately below the bridge, there are some cracking roach and chub (free fishing) along the short meadow down to the Falcon Weir. I caught my first-ever 2 lb roach in this very pool way back in 1957. It accepted a grain of stewed wheat, a killing summer bait on the Waveney, and there are still some big roach around for the taking in addition to good pike and chub. In 1993, P. Heywood captured the largest chub ever to come from the Waveney on rod and line. It weighed an incredible 8 lb 2 oz and confirmed my long-held belief that if ever an East Anglian chub was to break the British record it could well come from the Waveney.

The Falcon pool is very deep but shallows off at the tail, where the course bends downriver to Wainford Maltings. It is in this next mile of the Waveney that, in addition to good stocks of quality roach, one finds isolated shoals of those famously large upper-Waveney bream. These fish are beautifully coloured with blue black shoulders, bronze-golden flanks and fins of a mauve hue. They are so unlike their tidal, lower-river contemporaries, being virtually slimeless and able to fight hard. The average weight is over 4 lb, with specimens to over 8 lb.

I find the most rewarding approach for these super bream is to locate the shoals in summer during daylight, wearing polarising sunglasses, and to form some idea of their feeding-pattern and the route the shoal takes. They appear to wander among the weeds during daytime and select a deep hole somewhere along their particular route for the evening feed. A good plan is to pre-bait such a swim or two just before dusk with the intention of fishing when the light has really gone and the bream are less timid. Laying a piece of breadflake or paste on the groundbait carpet is my usual method, and I float-fish 'lift' style using a betalight float. This is an effective way of night fishing as one can maintain an interest all night long when there is a float to watch. Bites are nearly always a positive 'flat' or a glide away.

The Fleece Angling Club controls half a mile of the river on both banks immediately upstream from Wainford Mill. Below Wainford Maltings, the Cherry Tree Club has the first 100 yards on the Suffolk bank, which fishes particularly well in flood time, and the entire Norfolk bank all the way down to beautiful Ellingham Mill, with access from the A143 Great Yarmouth road in Broome, just past the Artichoke public house. As the river slowly bends for two miles to Ellingham, it is deep in parts and contains good-sized shoals of big bream with individual specimens topping 8 lb. The roach also average high weights; and there is a strong head of pounders. In addition, there are some good tench, a few perch and one or two really large pike among numerous lesser fish. Eels, of course, pave the bottom as they do throughout the Waveney, The upper Waveney ends at Ellingham where the course splits into three channels just upstream of the mill. These then rejoin a little downstream of the road bridges spanning them in what is now strictly speaking the tidal reaches, though little difference is noted this far upriver as regards flow, colour, etc.

Some of the fishing here is accessible provided one enquires locally for permission, with the exception of the two mill pools (private). There are some really large roach to over 2 lb, dace, chub, perch, good tench, pike and, at times, a shoal of good-sized bream makes its way upriver into this area, though the average size is not as high as around Wainford. Upon leaving Ellingham, the river bends slowly for three miles through marshland until it reaches Geldeston. Much of this section is accessible to those who obtain permission from local landowners and, in addition to roach and bream, there are numbers of double-figure pike, with specimens exceeding 20 lb and some chub to 5 lb-plus.

Cherry Tree Club members have access to some great roach fishing downstream of the bridge on the Suffolk bank and on the north bank at Dairy Farm. The club controls still more water further downstream at Shipmeadow (southern bank), with access off the A1116 road through Nunnery Farm. Before reaching the river, there are some good roach, tench and bream in the large dyke, and in the mainstream, which averages around 6 feet deep, roach are both prolific and of an excellent stamp, running to well over the pound. There is also a stock of bream and a strong head of pike, some reaching to large proportions.

Below the Cherry Tree's water on the same Suffolk bank, the river authority controls over two miles of excellent free fishing along Barsham Marshes, between Shipmeadow and Beccles, with access points via Puddingmoor Lane and Farm Road. On the opposite bank around Geldeston Lock, access is unfortunately rather limited. But for sport with both roach and pike during the winter, fishing is free along the dyke that starts in Geldeston village and joins the Waveney at Three Rivers. The Cherry Tree Club also control a length of the Norfolk bank at Geldeston down to three rivers at Dunburgh. From Dunburgh Hill on the same Norfolk bank a one-and-a-quarter-mile length down to Gillingham Beach is under the control of the Southwold and District Freshwater Angling Preservation Society. Membership is open. The secretary is Barry Reid (Tel: 01502 518198).

Despite the tidal influence in these last few miles before flowing through the town of Beccles, the Waveney retains that special friendliness for which it is perhaps best loved. In parts, it runs deep and quite narrow between beds of thick reeds and holds isolated, yet quite large shoals of bream to 4 lb, in addition to a prolific roach population.

Throughout the sheltered first half-mile upstream of Beccles town road bridge, where boatyards and hotels front the water, winter sport is particularly good – regardless of the weather – with quality roach predominating. Below the bridge, the quay at Beccles fishes particularly well from October onwards for quality roach and a few bream with float-fished casters producing the best results, though maggots take fish also, if somewhat smaller. There are also numbers of pike along this stretch, with some really big fish among the hordes of jacks. Whether roach or pike fishing the tidal Waveney, fishing from a dinghy produces the very best of results. Dinghies may be hired (without motors) locally from Aston Boats (Tel: 01502 713960).

Anglers may also launch their own small craft from the slipway on Beccles Quay, next to the Harbourmaster's Office. Depth really increases from Beccles Quay going downriver, depending on the state of the tide, with most swims holding between 8 and 12 feet of water through the middle of the river. On the southern bank is excellent free fishing as the Waveney winds through Beccles Marshes. The largest pike ever to be caught from the river came from the top of this stretch in 1980 to the rod of Dave Humphries and weighed 30 lb 1 oz. There is, in fact, a terrific head of pike throughout these tidal reaches, fed by massive shoals of roach and dace as the river twists down to the old railway supports, Aldeby Staithe and on to Worlingham, where the river authority owns a short but pleasantly wooded length of the southern bank. There are some really comfortable swims here with depths to 17 feet. Access is from Marsh Lane off the large roundabout out of Beccles, which bypasses Worlingham. Unfortu-nately, most of the Waveney in these lower reaches is simply inaccessible from the bank, which is a pity because, in addition to providing good sport during early and late sessions in the summer, winter fishing is really marvellous. So organising a boat back at Beccles and motoring downriver is well worthwhile. Besides good bags of quality roach and dace as well as the odd sizeable bream, I have taken lots of pike up to 25 lb from between Beccles and Worlingham and usually without seeing a soul all day after the cruisers have been put away from November onwards.

Below Worlingham down to Barnby and on to Burgh St Peter, fishing is of a similar quality all the way, although the flow gets strong and the water is more coloured, comparable to the lower Yare in the region of Buckenham Ferry, and the tactics of ledgering with a substantial amount of lead, in conjunction with plenty of stiff groundbait, work well. Bread is often preferred to worms and maggots, particularly if quality fish are sought. Maggots are a good winter bait though.

There are good stocks of bream between 2 and 4 lb and many roach with a high average size – in the 6 to 8 oz range. Naturally, there are hordes of eels and flounders also. Really huge bags of bream, often in excess of a hundredweight, with individual fish topping 5 lb, were once considered only ordinary catches from these lower reaches. However, as elsewhere, the Waveney no longer produces such numbers of bream. Today, a 50 lb bag is exceptional. Winding through lonely marshlands, the Waveney feeds Oulton Dyke, which leads to Oulton Broad (see The Broads), from its southern bank. There is excellent sport to be had in this area, particularly in the dyke at night during the summer months. Indeed, it is one of the best bream spots to be found in Broadland.

From Oulton Dyke, the course passes through wide bends onwards for four miles to Somerleyton, St Olaves and Haddiscoe, where the New Cut flows off from the Norfolk bank, joining the Waveney to the Yare at Reedham Ferry.

This straight, man-made channel offers two and a half miles of free fishing in deep water, which can flow very fast at times. It is spanned by the A143 Yarmouth to Beccles road 300 yards down from its junction with the Waveney, with access from the towpath running parallel along the northern bank from Haddiscoe Bridge. From this point downstream, there is just four miles remaining of this wonderful river before it enters the brackish Breydon Water.

These last few miles do harbour fish at times, depending on the prevailing tides and how far the salt penetrates upriver on the flood. However, one would do well to leave this section alone, for the fishing is always patchy.

History of the Broads Enigma

To tell the story of how Broadland evolved is not as simple as it might seem. Did the Broads originate from the deepest areas of valleys, formerly the bed of an enormous estuary feeding into the North Sea? Or did peat excavations during the Middle Ages help to create our now threatened playground of reed-fringed fisheries?

Historians disagree, with many conflicting ideas, as to exactly how this water playground arose for, due to gaps in the stratigraphical record, unresolved problems are numerous. In the eyes of some (particularly the older Broadsmen still living, who cut reeds or run boats), there will always be differences of opinion despite the efforts of Dr Joyce Lambert, whose comprehensive work undertaken in the 1950s favoured the explanation that such steep-sided islands of peat left around the margins of most broads could only have been made by the efforts of man removing peat for fuel to burn. Surely the name of 'Barton Turf' is a reminder as to its origin, and there are many other references to turbaries'.

As many of these excavations and the peninsulas they left were found to run in parallel lines and actually follow old parish boundaries, and as no mention of large expanses of open water was recorded before the fifteenth century, the case for man's involvement is almost beyond question. Samuel Woodward suspected there was an 'artificial' link in 1834, but not until the 1950s was scientific evidence amassed in abundance.

It is a fair assumption that most broads are no more than five or six hundred years old, although it has been suggested that digging peat for fuel and thus creating pits or broads (as they later became flooded) could date back to as early as the twelfth century.

That East Norfolk itself was one gigantic estuary only 1,000 years ago and, millions of years before that, actually part of the seabed, there is little doubt. The geological history of Norfolk runs side by side with data we were all given at school. During the Roman conquest, for instance, the estuary was so vast that strongholds at Burgh and at Caister were built to deter the attacks of invaders by sea, who might have sailed all the way inland to Norwich – and their fears were well founded. In 1004 Sweyn sailed a Danish fleet up to Norwich, which he plundered and burnt.

At this time, 'fingers' of the estuary went as far north as Horsey, while the mouth of the Yare extended from Caister to Gorleston, a distance of four miles. Sandbanks eventually formed in the mouth of the river over the succeeding years (to create Great Yarmouth), as the inland waters decreased and the estuary narrowed. The banking up of debris in the Yare estuary arose from the erosion of the cliffs to the north. Over twenty miles of the Norfolk coastline have been subjected to this erosion, with the sediment being deposited southwards by the great tidal currents, and, of course, it is still going on today. One look at the houses balanced precariously on the edge of the cliffs at Happisburgh and Mundesley tells the story instantly.

So, even from as recently as the time of Christ, a comparatively short period in historical and geological terms, the entire composition of East Norfolk and Suffolk has been constantly changing with water levels rising and falling, debris being displaced and banked, not to mention Man's intervention. Certainly, water levels must have been much reduced in the Middle Ages for peat to have been excavated from some of the broads as we know them today. Archaeological evidence from the Great Yarmouth area does in fact suggest that the sea-level, relative to the level of the land, was lower by 13 feet during the thirteenth century.

The Bure broads, for instance, like the Hoveton group, Decoy, Wroxham, South Walsham and Ranworth Broads, plus Rockland Broad on the Yare, although mostly now all silted to various levels of between just 2 to 10 feet of fishable water, must have at some time been excavated as deep as 20 feet. However, one wonders how the upper-Thurne broads like Hickling, for instance, were formed, because the bottom is, for the most part, hard and the depth but 3 feet. Was a thin layer of turf taken from this irregular-shaped complex and the diggings allowed to fill up? Or are these upper-Thurne broads completely natural?

The nearby and now landlocked broads of Filby, Rollesby and Ormesby also pose some interesting questions. Why is such an enormous sheet of interconnected waters, whether formed from old peat workings or simply once part of a deep estuary valley, now so cut off from the tidal influence? Was the Ormesby complex once filled through the tiny Muck Fleet Dyke (to the tidal Bure), then part of the estuary maze which bisected East Norfolk? Or has the land between (once all estuary) simply been back-filled or reclaimed by the silts of time? And what, I hear you ask, of those broads which are completely landlocked, some several miles from tidal water, like Alderfen Broad, Mautby Broad, Barnby Broad and Benacre Broad? Were they all once part of the giant estuary, or were they, too, merely localised peat workings later to become flooded? It is difficult to imagine broads like Alderfen once part of an estuary, but then, equally, it is hard to picture Norwich once totally beneath the sea. With regard to Alderfen, I quote from a paper by Dr J.M. Lambert which appeared in the *New Scientist* in 1960: '... even in the twelfth and thirteenth centuries turf was dug from deep pits. 'Alderfen pyttes' were so re-corded in 1209 and are presumably now represented by Alderfen Broad.' Dr Lambert also goes on to say of the Broads in general: 'That although field evidence shows the basins of the broads must have been dug out by Man, neither pollen analysis nor the stratigraphy of peats, muds and clays indicate with any precision when the excavations were made or when and under what conditions they were flooded and abandoned.' A highly intriguing puzzle indeed is the enigma of the Broads.

55

Of course, it is pointless wondering how they originated, when – if we are not careful and extensive dredging does not take place within the next couple of decades – generations of anglers (if there are any) in a couple of hundred years, may well be asking whether the Broads ever existed? And they might indeed have a point, for since the Broads came to be, vegetation has formed around their margins, considerably reducing their areas. Some broads have completely disappeared in just the few hundred years since they were dug, while others have merely 'decades left' before they too silt into extinction.

Unfortunately, it is a simple fact that the Broads are physically self-destructing. Those thick around the margins with carr or sallow, and especially alders, fare worse than others, as the debris of leaves and wood from the trees expedites the inevitable and helps hold the silt together. A typical example of this is the small portion of what was once Womack Broad in Ludham village. Part of today's relatively rapid deterioration lies in the fact that commercial usage of the Broads is linked almost entirely to the boating industry.

Since the last war, the number of power boats, both hire craft and privately owned, has dramatically escalated, although for the present their numbers have stabilised. Boat bookings over the past few years have even fallen, due no doubt in part to the recession and cheaper package holidays abroad. But the damage has already been done in so far as the angler is concerned. Erosion of the riverbanks is widespread because of power craft, with perhaps a little help from the burrowing of coypu, although these rodents have now been trapped almost to the point of extinction. During the holiday season the water is kept in a permanent state of turbidity, which, apart from cutting out light needed by rooted water plants to exist and for fish to spawn upon, results in a downriver movement of sediment. The consequence is that some of the broads are now silting up at the rate of over a centimetre each year.

It would be wrong to lump all of Broadland's problems onto the boating industry as we anglers tend to. As members of a society which requires an efficient disposal of its sewage, which demands a variety of vegetables available throughout the year, and which uses two gallons of water every time we pull the chain, we are all to blame. One of the major reasons for high phytoplankton production is the unacceptable levels of phosphorus entering the Broads' system through our treated sewage effluent. This is being cleared up to some extent by phosphate-stripping at the main sewage plant at Stalham, which feeds into the River Ant and then Barton Broad. However, phosphorus still enters the system from pig farms and from the surface run-off of herbicides and pesticides, although the highest percentage by far comes from treated effluent.

At this point, and at the risk of sounding contradictory, I must admit to having held the view that some of the Broads, now badly silted and seemingly coming rapidly to the end of their lives, have only deteriorated during the last few decades or comparatively recently. However, after delving into numerous books, this would appear not to be so. For instance, it would seem that both Rockland and Barton Broads, now extremely silted and shallow except for the boat channels, were no different around 1900. I quote from the book *The Norfolk Broads* by W.A. Dutt (1904): 'Rockland has an advantage over some of the more popular broads in its being unnavigable to the larger kinds of river craft. Its swampy shores helping to retain its primitive aspect.' Rockland today, to the penny. Nevertheless, most of the broads really are noticeably on the way out, and they can so easily be preserved from extinction. Proof of the pudding is Brundall Broad off the River Yare, near

Norwich, once badly silted and overgrown, which has been dredged and restored in depth to its former glory by private enterprise.

It is my personal view that teams of dredgers in permanent employment for the foreseeable future would be needed to keep Broadland in a reasonable state of repair, considering the commercial and natural pressures it bears. If it can be done by private enterprise, then surely the nation owes these medieval peat diggings continued existence.

There is at the present time much excellent work going on in the hope of restoring certain broads. The University of East Anglia have regular projects testing both fish and plant life, with perhaps the most successful of their work to date being the complete change seen on Alderfen Broad. First, all drainage dykes leading from the surrounding farmland by which surface run-off could enter the broad were blocked up. Then a separate 'outer' channel was dug around the perimeter to contain run-off with the herbicides and insecticides rich in nitrogen, phosphorus and potassium. This restriction of the food of green phytoplankton has brought about quite staggering results, turning pea-green water to clear. In 1982, for the first summer I can remember in over ten years of tench fishing on Alderfen, the water remained beautifully clear throughout the warmer months with a much-restored carpet of bottom-rooted weed, mostly hornwort. In time, it is hoped Alderfen's ecology can be restored to how it was back in the 1930s when the Norfolk Naturalists Trust purchased the broad, with the surface then a mass of beautiful white water-lilies. As far as the fishing is concerned, however, changing the water from pea-green to crystal-clear has created problems for the angler. Without lilies to shade the surface, fish retreat into the reeds around the margins and into the thickets of hornwort during daylight hours, whereas when the broad was thick pea-green, they fed with less caution, but then you cannot have everything.

The Norfolk Naturalists Trust started purchasing waters as far back as 1928 with Martham Broad. The Hickling estate was acquired in 1945, and now the trust has control of thirty nature reserves in Norfolk, one-third of which is Broadland – though not necessarily all water. It boasts 10,000 members and is one of the few organisations whose aim is to preserve the bird, animal and fish life of the region. I would like to have said that the Anglian Water Authority complied with its statutory obligation of maintaining and promoting fisheries, prior to the birth of the National Rivers Authority in 1989, but it did not. It started by ditching most of its non-tidal holdings in 1982 as a result of economic shake-ups at headquarters in Huntingdon and sold anglers down the river thereafter. Let's hope the NRA can do more for the rivers of Broadland and throughout the country.

Going back in time through the old record books of Broadland is quite fascinating. Yet by and large not everything has changed during the past 100 years – at least not in terms of the tackle and fishing techniques. We have simply become more sophisticated because there are far fewer fish about.

But what of Broadland in its heyday? Was the fishing really as good as we have been led to believe? Well, from talking to some of the old watermen who have cut reeds and rented out boats all their lives, it most certainly was. At the turn of the century, fishing was so good that inns and hotels catered especially for anglers, with boats readily available almost everywhere, which is more than can be said of today's facilities.

I don't, however, think we would fancy the rods then in use, made from greenheart and lancewood, in lengths from 12 to 14 feet. They weighed not ounces but pounds in those days. Reels were wooden centre-pins, a 3-inch diameter being most

57

popular, holding 30 yards of line, mainly of plaited silk, while terminal tackle consisted of separate gut casts and hooks tied to even finer gut. Floats were manufactured from bird quills – pelican, goose and crow – with porcupine and Norfolk reed floats also popular. Incidentally, if you have never tried making and using Norfolk 'reed floats', you don't know what you're missing. The materials are even free. As for baits, worms were far more widely used than today, both brandlings and lobs being considered the premier bait for bream, as was a large lump of breadpaste. Gentles, as they were commonly called, were just another bait, and not, as many now see them, the only way to catch fish. Babbing or bobbing for eels was practised by many marshmen, using a bunch of lobworms threaded onto wool and lowered on the end of a line and pole. Again, this is something today's anglers might like to try their hand at. It is great fun.

Groundbaits were mainly concocted from boiled wheat, rice and barley meal, although even in those days, mixes to which just water was added were sometimes available from the tackle dealers. For ledgering, the old pierced bullet seemed to be the order of the day, and most anglers used a two-hook rig. While during the last few years I cannot recall being asked for them, up to the end of the 1970s the occasional elderly angler still enquired in my shop for two-hook river paternosters with wire booms. Honestly!

It would seem that at the turn of the century, 5 lb bream were commonplace, and catches of this prolific Broadland fish were rated in stones rather than pounds – 20-stone hauls between two anglers being nothing out of the ordinary. They were even eaten, as, of course, were many of the pike caught. With fish everywhere the need for conservation did not exist.

Fishing was mostly by boat, moored to long, stout poles, which in the rivers were always parallel to the flow about a third of the way out. The only river traffic was wherries taking coal to the towns and mills and returning with grain. For an angler it must have been a wonderful life when you think about it, with quality bream as thick on the ground as roach, and with rudd and perch everywhere, not to mention the pike fishing. It would appear, however, that in terms of overall size (with the exception of those particularly large upper-Thurne broads' pike – an entity unto themselves) pike were on average no larger than they are caught today. There were simply a lot more of them because the fodder-fish shoals were so numerous. A popular pursuit was dry fly-fishing for rudd on Barton and on Hickling, using thick-bodied patterns such as the Palmers, Coachman, Black Gnat and Governor, etc. A bunch of six to eight maggots cast like a fly was also used with effect. Old Archie Taylor of Rockland Broad, now sadly passed on, always used a maggot-tipped fly when he was not cutting reeds, accounting for roach and sometimes rudd to over 2 lb from Rockland at least up to the early 1970s. I can remember him now, putting out on the broad with his old cane fly rod during the worst of weather (while I was piking) to take the odd roach.

The old record books show oddities like a salmon taken from a flooded marsh near Norwich in 1886 (sea trout still run up to the city but cannot migrate upstream), and going back still further a sturgeon weighing 11 stone was taken from the Waveney above Beccles in 1753. Some of the old angling writers like A.J. Rudd even mentioned the burbot, but not in enough detail for us to form a picture of their distribution. The same writer also mentions that even as early as the turn of the century, common or wild carp were plentiful in parts of Broadland, particularly the River Yare. I wonder what happened to them. Did they originate from the monasteries such as St Benet's Abbey? The late Bill Cooper recalled the days back in the 1920s and 1930s when there was a holding pen alongside the stagings on Ormesby Broad for anglers to retain their nets of large bream, so holiday-makers could see the catches. Ormesby, in fact, produced some huge bream in that period. A cased specimen of 12 lb was displayed in the Eel's Foot Hotel until a few years a go. A display of antique fishing tackle, donated by Bill Cooper is on show at Gressenhall Museum, near Dereham.

The real heyday of the Broads was the twenty-year span of the 1950s and 1960s. As the fishing became more widely known through the angling press, and as anglers in poor fishing areas travelled further afield, the Broads' fishing really took off. They came from Coventry, from Sheffield, Birmingham and London in their droves. Catches of bream were fantastic, with weekly catches in excess of 1,000 lb to anglers who fished at night.

Although it must be said that the daytime sport was so wonderful no-one needed to lose sleep.

The Broads rightly gained the reputation of being the finest fishing in Britain. The Hickling-Heigham Sounds complex was simply fantastic. Wherever you went and no matter how you fished, you caught sparkling roach and rudd, bream of all sizes and mountains of perch, with tench and pike available to those who specialised. After an apprenticeship on the hard-fished, canalised River Lea in North London, my first week's holiday at Martham in the late 1950s was a revelation.

The upper-Thurne system is still unique and like no other Broadland complex in that the water is all extremely shallow with a high saline content which enters through seepage and through land-drainage pumps via the salty marshes. Readings of ten per cent salt have in fact been recorded in Horsey Mere. In this

Nowadays anglers return their pike. This massive haul from Rockland Broad at the turn of the century would have been eaten

59

saline environment live brine shrimps, a valuable food source readily available to young roach, rudd and bream at every stage of their growth. I am convinced this is why everything grows so fast and so large in these broads, perhaps even the pike, which consequently never have a lack of the right-sized food throughout their lives – from 3 oz tiddlers to 30-pounders.

Sport was also good on all the other broads, of course, particularly Barton for pike, bream and perch, and not forgetting Oulton Broad for those truly giant perch. All the Bure-fed broads were also crammed with fish, but the fact remained that the upper-Thurne complex took the honours because it was outstanding.

To give a date for when the fishing actually first started to decline is impossible. There have been numerous localised setbacks in just these last 100 years, usually as a result of the sea breaking through the defences at Horsey, affecting the Thurne-fed broads – something the sea has been doing for over 200 years. In the late 1700s there were enormous fish kills caused by breaks in the sand hills at Horsey with salt-water covering the marshes for several miles inland. Since then, of course, acre by acre all over Broadland, swamps have been turned into rush marshes and marshes into grazing ground by banking up the tidal rivers and pumping water off the land. Steam- and wind-powered pumping mills were also used to free the marshes of regular rain floods, but today, so far as the fishing is concerned, pumping water off the land is too effective by far. One look at the horrible 'orange' colour of Waxham Cut, which runs into Horsey Mere, tells the story. The thick suspension of iron oxide sediment simply covers everything and deters rooted plants from growing by cutting out the light they need. Altogether, there has been a tremendous decline of aquatic conditions in the Broads since the Second World War. In modern times, I suppose more happened to start a downhill trend in the late 1960s than at any other time previously recorded. For starters, Alga prymnesium hit the upper-Thurne system in 1969, decimating the entire stocks and putting an end to unquestionably the finest fishing in England, just a year after Horsey Mere had produced the record pike of 40 lb 1 oz to the rod of Peter Hancock. Incidentally, although prymnesium, which releases a powerful toxin to interfere with fishes' gills, struck so disastrously in 1969, it might have been responsible for fish kills as far back as 1911. Other outbreaks have occurred since in 1970, 1973, 1975, 1982, 1984, 1985, 1986 and 1987. In addition to the huge pike, specimen rudd, perch, bream and tench were also prolific in the upper-Thurne system and all perished. Also in the late 1960s and throughout Broadland came both the national roach and perch diseases. Those massive perch of Oulton Broad, from where Sid Baker of Norwich caught the once English record, were wiped out, as were perch all over East Anglia. Even now, years later, perch are still making a painfully slow recovery throughout the river systems.

With roach, however, the future looks more promising, due to some consecutive good years for spawning during the mid 1970s. But roach were terribly thin on the ground after the national disease. As if roach and perch diseases, plus prymnesium outbreaks were not enough, Broadland has had to combat escalating pressure from angling, from motor boats and from a reduction in areas where fish can spawn, in addition to the previously mentioned unacceptable levels of phosphorus. Small wonder there has been a massive decline. I have heard it said, and recently too, that taking the Broads as a whole there are not a quarter of the fish present now as there were twenty years ago – and it would take a brave man to disagree, although there are quite a few signs to be pleased about for the future.

I see an immediate future with excellent roach and pike fishing, plus bream from certain parts of the tidal rivers and in particular the Rollesby, Ormesby and Filby broads. These super waters offer the most consistent fishing in Broadland today. Here and there for the angler who specialises there will be big tench, the odd carp and a sprinkling of rudd. Provided prymnesium does not rear its ugly head in a catastrophic manner again – and who can tell – I envisage the upper-Thurne complex of Heigham Sound and Hickling Broad to come on really strong again – as it has each time massive fish kills have occurred. Overall, I think the most consistent fishing will continue to be on the tidal rivers as it is at present with the Bure, Waveney and Yare – roach and hybrids providing the bulk of the sport, with pike in plenty. I, for one, certainly look forward to the foreseeable future with optimism.

Having written the above in 1985 for the third edition of this book, I am sad to say in this fifth edition that nothing has really improved, the biggest setback to the Thurne system being the estimated 100,000 roach and bream which died in March 1988 due to a surge of salt-water trapping them in the boatyards at Potter Heigham. There were further fish kills due to salt in the autumn of 1992 at Potter Heigham and for the first time ever in the boatyards at Horning in 1993. As we enter the next century, the biggest threat to Broadland, indeed to all low-lying land within Norfolk and Suffolk, is global warming. Since the bad floods of 1953, sea-levels have in fact risen by up to 6 cm, which means that a catastrophe is there waiting to happen whenever a fierce and prolonged north-westerly gale coincides with strong spring tides. This combination could at any time within the next fifty years create a major disaster to the entire ecosystem of Broadland as we know it.

How to Fish the Broadland Waterways

While this book is not intended to be instructional, it will no doubt be read by beginners and holiday anglers alike, whose knowledge of basic techniques could be rather limited. So, because the Broadland waterways with their strong tidal influences are so different from the venues most anglers fish, I think some hints on local techniques and end tackles will not go amiss.

To start with, it pays to accept that, unlike currants in a well-baked cake, fish are certainly not spread evenly throughout the Broads. Just like people, they prefer to live in locations which suit them and where food is within easy reach. This may sound an over-simplification but, generally speaking, river fish have their food brought along with the current every day, while those inhabiting the large, static, even-depth broads, such as Hickling, tend to graze over the bottom, covering much more ground. Bream shoals, for instance, may roam hundreds of yards in just a few hours so they need to be tracked down visually by looking for things like patches of bubbles or fish actually rolling on the surface. Alternatively, try pre-baiting just before dark with a carpet of mashed-up stale bread, well-soaked and stiffened with a cereal groundbait, and then plan to fish through the night, or at least till bites cease.

Of course, river fish roam, too, but on a day-to-day basis seldom anything like as far as those living in still water. So when after roach or bream in the tidal rivers, any swim is worth persevering with if signs of fish are present – or if fish have been caught from the same spot the day before. During the winter months, the roach shoals in particular occur in

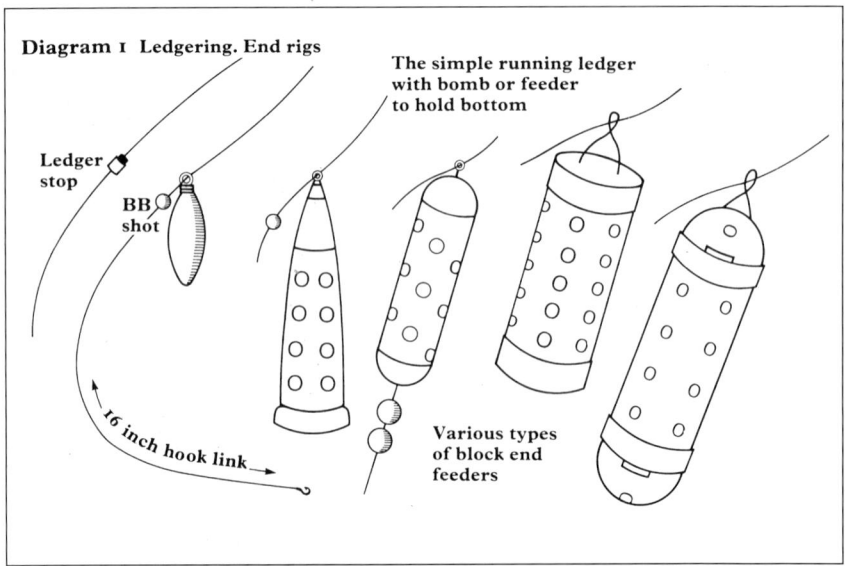

Diagram 1 Ledgering. End rigs

hot-spots. Enormous concentrations of fish, which occupy the lower tidal reaches throughout the summer, migrate upriver to evade the salt tides once the really harsh weather has set in. This is why sheltered town areas, such as the Bure at Wroxham and Horning, or Beccles on the Waveney, are crammed with fish from December onwards.

The holiday angler, however, can rest assured that by the time 16 June comes round again these same fish will once more be spread out throughout the middle to lower reaches, where they provide excellent, consistent sport during the summer and autumn. Fishing these tidal reaches, where depths can vary anywhere between 8 and 20 feet, can pose real problems for those not used to a deep, fast river. Of course, by far the easiest way of getting the bait down on the bottom, right where the fish are, is to ledger with a heavy block end swim-feeder, using a sensitive quiver-tip bite indicator which screws into the tip ring. The feeder's secret is that, once filled with maggots or casters, it delivers the hook bait right next to the loose feed, so bites come quickly and more regularly. Regular casting is necessary to concentrate a good shoal of roach or bream, so at least a couple of pints of maggots are needed for a session lasting several hours.

Don't cast straight out across the current, but downstream and across. In fact, over the very spot where you intend the feeder to hold bottom. Otherwise most of the maggots will be deposited in a long line across the river as the feeder bumps along before coming to rest. Keep the rod tip as high as possible to minimise water pressure against the line and watch the quiver-tip carefully. Any sudden jerk, either forwards or backwards, once the feeder has settled properly, should be considered a bite and worth striking. Sometimes, it could merely be the feeder repositioning itself in a strong flow, but then a fish may have grabbed the bait and dislodged the feeder, causing the tip to 'jerk' or 'nod' backwards. So strike anyway.

Due to the immense water pressure, which can rip a tiny hook out of a fish brought upstream too quickly against the flow, stick to sizes 14 and 16, going smaller only if bites are not forthcoming. Tidal-river fish are nowhere near so hook conscious or shy biting as their clear-water counterparts, so tackle can be what many would call on the heavy side. A reel line of around 4 lb test is ideal, with hook lengths from 1½ to 2½ lb. If seeking large bream on size 6 and 8 hooks holding a large lump of breadflake, then stick to the 4 lb line right through, but be prepared to vary the hook link from a basic 16 inches long down to say 6 inches if bites are really 'twitchy'. Alternatively, don't be afraid to increase the hook link to 4 feet when fish are taking the bait 'on the drop', just before it settles on the bottom. As in Diagram 2.

Swim-feeders, or a simple bomb ledger, can run directly on the line as in Diagram 1, being stopped with a single BB shot or a ledger-stop at the desired distance from the hook. Better still, make a simple, fixed, lead paternoster as in Diagram 2, using a size 10 swivel as the junction. Both hook and bomb or feeder links may be altered in seconds without dismantling, and bites are registered in exactly the same way as with a running ledger. The beauty of the 'paternoster' or 'fixed lead' is that you don't need to keep worrying whether it is still running or not, because it does not matter anyway.

For ledgering where the flow is gentle or next to nothing, as on most of the broads and at the upstream end of the tidal rivers, a screw-in quiver tip will provide a more sensitive bite-indicator. A ledger-bobbin which is fixed on a retainer cord and clipped on the line between reel and the butt ring works well also. See Diagram 3. Both provide valuable 'slack' to a biting fish, which responds by sucking the bait in with much more confidence. Groundbait, either cereal-based or loose feed such as maggots or casters, may be either thrown or catapulted in, without the use of a feeder, using a small ½ oz bomb or a couple of swan shot on the lead link to aid casting and hold bottom.

So much for presenting the bait on the bottom. Now what about some float-fishing to offer the bait on the move, tumbling just above the bottom, simulating how the current deposits it? The most effective way of trotting at close range is with a stick-float (see Diagram 4, Fig. 1). Spread the shot fairly evenly down the line between float and hook, using a smaller shot, either a dust or a No. 6 around 18 to 20 inches from the hook. Plumb the depth carefully and set the float slightly over depth. The real secret of stick-float-fishing is actually to overshot the float so it is almost sunk. Then, as it is pulled along by the current, keep it gently in check. Try not to 'over-control' or it will drift off course and be presenting the maggots along a different course from where you have thrown in the loose feed. This calls for careful manipulation of the tackle and a delicate touch, but it is a deadly way of catching roach and dace. Every so often, hold back a little on the float to make the bait swing enticingly upwards (as in Diagram 4, Fig. 2). Bites can then be expected almost any time as the bait drifts down again, often within a second of the float continuing its trot through. On some days, roach will only take a bait which is being slowed down by holding back hard. So don't be afraid of fishing well over depth and easing the float down really slowly. Where the current is even-paced and the water, say, less than 8 feet deep, a stick-float carrying six No. 4 shot or three No. 1 is adequate. But step up for one holding between 3 and 5 BB where the depth is greater and accompanied by a strong flow. If in doubt, always choose a float carrying more lead than the flow would indicate, rather than less.

For fishing in windy conditions – and always at distances, say, further than two rod lengths, whether on still or running water – the floats to use are wagglers: either straight peacock or sarkandas wagglers, and with a body to hold extra shot if required. These are always fished bottom end only (except when laying-on) either by locking either side of the bottom ring with a split shot, or with a couple of float bands (see Diagram 5, Fig. 1).

In a slow flow, concentrate most of the lead in these two locking shot with the minimum spread down the line. Whereas for fishing a medium flow, where you need to get the bait down quickly, keep all

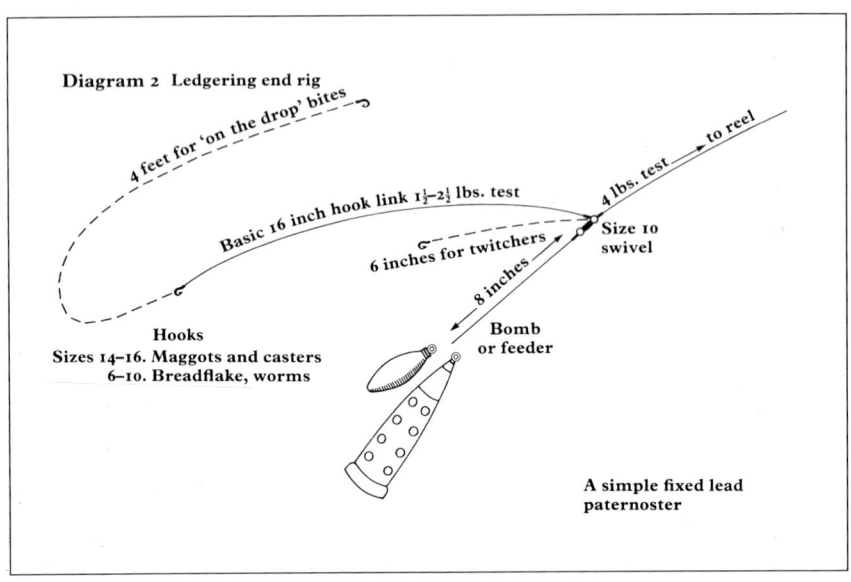

Diagram 2 Ledgering end rig
4 feet for 'on the drop' bites
Basic 16 inch hook link 1½–2½ lbs. test
6 inches for twitchers
8 inches
4 lbs. test to reel
Size 10 swivel
Hooks
Sizes 14–16. Maggots and casters
6–10. Breadflake, worms
Bomb or feeder
A simple fixed lead paternoster

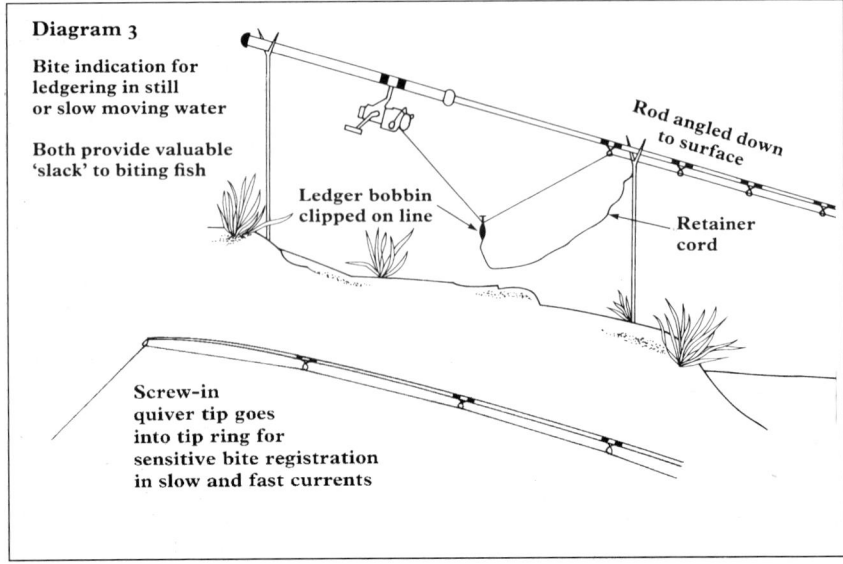

Diagram 3
Bite indication for ledgering in still or slow moving water

Both provide valuable 'slack' to biting fish

Ledger bobbin clipped on line

Rod angled down to surface

Retainer cord

Screw-in quiver tip goes into tip ring for sensitive bite registration in slow and fast currents

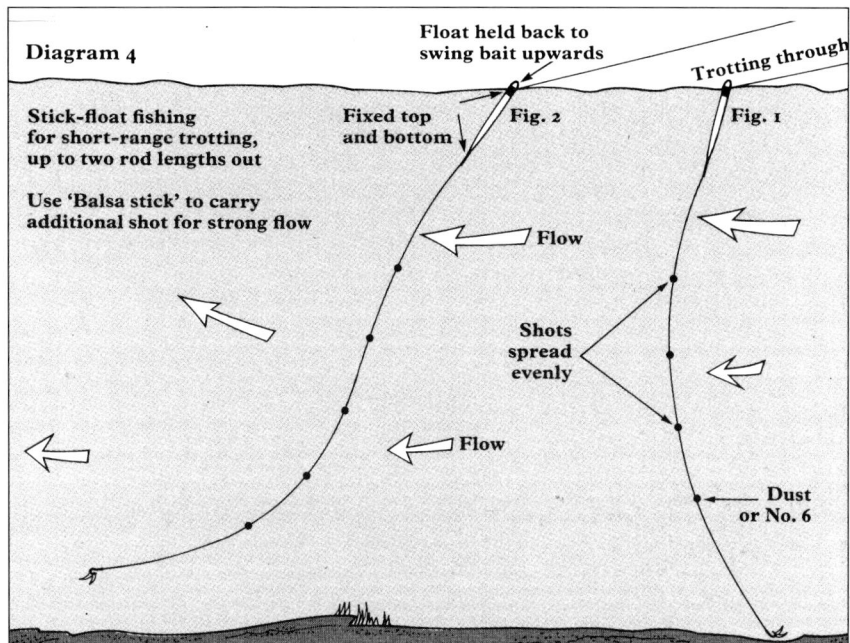

Diagram 4

Stick-float fishing for short-range trotting, up to two rod lengths out

Use 'Balsa stick' to carry additional shot for strong flow

Float held back to swing bait upwards

Fixed top and bottom

Fig. 2 — Fig. 1

Trotting through

Flow

Shots spread evenly

Flow

Dust or No. 6

the shot spread down the line as with the stick-float (see Diagram 5, Fig. 2). In really fast water, don't bother with spreading it too evenly. Bulk most of the shot at around mid depth and then graduate down to the hook (see Diagram 5, Fig. 3).

The float should not be checked as with the stick (except when straightening the line) but simply allowed to trot through smoothly at current speed with the bait trundling along well behind. As the float really precedes the bait when waggler fishing, be prepared for a long sweep-through strike, to set the hook, particularly if long-trotting, or fishing 30 to 40 yards out into a broad. Of course, the bait does not always have to be set to fish just above bottom. There will be times during the summer months when the roach and even bream will be well off bottom and will want to take the bait at the level at which they are swimming. So experiment at different depths till bites come. To revert to fishing on the bottom to encourage 'lift'

bites (as in Diagram 5, Fig. 4), fix a small shot 4 inches from the hook and set the float to fish a little over depth. This is a good general rig for static water on the Broads; for casting extra distances use a bodied waggler, which carries more shot.

To lay the bait hard on the bottom in a river (often called stret-pegging) fix a straight peacock waggler on the line with a band at both ends, just like a stick-float, and fix just one large shot, an AA or swan, 6 inches from the hook (see Diagram 6, Fig. 2). If extra shot are required, condense them into a mini-ledger (as in Diagram 6, Fig. 1), because shot down the line are not required. The secret of stret-pegging is to fish with the float lying perfectly flat, and set at least a couple of feet over depth. In strong currents it will need to be fished 5 or 6 feet over depth or even more. Just consider how the line is curved by the force of the current in Diagram 6, Fig. 2, and you can see why. Always cast downstream and across so the float comes

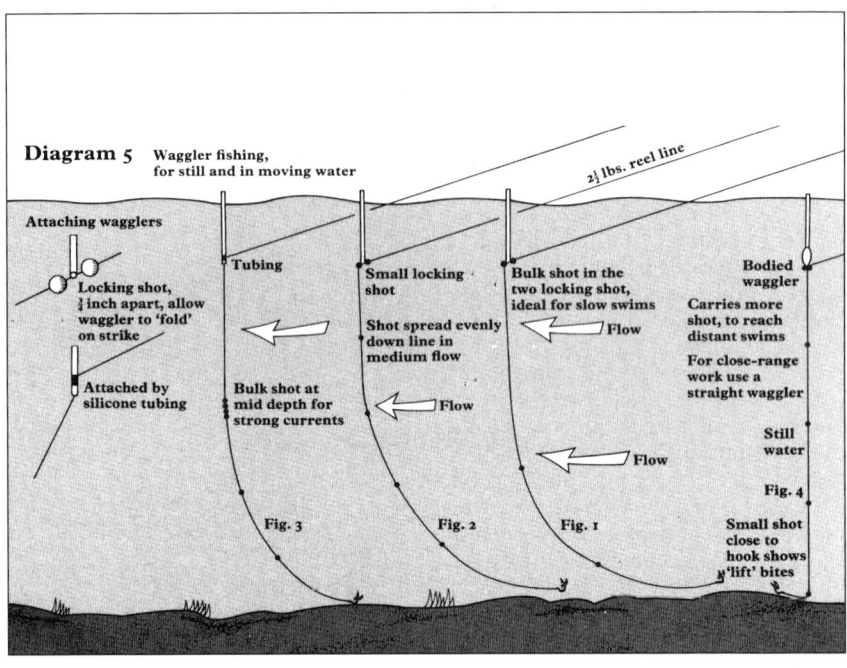

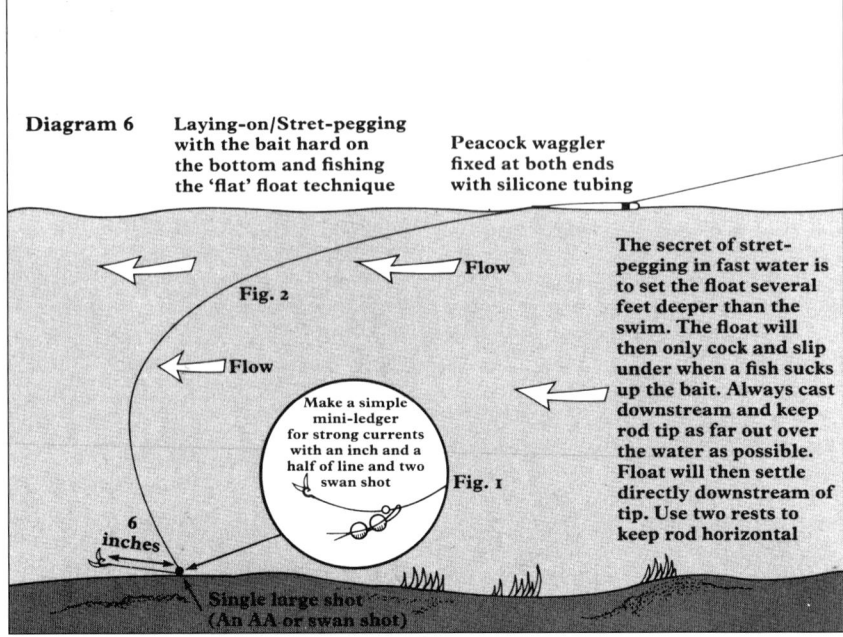

to rest directly down from the rod tip, although the bait might be situated a little further out. Bites are invariably bold, with the float simply cocking and slipping straight under without any prior warning, other than an occasional 'shake' from the float.

This method of stret-pegging, laying-on, float-ledgering – call it what you will – is a killing method of presenting a static bait. It works on a whole variety of occasions when one is after river fish, from the roach and bream of the Broads to taking specimen roach, bream, chub and barbel from the upper reaches of the Bure, Wensum, Yare and Waveney. What is more, simply by gluing a powerful beta-light element into the tip of the float, this is a method which can be used after dark to take those extra-shy whoppers. From the upper Wensum alone, stret-pegging after dark has produced for me double-figure barbel, chub to nearly 6 lb and countless roach over 2 lb. So I have numerous good reasons for recommending it. Try it for yourself and see.

BOAT HIRE AND SLIPWAYS WITHIN TIDAL BROADLAND
where anglers can launch their own dinghies

BROADS
Barton Broad (leading to River Ant)
Slipway opposite Barton Angler Hotel; launching costs £2. Telephone Mr Booth on 01692 630644, who also rents out angling dinghies at £8 per day.

Great Ormesby Broad (Eel's Foot Broad)
No boat launching. Angling dinghies can be hired from The Eel's Foot Hotel at £7.50 per day (telephone C. Walch on 01493 731441) or from Mr Barnes at £8 per day (Tel: 01493 368142).

Hickling Broad
(leading to River Thurne)
Slipway at Whispering Reeds boatyard costs £4. Tel: 01692 598314 Whispering Reeds also rent out angling dinghies at £8 per day.

Oulton Broad
(leading to River Waveney)
Slipway situated in Colman's Dyke at the rear of Nicholas Everet Park. Launching is free.

Rockland Broad
(leading to River Yare)
Slipway is adjacent to the dyke in Rockland St Mary with key to gate across slipway available from R. Dye, Tel: 01508 538256. Cost for launching is £2.

Rollesby Broad
No boat launching. Angling dinghies are for hire from Paul or Debbie at the Kingfisher Jetty at £7.50 per day. Tel: 01493 748724.

Wroxham Broad
(leading to River Bure)
Slipway is adjacent to the Yacht Club car park at the Broad. A small charge is made to anglers launching their own dinghies. Telephone the Yacht Club on 01603 782808. Wroxham and District Angling Club boats are kept here at Hospital Farm and available for hire to non-members at £5 per day. Tel: 01603 401062.

WAXHAM CUT
(leading to Horsey Mere)
During the winter only Mr Matthews has two boats for hire. Tel: 01692 598630.

RIVERS
River Ant – Stalham Staithe
Slipway at Richardson's Boatyard costs £5. Tel: 01692 581081.

River Ant – Wayford Bridge
Slipway is adjacent to Urwin's Day Boats, and anglers may launch their own dinghies free of charge. Anglers' dinghies cost £8 per day from Urwin's. These are bookable in advance only. Tel: 01692 582071.

River Bure – Horning
Slipway adjacent to the Swan public house, costs £5 with the key available from Ralph's Newsagent of Lower Street. Tel: 01692 630434. Can only be used 6.30 a.m.– 6.30 p.m.

River Bure – Wroxham
No boat launching. Angling dinghies can be hired at £5 per day from Summercraft. Tel: 01603 782809.

River Chet – Loddon Marina
Slipway at Mistral Craft costs £2. Tel: 01508 520438. Angling dinghies for hire at £8 per day from Loddon Boatyard. Tel: 01508 528735.

River Thurne – Martham Ferry
Slipway at Martham Ferry Boatyard costs £2 and is open all year round. Angling dinghies available for hire. Tel: 01493 740303.

River Thurne – Potter Heigham
Slipway at Phoenix Fleet Boatyard costs £2 all year round. Motor Boats for hire at £30 per day, including motor. Tel: 01692 670460.

River Waveney – Beccles Quay
Slipway adjacent to Yacht Station. Tel: 01502 712225 is free but only from April to November. It is boarded up during the winter months and not usable.

River Waveney – Beccles
Slipway at Aston Boats costs £6 Angling dinghies to hire cost £6 per day. Tel: 01502 713960. Open all year.

River Waveney – Beccles
Slipway at Hipperson Boats costs £4. Angling dinghies cost £6 to hire per day. Tel: 01502 712166. Open all year.

River Waveney – Burgh St Peter
Slipway at the Waveney Inn public house costs £3 all year round. Tel: 01502 677217.

River Yare – Riverside Estate, Brundall
Slipway of Fencraft costs £5. They also rent out angling dinghies at £8 per day. Tel: 01603 715011.

River Yare – Thorpe St Andrew
Slipway of Griffin Marine costs £4. They also have angling dinghies for hire at £8 per day. Tel: 01603 33253.

River Yare – Brundall Bay Marina
Slipway at Broadland Boat Centre costs £5. Tel: 01603 716606.

River Yare – Reedham Ferry
Slipway controlled by Reedham Ferry Inn public house. The cost for launching is £3. Tel: 01493 700429.

River Wensum – Friars Quay, Norwich City Centre
Slipway is behind riverside flats. Launching from this steep slipway is free. Cars must not be left adjacent to slipway.

River Wensum – Bishopgate Bridge, Riverside Road, Norwich
Slipway adjacent to the Red Lion public house may be used free of charge by customers. There is a charity box for others. Telephone the landlord, J. Barlow, on 01603 620154.

THE BROADS

Alderfen Broad,
Neatishead, Norfolk
More a lake than a broad, Alderfen is situated close to Barton Broad. For the most part of its 25 acres the broad is fairly shallow, averaging between 2 and 4 feet in depth, and is completely fringed with extensive beds of Norfolk reed and lesser reedmace. To contact the tench here, which average close on the 4 lb mark, it is advisable to moor up to within casting distance of the reeds and to float-fish as

close as possible. Favourite baits to sort out the quality tench, which run to over 7 lb, are breadflake, lobworms and sweetcorn. When hooked close to reeds, these tench really take some holding. So don't fish too light. A reel line of 4 to 5 lb test, with hooks tied direct, is advisable. Fishing is by boat only.

In addition to roach, rudd, perch, some good pike and plenty of eels, there are some isolated groups of exceedingly large bream from 6 lb upwards, reaching into double figures. The largest taken on rod and line weighed 10 lb 7 oz and was caught by P. Mason in 1990, but when catastrophic oxygen starvation affected the water a short while later sadly over 100 huge bream to over 13 lb died.

Route: Permits to fish this excellent water may be obtained from Wroxham Angling Centre, Wroxham (Tel: 01603 782453). Visitors are given advice on where to fish and are issued with a map of how to reach Alderfen, but first take the A1151 road from Norwich to Wroxham.

Barton Broad, *Norfolk*

Barton Broad covers some 150 acres and is fed by the tidal River Ant which furrows down the centre of the broad and is well marked for navigation. The Ant leaves Barton a little south of Pleasure Hill Island, which is navigable on both sides. Through the western gap between the island and the reedy shore, a broad dyke leads off to the Old Gay Staithe and the Barton Lodge Hotel, where fishing boats are for hire from Bill Booth at £8 a day (Tel: 01692 630644). Mr and Mrs King, who manage the hotel, cater especially for anglers. There is a £2 charge for non-residents wishing to launch their own boats from the hotel slipway.

Further along the dyke, close to Neatishead village, there is excellent fishing, particularly on mild days during the winter months. This is because big roach and rudd join the bream shoals and often leave the broad itself to avoid the salt tides, which may penetrate high up the River Ant. Caster and maggot baits prove most fruitful in this dyke.

Where the Ant enters the broad at the northern end, a dyke leads off to Barton Turf Staithe and Inn. All fishing on the broad is by boat and the visitor should make sure that either mooring poles or weights are on board, before leaving the boatyard.

Remember also, always row slowly and with the least amount of noise when approaching your swim. Avoid clanging things like bait tins and vacuum flasks on the decking, for these vibrations are the quickest way to ensure poor sport. Also, try to moor as far away from your intended swim as casting permits.

There are many spots to fish on the broad. One has the option of fishing the actual boat channels in up to 6 feet of water or a pick of the countless bays and inlets on either side of the boat channel, where depth varies between 2 and 4 feet. Favourite locations are around 'Turkey Hole', the 'Jungle' and 'Red Mill Bay'.

The bream may be taken from almost anywhere. For starters though, try casting to the edge of the boat channel from the shallow water and encourage them to feed by offering some light cereal groundbait. Bread and maggots are the most popular hook baits, but the bigger bream and tench sometimes show a preference for worms. Watch out for eels though. Laying well on the bottom with float tackle will nearly always sort out the quality fish, while 'bream flats', roach and the occasional rudd are oftentaken on the drop.

It pays to experiment if bites are not forthcoming and even to consider leaving a baited swim should sport not materialise. It will be found that early morning and evening sessions are particularly worthwhile, and anglers who fish through the night often take huge bream hauls. Most fish weigh from around 12 oz up to 4 lb, but much larger bream do exist.

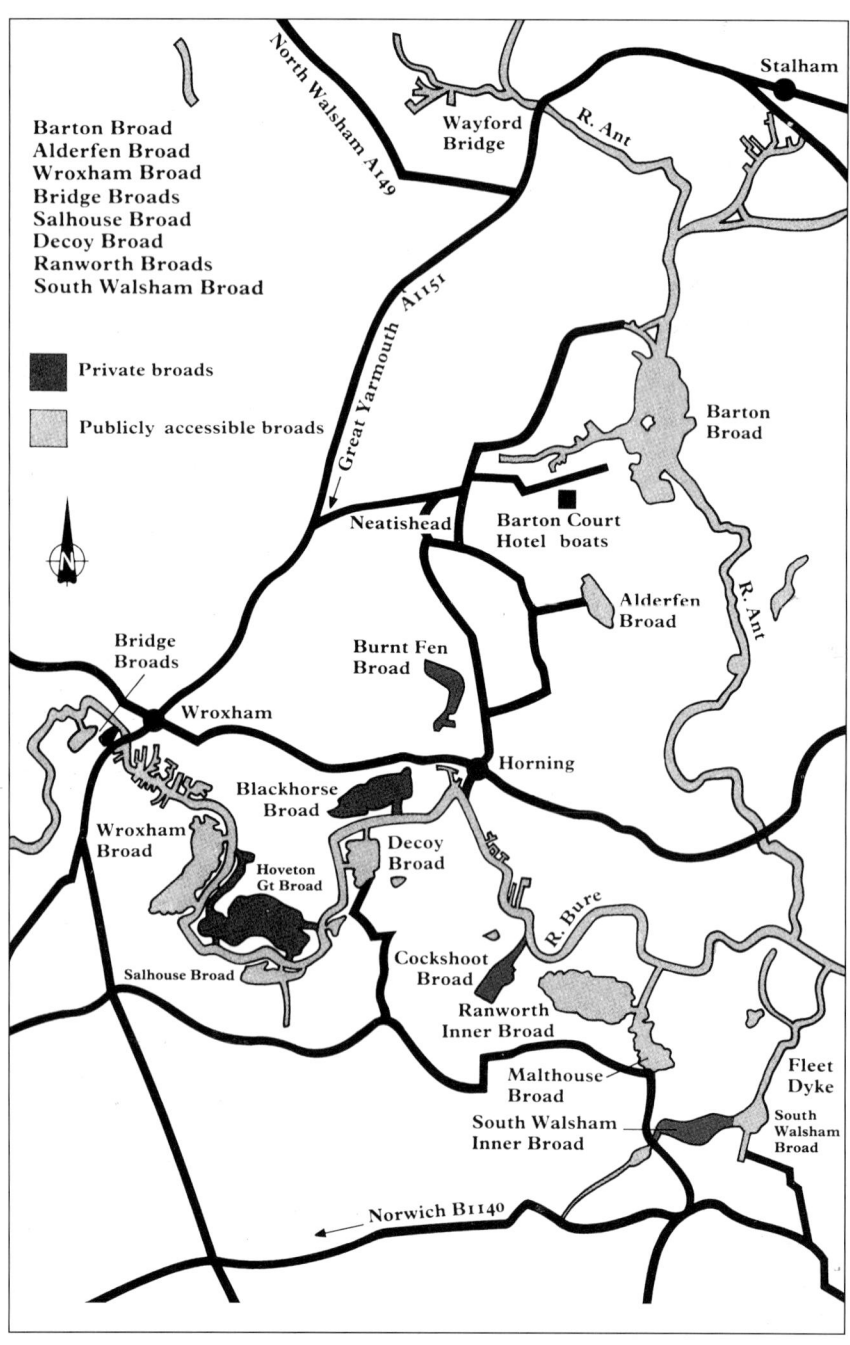

Barton Broad, fishable by boat only

Tench of reasonable size are periodically taken close to the reed islands or among the patches of surface weed.

Winter pike fishing can prove a little inconsistent on the broad proper. Best prospects are in and around Neatishead Dyke and particularly around Cox's Boatyard and up the River Ant all the way to Wayford Bridge.

Route: To reach Barton Broad from Norwich take the A1151 to one and a half miles beyond Wroxham and then take the Neatishead road. In Neatishead, keep straight ahead to reach the Barton Lodge Hotel and boats or turn left to follow the signposts to Barton Turf and Staithe.

Bridge Broad (West),
Wroxham, Norfolk
This 2-acre, irregularly shaped western end of Bridge Broad (divided off from the eastern end), and sometimes called Little Bridge Broad, is full of nooks and crannies and averages about 4 feet deep. There is a prolific head of roach and hybrids plus some good pike during the winter months. Access is only by boat from the River Bure just a few hundred yards upstream (via the southern bank) of Wroxham Bridge, immediately beyond the railway bridge. Fishing dinghies are available from Wroxham from Summercraft. Tel: (01603) 782809.

Decoy Broad,
Woodbastwick, Norfolk
This large sheet of water covering over 30 acres is controlled by the Norwich and District Angling Association and is for members only. Membership is available from the secretary, C. Wigg, 3 Coppice Avenue, Norwich (Tel: 01603 423625) or local tackle dealers. Boats are bookable in advance from the secretary only.

There is a little bank-fishing possible from the staithes but boat-fishing is advisable because of the enormous amount of good fishable water which can be covered. There is a deep area through the centre of the broad and shallow water with large lily beds around the perimeter where the bottom is largely of mud. The colour tends to fluctuate due to the influx of water from the River Bure which feeds the broad.

Decoy holds a head of bream in the 1½ to 4 lb range that are not always easy to track down and a prolific head of roach under the pound. Summer sport with light float tackle can be excellent, provided the broad holds some colour. Also, there is always a chance of contacting a tench, which run to over 4 lb. Other species are eels, a few perch and some cracking pike. Among a fair head of jacks plus fish running into double figures there are one or two real whoppers, the best being a 32-pounder from 1982.

Route: Take the B1140 to a distance of about six miles beyond Norwich and turn left at the signpost to Woodbastwick village at Primrose Corner and proceed along the road skirting Woodbastwick church. Turn left at the cottages at the bottom of the hill. Follow the sign to Decoy Broad and park in space provided behind cottages.

Hickling Broad and Heigham Sound, *Norfolk*

The area of Hickling Broad and Heigham Sound covers some 700 acres. The two are joined together by Whiteslea, and boats may navigate between them via Deep Dyke. This entire area is linked with the coloured and tidal waters of the River Thurne so that the further north one travels the clearer the water becomes.

The best sport is usually to be had well away from the boat traffic and the never-ending swell it produces in and around the countless reedy bays and inlets, although the boating channel can really come alive after dark.

Depth other than in the boating channel seldom exceeds 4 feet, and there are large patches of weed, not always apparent whenever the broad is coloured by algae bloom. Hickling, largest of all the Broads, contains vast quantities of roach from a couple of ounces up to a pound with ever-increasing numbers of beautiful rudd. There are also a few perch and tench plus some big pike among hordes of jacks. The bream here grow large, averaging between 4 and 6 lb and, on the right day, catches of over 100 lb are not uncommon. One of the largest recent catches, over 1,000 lb of bream to 7 lb, was made in 1994 by four holiday-makers boat-fishing at night during a three-day stint.

These large bream, which can often prove difficult to track down if the surface is ruffled so that bubbles and the odd rolling fish are not evident, are sometimes scared off by heavy groundbaiting. So it pays to go easy by fishing at a distance and loose-feeding with a catapult, unless night fishing, when the shoals usually move over a cereal carpet some time during the hours of darkness. Good areas are along the western shoreline near Catfield Dyke and at the southern end near the mouth of Deep Dyke.

In Deep Dyke itself, there is good sport from bream after dark as they move through from Heigham Sound. Regular groundbaiting throughout the night, with breadflake or lobworms on the hook, accounts for large bream catches, including the occasional hybrids in the 2 to 3 lb range. I have enjoyed some super evenings here, and always around dawn the bream suddenly switch off the feed and the roach come on until the cruisers start ploughing through.

The point where Deep Dyke merges with Heigham Sound is also a good bream and roach area. Nearly all over the Sound there is more colour than one finds on Hickling. Fishing near to the actual boat channel between the marker-posts and the reed islands can be good at times and, when the boat traffic has ceased, the channel itself fishes well, particularly at night.

Travelling further south towards the bottom of the Sound, where it funnels into Candle Dyke, the depth is slightly better and some good roach bags are

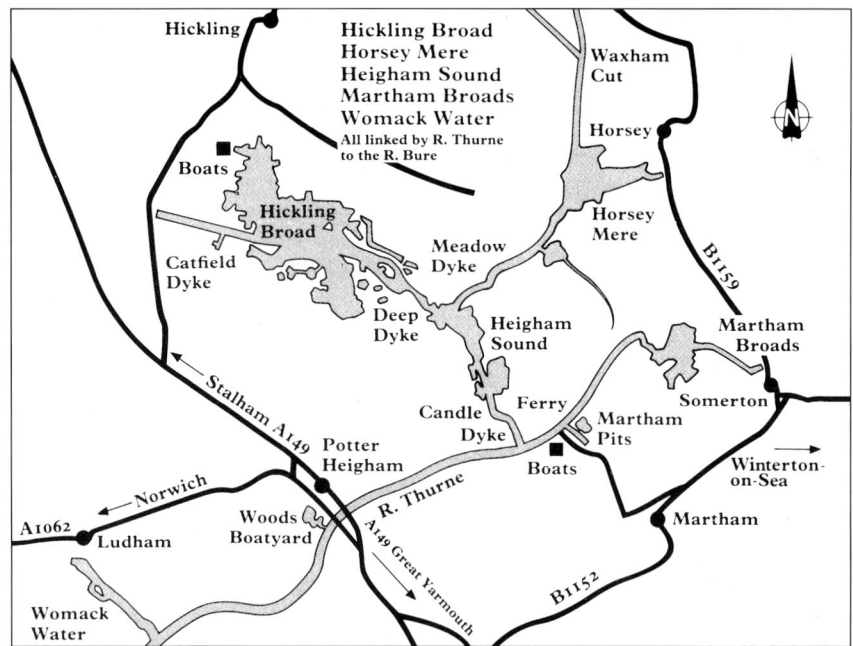

taken all along this reach during the autumn, right the way down, past the old eel set to the junction with the River Thurne. There are good bream bags here for night hawks, even during the winter months and, of course, pike fishing is excellent.

In recent years, several pike over 25 lb have been taken on ledgered deadbaits in this vicinity, but there are numerous jacks to wade through.

There is a little bank-fishing at the start of Candle Dyke and along parts of Deep Dyke, but just about everywhere else is surrounded by marshland thick with Norfolk reeds. It is, in fact, the epitome of how a Norfolk broad should look, and fishing is exclusively by boat. One may either hire a boat from Martham Ferry and navigate along the Thurne, up through Candle Dyke into Heigham Sound, or obtain one from the northern end of Hickling and start from there. The actual distance by boat from the top end of Hickling to Martham Ferry is the best part of four miles. It is therefore advisable to put some thought into planning a fishing trip and hire a boat well in advance.

Boat Hire: In Martham, Ferry Boatyard (Tel: 01493 730303) have six fishing dinghies available. In Hickling, the Whispering Reeds Boatyard (Tel: 01692 598314) have eight boats available.

Route: From Norwich take the A1151 to Wroxham and the A149 to Potter Heigham. Cross the Thurne on the A149 and take the B1152 at the next crossroads into Martham. For Hickling and the boatyards, turn north onto the A149 and follow the signposts.

Horsey Mere, *Norfolk*

Horsey Mere is a nature reserve of approximately 100 acres, linked to the tidal waters of the River Thurne via Meadow Dyke, situated at the top of Heigham Sound. There is also a dyke which is part-source of Horsey and which

73

enters at its northern end, known as Waxham Cut.

Horsey offers similar fishing to Hickling Broad in that it is generally shallow and may be quite clear at times with prolific summer weed growth. There is a good stock of roach, rudd, perch and bream with numbers of fish in the 6 to 7 lb range. A 10½-pounder was taken here by C. Barker in 1994.

However, Horsey has always been most renowned for its fine head of specimen pike. The 40 lb 1 oz pike caught here on a dead roach in 1967 by Peter Hancock once held the English record, prior to the stocks being wiped out by prymnesium in the late 1960s. Sport with large pike is now back to an enjoyable level again, and most winters see at least one monster over 30 lb being caught.

The fishing is controlled by J. Buxton of Horsey Hall, and anglers may fish the broad by boat from 16 June to 31 October. There is then a long pause for the conservation of wildfowl until 1 March, when the mere reopens to anglers until the end of the season. Pike anglers should note that livebaiting is not allowed.

There are no boats for hire at Horsey, so anyone wishing to boat-fish must make the long journey up through Meadow Dyke from either Martham or Hickling.

Boats: Contact Whispering Reeds of Hickling (Tel: 01692 598314) or Martham Ferry Boatyard (Tel: 01493 740303). Boats, during the winter only, are also available from Mr Matthews at Waxham Cut (Tel: 01692 598630).

Once on Horsey Mere, a warden will come round to boat anglers. A charge of £1 per rod is made. There is also a small amount of bank-fishing from Horsey Village Staithe (anglers can fish here all winter through), where tickets costing £1 per rod (two rods only) are available from either the Staithe Stores (summer months only) or Mr Applegate of Farm House, Horsey (Tel: 01493 393511).

Route: To reach Horsey Staithe by road, take the A47 from Norwich to Acle and then the A1064 and B1152 into West Somerton. Turn north in the village onto the B1159, which leads direct to Horsey. The hall and staithe are close to the road.

Little Ormesby, Rollesby, Lily, Great Ormesby and Filby broads, *Norfolk*

Covering over 800 acres, these broads form the largest complex of angling waters in the whole of Norfolk. What is more, they are not connected to a tidal channel and therefore not overrun by holiday craft. The only boats allowed are a few sailing dinghies and the craft of anglers. In fact, because the banks are marshland and thickly reeded, only boat-fishing is possible, although there are several good bankside swims adjacent to the two roads which bisect these broads (see map).

Route: To reach the A149 road separating Little Ormesby Broad from Rollesby Broad, take the A1151 from Norwich to Wroxham and on to Stalham. Carry on along the Stalham bypass over the River Thurne at Potter Heigham and on to Ormesby St Margaret.

To reach the A1064 road separating Filby Broad from Great Ormesby Eel's Foot Broad, take the A47 from Norwich, passing through Acle, and follow signposts to Filby.

Little Ormesby (Sportsman's) Broad, *Norfolk*

This, the most northerly of these five broads, is completely reed-fringed and fairly deep through the middle section. At the junction of the long, eastern arm, there is around 9 feet of water close to the water tower, a favourite winter piking area, but the arm itself eventually shallows off to between 3 and 4 feet. As for roach fishing, there are massive shoals throughout the entire complex to provide excellent sport during the summer months, when there tends to be more colour in the water.

There are some really big tench, best

sought along the reedy margins, and good-sized bream shoals with individual specimens over 8 lb. Pike are numerous, and 20-pounders are regularly taken from October onwards. When there is a good blow on, go for static or twitched deadbaits. In cold, clear-water conditions, free-swimming or paternostered livebaits sort out the better fish. T. Wilson took a 32 lb pike here in 1989.

To fish this broad, boats must be rowed beneath the A149 road bridge from Rollesby Broad. Contact Paul or Debbie at the Kingfisher's Jetty by the roadside at Rollesby Broad (Tel: 01493 748724), who have fourteen fishing dinghies for hire at £7.50 a day. Anglers may not launch their own boats to fish this group of broads. Only electric outboard motors are allowed.

Rollesby Broad, *Norfolk*

This wide, reed-fringed sheet of water varies from 3 feet deep in the margins, where specimen tench are to be located, to over 10 feet deep through the middle channel at the road end. Mixed catches of roach, hybrids and bream are taken on light float tackle, baiting with either maggots, casters or breadflake in conjunction with a little cereal groundbait. Pike fishing hots up during October, when the temperatures start to fall, and among numerous pike running into high double figures there is a good sprinkling of fish between 20 and 25 lb. Fish the reedbeds early on and the deeper water once winter has really set in.

All methods work well, but deadbaits invariably produce the biggies. Once the more common baits such as herring and mackerel have lost their effectiveness, give oddities such as eels, smelt, sand eels and brown or rainbow trout a try. The pike definitely 'group up' on these broads, probably because shoals of bait fish are somewhere close by. So don't be in too much of a hurry to move when the first pike has been taken.

Lily Broad, *Norfolk*

A lovely, intimate little broad averaging between just 3 and 5 feet deep. After rowing down Rollesby's western shoreline or

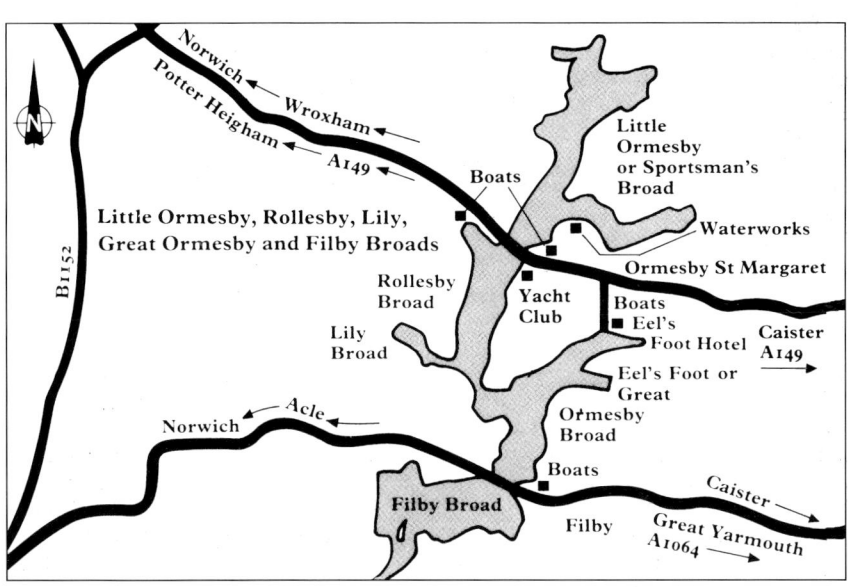

coming across the bottom end of Great Ormesby (see map), 'Lily' is reached, and once inside there is a definite feeling of friendliness. The southern bank is mostly alder-carr, and the best areas are through the middle or along the reed-lined margins of the northern shore. Good stocks of roach and bream plus a few tench and rudd are to be found here, along with a most prolific head of pike running well into the 20 lb bracket.

In the strongest winds, calm water can always be found and float-fishing with maggots or casters over a carpet of loose feed produces some good mixed catches, especially when the water holds a fair colour.

Great Ormesby (Eel's Foot) Broad, *Norfolk*

To fish this long, 100-acre broad, boats may be hired at the northern end from the Eel's Foot Hotel, who have fifteen boats available at £7.50 a day (Tel: C. Walch on 01493 731441), and at the southern end from the café, who have thirty boats available at £8 a day (Tel: Mr Barnes on 01493 368142).

Some huge catches of bream come from this broad with individual specimens topping 10 lb. Favourite areas are at the southern end, where it merges with Rollesby, and off Jerusalem Bay, halfway down the eastern shore. Tall reeds grow from the shallows all along the margins, and there are numerous little bays and inlets, all worth exploring for tench and bream, not to forget the pike, which are widespread. Working a livebait or plug along the reeds is an exciting way of catching pike here, but as with all these broads, a static deadbait either hard on or suspended just off bottom catches the whoppers, with perhaps a paternostered livebait running a close second.

Filby Broad, *Norfolk*

This is the most southerly of the complex and particularly during westerly winds, the most coloured. There is no boatshed on the broad, and anglers must row beneath the A1064 road bridge, after hiring craft from the café in Great Ormesby (Tel: Mr Barnes on 01493 368142).

Filby is heavily reed-fringed all the way round with the deepest area about 100 yards directly out from the road bridge. It is a consistently productive area for pike during the winter months and for both roach and bream through the summer. When there is a good colour, roach can be readily taken in good bags with fish topping the pound all over the broad. The largest bream, however, which run to over 8 lb can prove elusive at times. Eels to 6 lb have been caught here.

The best pike fishing is when the broad has a good ripple on it, and I personally rate the chances of really big pike turning up when a stiff south-westerly or westerly rips down the entire length. The best fish in recent years weighed 31 lb and was caught by Derek Allen in 1983.

Once again lures and livebaits produce more, but deadbaits generally seem to produce the largest pike in these broads.

Martham North Broad, *Somerton, Norfolk*

There are two smallish, private broads at Somerton and they lie immediately to the north and the south of the River Thurne, which bisects them. Both are owned by the Norfolk Naturalists Trust (NNT) and are weedy, gin-clear and shallow. Both are also strictly private to anglers. However, during recent years, the NNT has tried an experiment from October through to February by allowing just limited numbers of pike anglers to sample the fabulous pike fishing. There are only two boats allowed each day, and fishing is on Thursday, Friday and Saturday only. Naturally, these permits must be booked well in advance by writing to the NNT, 72 The Close, Norwich NR1 4DF, with a stamped addressed envelope for a permit application form. This should then be sent with a stamped addressed envelope to the warden, R. Starling, 1 The Street, Somerton, Norfolk, including the fee of £5 and a selection of preferable days. It is a bit of a rigmarole to secure a permit, but the pike fishing on Martham North Broad could prove well worth the effort, as fish over 30 lb are caught each year. It must be pointed out, however, that permission to fish by the NNT will only continue so long as anglers abide by the rules by which the permits are granted, which includes no livebaiting and no artificial lures. Only deadbaiting for pike is allowed and the use of two rods only. Anglers must also tie up only to mooring stakes provided and not fish just anywhere on the broad.

The broad can only be reached by boat from the River Thurne from Martham Ferry. Boat hire is available from Martham Ferry Boatyard (Tel: 01493 740303). Anglers may also launch their own dinghies at the end of Martham Dyke. Note that dinghies may not be launched from Somerton Staithe, which is private.

Route: To reach Martham Ferry dyke, take the A47 from Norwich to Acle and then the A1064 and B1152 into Martham village. Take Staithe Road, which leads directly to the dyke and boatyards.

Oulton Broad, *Lowestoft, Suffolk*

Oulton Broad is a large sheet of water in excess of 100 acres that is connected by a dyke to the tidal River Waveney. It is situated in the suburbs of Lowestoft and, due to this location, has in recent years become a playground for holiday-makers. Much of the broad, especially at the weekends, is taken up by pleasure boats, hydroplanes and water-skiing enthusiasts, but there is still enough water for the angler, and from October onwards he has virtually the entire broad to himself.

For many years Oulton was without question the finest perch fishery in Great Britain. The British record weighed 4 lb 12 oz and was caught here in 1962 by Sid Baker of Norwich. However, this glorious era of monster perch ended around 1968, when fishing in general started to deteriorate. Today a 4 lb perch is as rare from Oulton as it is anywhere, but perch are now commonly taken up to a pound plus, along with roach of a good average size. Occasionally, a tench turns up, but for specimen fish from the broad, anglers now turn to bream, which are taken during the summer months to close on 9 lb. The average size is in the 4 to 6 lb range. There are also plenty of eels and flounders which eagerly devour maggots and worms.

This is possibly a good reason for persevering with either bread or stewed wheat baits, but anglers seeking a real challenge might like to try luring one of the many mullet which invade the broad each summer? These super fighting estuary fish often fall to bread paste or maggot baits on light float tackle, and individual specimens may reach 5 lb or more.

Pike are not so evident as they are on much of the River Waveney, but towards the end of the season a big one from the broad is not unlikely, the best area being the huge, reed-fringed bay along the south-western shore and in the north bay.

All over the broad there is a general lack of weed growth and the bottom is largely of firm mud or clay, consequently the water is always well coloured. The depth fluctuates with a 2-foot drop in tides, and there is an average depth of around 5 feet.

For mixed catches, popular swims are found along the reedy margins of the North Bay, at the top of the eastern end, known locally as 'Dead End', and in the dyke at the western end, which connects Oulton to the River Waveney. There is excellent fishing here and all the way up the Waveney. In fact, the fishing in this area is possibly better than in the broad itself.

Night fishing for bream in Oulton

Dyke can produce good bags during the summer months, with individual specimens topping 6 lb. There is a little bank-fishing, but fishing from a boat is more rewarding. Anglers dinghies with or without motors may be hired from Knight's Creek Boatyard Ltd (Tel: 01502 572599) who have ten boats. Mr Hunt, the owner, specialises in fishing holidays and also rents out caravans to visiting anglers.

Route: Take the A146 from Norwich, which actually separates Oulton Broad from Lake Lothing in the town of Lowestoft.

Ranworth (including Malthouse) Broad, *Norfolk*

Ranworth Broad covers a 100 acres, fed by the tidal River Bure. It has both 'inner' and 'outer' sections which are separated by a series of stakes and a chaingate. This is to protect the inner broad, which is actually a wildlife reserve and the larger of the two sections. Ranworth 'inner' is fairly shallow all over, with no more than 5 feet of water, and is usually of good colour.

The fishing is controlled by Norwich and District Angling Association, and boats are available from the association through tackle dealers or the secretary, C. Wigg, 3 Coppice Avenue, Norwich (Tel: 01603 423625).

Fishing commences on 16 June, and the inner broad offers good mixed bags of roach, bream and hybrids in really peaceful surroundings. It then closes from 30 September for the flighting season until 1 March, when it reopens until the 14th. During this fortnight, pike fishing is sometimes rewarding, and the chance of contacting a big one is always on, the best fish ever being a 31½ lb monster taken in 1987 by Bill Giles.

These big pike are lured by deadbaits, rather than spinners or livebaits. I think this is due to the thick, coloured water of the inner broad, where the scent of a herring, sprat or mackerel is much easier for the pike to home in on. Float-fishing the bait is often rewarding, particularly during windy conditions, which appear ideal for success.

The outer section, where the Bure is joined to the broad by a long dyke (also with excellent fishing), is known as Malthouse Broad. Fishing is free from the staithe and from the dyke as well as the Bure itself, but during the summer months boat traffic spoils serious daytime angling. Early morning and late evenings can produce fair bream and roach to baits presented hard on the bottom over a groundbait carpet. Night fishing is good, but winter fishing is a far better proposition on this part of the broad.

Route: From Norwich take the B1140 to Panxworth. The Ranworth road is then well signposted and leads alongside the broad by the Maltsters Inn.

Rockland Broad, *Norfolk*

Rockland Broad covers over 40 acres and is completely surrounded by marshland and fringed with tall reeds of the Norfolk

Rockland Broad – superb piking

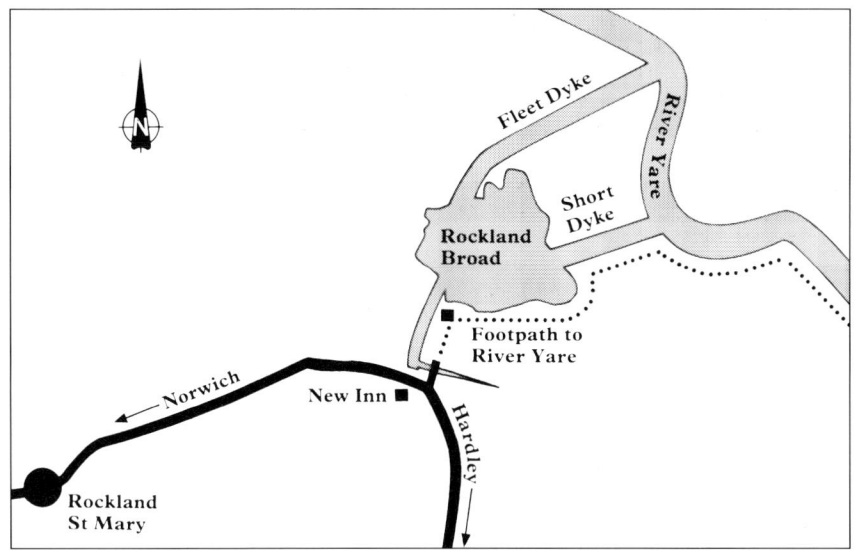

thatching' variety. At the start of the boat dyke at the southern end of the broad, adjacent to the road and the New Inn, Rockland Beck flows in from Poringland (see map), while at the northern end two separate navigable channels called Fleet and Short Dyke lead off Rockland into the tidal River Yare. There is a tidal rise and fall of around 3 feet and occasionally a particularly low tide may leave boats high and dry. Visitors are therefore warned to be careful of mooring. In any event, the best fishing is usually in or around the boat channels in the deeper water.

Being weedy with huge expanses of water-lilies in summer, the broad is a feeding-ground for fish that come up from the Yare on the flood tide, like roach and bream. At this period fishing is often at its best. Good-sized bream are widespread, with perhaps the chance of a real specimen. So too are roach, and generally one takes fish of a high average size. This is found to be the same in both the dykes leading into the Yare and especially in the fast waters of the Yare itself. Tench live in the weedbeds, and occasionally one or a brace are taken. Although they average on the large size, they are never common, but the eels at Rockland are and so, too, are flounders.

Apart from a few rudd and perch, pike are perhaps the favourite quarry of Rockland fishers, and one generally needs to wait until the end of September for the weeds to rot and vanish and for the water to clear a little before pike fishing is worthwhile. Whether the thick muddy water of the summer months keeps them in the river or just makes them disinclined to feed is debatable, but wintertime certainly improves one's chances of catching them. The average size is quite good, and double-figure fish are common, while fish in excess of 20 lb are on the rare side. However, a fish said to weigh 31 lb was caught way back in 1912.

All methods of pike fishing work well on Rockland, though livebaiting has the edge and usually sorts out the better-sized fish. Light to medium tackle is recommended, especially when spinning around the margins for the countless jacks. Beware of the tough lily roots though.

Apart from a little bank-fishing along Short Dyke, to which there is a public

79

footpath from the village (see map), Rockland can only be fished from a boat. There are none locally available, but anglers may launch their own craft from the slipway in Rockland Dyke for which a small charge is made. Contract Mr Dye (Tel: 01508 538256), who provides the key for unlocking the gate across the slipway for the owners, Rockland Poors Trust.

Route: From Norwich, proceed along the southern (A47) bypass and take the A146 Lowestoft Road. Then exit at the sign for Whitlingham, Kirby Bedon and Bramerton. This road goes through to Rockland St Mary, with the dyke on the left, just past the New Inn on the right.

Salhouse Broad, *Salhouse, Norfolk*

Salhouse Broad lies between Wroxham and Woodbastwick on the southern bank of the River Bure. It has two separate entrance dykes leading into the Bure for the angler to navigate his boat through. Once on the broad, there is a small charge which is collected by the warden. There is also some bank-fishing, for which a charge is also made, and unless one arrives by boat from either Wroxham or Horning one must reach the broad by road via the village of Salhouse. However, the final stage necessitates a long walk.

Depth averages around 5 feet, and there is some good general fishing to be had on light float tackle with roach, hybrids and bream plus the odd perch and tench. There is also a reasonable head of pike on Salhouse, including fish of over 20 lb. However, perhaps because of the location which involves a fair row from Wroxham, Salhouse Broad is comparatively little fished, especially in the winter.

Deadbaiting or livebait paternostering should pay off well here for there is good colour and the bottom is not too silty, with little weed to worry about.

Boats may be hired through the Wroxham Angling Club. Contact the secretary, Bob Westgate (Tel: 01603 401462). The boats are moored on Wroxham Broad adjacent to Hospital Farm and cost £5 per day to non-members or £2 per day to associate members. To become an associate member of the Wroxham Angling Club costs just £15 yearly, which is well worthwhile for those wishing to boat-fish regularly.

Route: To approach the broad from the road with a view to bank fishing, take the A1151 from Norwich, turning right at the signpost to Salhouse village, which is just before Wroxham. Alternatively, follow route directions for Wroxham Broad if you intend to take out a Wroxham Angling Club boat moored on Wroxham Broad.

South Walsham Broad, *Norfolk*

South Walsham Broad is similar to Ranworth in as much as it also has an inner and outer section. The inner part, substantially larger than the outer, is private and barred to anglers. The outer section is fairly shallow, and fishing is almost entirely from boats. Much of the bankside is privately owned, except for the right bank of Fleet Dyke and the village staithe, where anglers may bank fish and launch their own boats.

The dyke offers good fishing and is between 4 and 7 feet deep. It joins the broad to the River Bure, where the fishing is also good and the depth greater. River traffic after 8 a.m. during the summer months is heavy, and the fishing, as a result, difficult. Night fishing is exceptionally good here, almost anywhere along Fleet Dyke.

Species to be expected on the broad are bream, roach and some hybrids and good pike. Winter piking is very good indeed, but the broad is prone to salt tides. Bream are the predominating species, and may run up to the 5 to 6 lb mark, with an average weight of between 2 and 3 lb, although there are numerous skimmers to wade through.

Route: Take the B1140 from Norwich, going beyond the town of South Walsham. The first left turn out of town is signposted to the broad and staithe.

Surlingham Broad,
Surlingham, Norfolk

Surlingham Broad lies on the southern bank of the River Yare between Postwick and Strumpshaw and is directly opposite Brundall on the north bank. Over the years, it has been grossly reduced by silting, and local people talk of its area once being ten times its present 18 acres. However, although on ebb tides much of the broad is just a maze of mudflats, good-sized roach and a few bream enter the broad via the two connecting dykes on the flood tide. So angling is certainly a viable proposition, although boat-users are warned to observe the state of the tide before mooring.

There has been a little dredging work in recent years at the mouth of the dykes, where one enters the broad from the Yare, and these spots, especially along the downstream dyke, are exceptionally good for mixed catches. Night fishing can be particularly rewarding, but wherever anglers fish on the broad they are requested to bear in mind that the broad is, in fact, a nature reserve. The nearest slipways for boat-owners are at Coldham Hall and at Surlingham Ferry. One may also hire boats from Brundall to reach the broad and to fish the tidal Yare.

Route: To reach the town of Brundall from Norwich, take the A47. To reach Surlingham Ferry, take the Rockland St Mary road from Norwich, turning left at Bramerton to the village of Surlingham.

Womack Water, *Ludham, Norfolk*

Womack Water is a most attractive narrow fishery of about three-quarters of a mile which leads off the northern bank of the River Thurne, just one and a half miles upstream of Thurne Mouth. It is, in fact, a lengthy collection of bays, inlets and an island, with what is left of the old Womack Broad, at the north-western end, close by the public staithe. Boats may tie up here, and there is a mooring fee. Bank fishing is free from the staithe and also from the half-mile stretch, starting at the County Sailing Club, right down to the junction of the Thurne. There is a slight draw on the water, which is always well coloured, and depth varies between 3 and 5 feet, with odd holes around the island and boat dykes.

Sport can be patchy, but there are many 'bream flats' present, with better-sized fish up to the $3\frac{1}{2}$ lb mark. Roach are quite widespread, and some good bags, including the odd big hybrid, have been taken from the staithe in recent years. Eels, of course, are plentiful, as they are all over Broadland. There appears to be a deficiency of pike here though, with just the odd fish running into double figures taken during the winter. Night fishing is good for bream with bread baits for the better fish and maggots or worms for sheer numbers, although meaty baits are prone to attract eels during the summer months. Winter fishing is very good, especially when the Thurne is full of floodwater, and some nice roach are taken on light float tackle, with maggots or casters proving effective.

Route: To reach Womack Water, take the A1151 from Norwich to Wroxham, then the B1354 to Ludham village, where a well-signposted lane leads to the staithe.

Wroxham Broad, *Norfolk*

Fed by the tidal River Bure and the home of the Norfolk Broads Yacht Club, Wroxham Broad covers well over 100 acres of good fishing.

The centre of the broad is deepish and generally left well alone from an angling point of view, particularly when the yachts are racing. There is a little bankside fishing close to the moorings of the Yacht Club but the visitor would do well to go afloat and explore the countless weedy bays and inlets in the shallow water at either the northern or southern ends of the broad.

Wroxham Broad holds an immense head of quality roach, and 20 lb bags are not uncommon. It fishes well all summer through up until the first hard frosts; and among the roach are odd hybrids, perch and bream. In recent years, the bream have been difficult to track down, but the occasional bag including fish over 4 lb is taken by anglers who night fish. The broad undoubtedly holds some very large pike as fish between 25 and 30 lb are taken each winter from the River Bure, close to the two entrances. These fish obviously migrate and follow the roach shoals from river to broad, so there is much scope for those willing to specialise.

Boats may be hired in Wroxham and rowed down the Bure into the broad via either of the two connecting dykes. Alternatively, there is a charge to boat owners wishing to launch their craft from the picnic area adjacent to the Yacht Club.

Dinghies (all licensed for outboard motors) owned by the Wroxham Angling Club are actually moored on Wroxham Broad adjacent to Hospital Farm and are available to non-members at £5 a day. These provide wonderful access to both broad and the River Bure for pike anglers during the winter months. Club secretaries may also hire these boats for fishing matches. Apply to the secretary, Bob Westgate (Tel: 01603 401062). Norwich tackle dealers also hire out these boats.

Route: To reach the Yacht Club from Norwich, take the A1152, turning right just before Wroxham and following the signpost to Broad House and on to the club. To reach the Wroxham boatyards, carry on along the A1152 into the centre of Wroxham.

STILLWATERS

In the first edition of this book, way back in 1973, I wrote that 'Much of the finest fishing exists in the unlimited acres of ponds, gravel pits, lakes and meres, all isolated from boats, pollution and water abstraction, not only of today but particularly for the future. Since that time over twenty years have elapsed and, in addition to my hair turning from dark brown to silvery grey, the balance has indeed swung away from river fishing and changed no less drastically. We cannot prevent the sands, or more appropriately the silts, of time from slowly strangling our waterways.

To maintain a stabilised situation with present fish stocks in our rivers is, I feel, the very best we can hope for. Indeed, there are even some actual improvements, such as the proliferation of good-sized chub throughout the upper reaches of the rivers Yare, Bure, Waveney and Wensum, albeit perhaps at the expense of the roach.

Personally, I would sooner be long-trotting a fast river for roach than enjoying any other kind of fishing, but, then again, I would rather enjoy the fruits of a well-stocked carp lake or pit than have no access to fishing at all. This swing away from rivers to the excitement and quality of stillwater fishing now available is proved by the fact that there is now a choice of no less than 289 different waters in this chapter, compared to 190 in 1989, and just 37 way back in 1973.

Many of these lakes and meres are situated in public parks, private estates or adjacent to country mansions where fishing is available only on the strength that anglers will respect other people's property. Similarly, many of the gravel pits are club or syndicate controlled, with day tickets available to all anglers. It is therefore essential and up to each individual to respect his fishing and the fishing of others, be it a tiny pond or a secluded lake, by adhering to the country code of leaving no litter and in general leaving the bankside as it was found. Lastly, in an effort to make the whereabouts of accessible fishing available to all, should any reader know of day ticket or club waters not mentioned in this chapter, perhaps he or she would be kind enough to contact me: John Wilson, John's Tackle Den, 16 Bridewell Alley, Norwich NR2 1AQ. Tel: 01603 614114.

Close Season Laws

Anglers should note that in 1995 the close season laws applying to stillwater fisheries, i.e. ponds, pits, lakes and reservoirs were changed. The statutory close season for all river systems, including the Norfolk and Suffolk Broads from 15 March until 15 June inclusive, still stands. However, during this period, fishing is now allowed in stillwaters provided the owner of the fishery concerned decides to waive the close season rules, as the NRA has done. Many fishery owners are, however, sticking to the 'statutory' close season in order to give their waters and accompanying wildlife a rest, so always check by asking the manager or owner of the stillwater you intend fishing about close season rules before setting off. Do not automatically assume that close season fishing is allowed.

STILLWATERS – DAY TICKET

Aldeby Hall Farm Pits, *Aldeby, Norfolk*
These are a secluded and most interesting collection of five small pits offering a variety of species, including rudd, crucian carp, tench, bream and a strong head of king carp reaching to 20 lb-plus. They provide ideal fishing for youngsters with wooden stagings in all swims, some of which cater especially for disabled anglers. Depths vary between 2 and 8 feet and the water is always well coloured. There is adjacent car-parking and toilet facilities. For additional information telephone 01502 677648. Day tickets are available from the bailiff who calls round. These cost £4 for adults and £2 for juniors, senior citizens and disabled anglers. A special £50 season permit is also available. There is a caravan site only one mile away at Toft Monks.

Route: Take the A146 from Norwich to just before Beccles, turning onto the A143 at a large roundabout. A mile further on, turn right to Aldeby and, one mile further on again, look for a track on the right going through the fruit farm. Proceed down the track (actually an old railway track) and half a mile further on the pits are on the left, bordered by woodlands.

Alton Water Reservoir, *Holbrook, Suffolk*
This 350-acre water is unique as the only reservoir within the counties of Norfolk and Suffolk and the first developed coarse-fishing reservoir in Great Britain. It was started in 1972 as a water storage project for the Ipswich area. The Gipping Angling Preservation Society and its present manager, George Alderson, were from the outset involved in helping to make this sheet of water into a natural fishery. However, Alton has materialised into much more because, due to its size, other activities are catered for, such as sub-aqua, sailing, etc., and nature reserves have been provided. Called the Alton Water Users' Association, the management control these various segments and have designated certain locations around the perimeter for particular interests (see map).

The reservoir was opened for fishing in 1981 and has steadily grown in popularity ever since. Almost everywhere there is a depth of between 8 and 12 feet just three to four rod-lengths out and unlimited bank space. It provides excellent summer to autumn sport with roach of all sizes,

83

including fish topping the 2 lb barrier. It suits the matchman and specimen-hunter alike. There is also a tremendous head of bream in all weight ranges, from skimmers to fish between 4 and 7 lb, plus some incredibly large roach/bream hybrids, which have been caught to over 4 lb. Other species include perch, tench, rudd, big eels, crucian carp, and there is an excellent head of pike going to 25 lb-plus.

Access to the reservoir is from Coxall Road to car park No. 3 and via a private road to Birchwood cottages or from the B1080 at Holbrook to the main entrance. (For other access roads, see map). Anglers must at all times use the car parks provided and note that tickets are not sold on the bank. These must be arranged in advance.

Day tickets cost £2.50 from the tackle shop in the main car park, from Stutton post office, which is only 200 yards from the main gate, and from all local tackle shops.

Route: To reach Alton, take the B1080 or the A137 from Ipswich with access via Tattingstone and Holbrook respectively.

Attleborough Fish Farm Lake,
Besthorpe, near Attleborough, Norfolk

This is a three-quarter-acre, kidney-shaped, former clay pit, well-established with two islands and just nine prepared swims. The water is always well coloured, and depths vary between 4 and 10 feet. There is a head of carp to over 20 lb as well as tench, perch, roach, crucian carp and various koi.

Fishing is from dawn until dusk only.

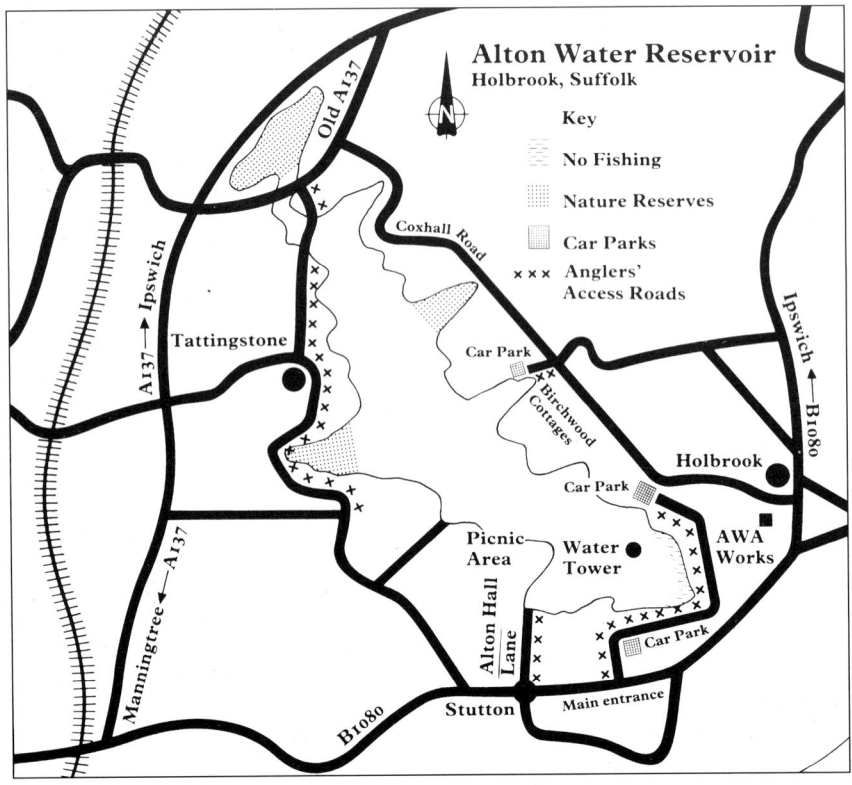

Day tickets cost £4 and must be obtained in advance from J.M.P. Tackle of Leys Lane, Attleborough (Tel: 01953 455282).

Route: Take the A11 from Norwich and take the first right turn on the Attleborough bypass marked 'Silver Street'. At the first T-junction, turn left and continue for one mile. The entrance to the farm shop complex and lake with adjacent car park is then on the right-hand side.

Barford Lakes, *Barford, Norfolk*
This fishery comprises three man-made gravel pits, each with depths fluctuating between 5 and 14 feet. The 'pleasure lake' is keyhole-shaped, over 2 acres and holds perch, roach, bream, rudd, tench, crucian carp and a good stock of king carp running into double figures as well as ghost koi. Day tickets at £5 are available from the office prior to fishing. Toilet and disabled angler's swims. No night fishing.

The other two lakes are oblong and rectangular in shape, hold 30-peg and 15-peg swims and are 1½ and half an acre in area respectively. These are only available for matches. The stocks include roach, perch, rudd and tench plus a prolific head of small carp. Match bookings at £5 per peg in advance only from Alan Thomson (Tel: 01603 759624).

Route: From Norwich, take the B1108 Watton road into Barford and turn right opposite the Cock public house. Proceed to the T-junction and then turn right and go through village. Half a mile further on, look for fishery signposts at the entrance lane on the right.

Barham Pit, *near Claydon, Suffolk*
This 4-acre gravel pit has two small islands, and depths vary from 7 to 12 feet. The pit contains a strong head of roach, rudd, tench and bream plus carp to over 20 lb – a water which is popular with both match anglers and specimen-hunters.

Day tickets cost £2 dawn till dusk or £4.50 for 24 hours and must be obtained in advance from Breakaway Tackle of Ipswich (Tel: 01473 741393).

Route: From Ipswich, take the A14 and branch onto the Claydon road (old Norwich road). Turn left into Pest House Lane, which leads directly to the pit, which is one amongst a large complex.

Bartles Lodge Lake, *Elsing, Norfolk*
Set in beautifully landscaped countryside, this spring-fed, man-made lake of around an acre has a tree-clad centre island and a variation in depths between 2 and 8 feet. There is a prolific head of roach, rudd and small tench plus koi, ghost koi and king carp running into double figures. This is real bran-tub fishing, where simple techniques and baits are encouraged. Boilies are banned.

An adjacent stable block has been converted into farmhouse accommodation for up to sixteen anglers, with meals provided. A bar and refreshments are available to all. Children under fifteen are not allowed to fish unless accompanied by an adult.

Day tickets at £5 are available from the bailiff, who calls round, and from the house adjacent to the fishery. For further information, telephone 01362 637177.

Route: From Norwich, take the A1067 Fakenham Road and turn left opposite Bawdeswell Garden Centre towards Elsing. Cross over the bridge spanning the River Wensum and turn right to the village. The lake is then next to the Mermaid public house opposite Elsing church.

Blickling Lake, *Aylsham, Norfolk*
Blickling is a long, wide, open water of over 20 acres, set in the grounds of Blickling Hall, owned by the National Trust. It is shallow and weedy at the hall end, with an average depth through the middle of around 6 feet all the way up the lake to the dam end, where depth increases to over 10 feet in the middle. The most popular spot is naturally off the dam wall, where a thick spinney shelters anglers from northerly winds. The

85

lake holds a good head of roach to over the pound, plus the odd perch and crucian carp, but the bream are what most anglers come to Blickling Hall for. In addition to huge shoals of skimmers from a few ounces upwards, there are really strong shoals of fish between 4 and 7 lb, 100 lb catches being quite common. The occasional bream over 10 lb is also taken. There are also some good tench and mirror carp weighing into double figures. Pike fishing here is excellent, both for numbers and for big fish to over 20 lb. Pike fishing is not allowed until 1 October. No night fishing. Wheelchair anglers are well catered for at Blickling with two special stagings and over 100 yards of level banking along the dam wall.

Day tickets cost £3.50 (£1.50 for juniors and senior citizens from Monday to Friday only) from the bailiff who calls round. There are also a few season permits available. Contact Mr Cooper on 01263 734181 for additional information.

Route: Take the A140 from Norwich to one mile beyond Aylsham by ignoring the bypass and going through the town, taking the road on the left to Blickling, immediately before Ingworth road bridge. After a short distance, bear right and keep straight ahead for half a mile. This leads directly to the northern end of the lake and car park on the left.

Blue Waters (Swan Lake), *Woolpit, Suffolk*
This picturesque flooded brick pit of some 2 acres shelves down to over 20 feet in places, and the water is nearly always extremely clear. Species include roach, rudd, perch to over 3 lb and pike, plus a good head of bream to 6 lb.

Day tickets cost £1.50 from the bailiff who calls round to anglers. Fishing is controlled by Mr Baker (Tel: 01359 240293) for additional information.

Route: Take the A14 Stowmarket road from Bury St Edmunds and turn right to Woolpit. Just before Woolpit village, turn left and proceed down a 'no through road' (old Stowmarket road). The lake is then 600 yards further along on the right, hidden behind laurel hedging.

Bodham Pond, *Bodham, Norfolk*
This is an old marl pit of around half an acre with steep banks. It is deep one end and can be extremely weedy at times. It holds a good head of crucian carp and the occasional wildie plus tench and rudd.

Day tickets cost £3 (£1.50 juniors) from the post office within Bodham Village Stores (Tel: 01263 588209).

Route: From Norwich, take the B1149 to Holt, turning onto the A148 to Bodham. In the village, turn right and then sharp right again down to a T-junction. Directly opposite is a lane with the pond, situated 200 yards along on the left.

Booton Clay Pit, *Booton, Norfolk*
This triangular, beautifully wooded old pit of about 4 acres has water that is usually well coloured and for the most part quite deep, with long peninsulas of reeds topping the shallow bars. It holds a prolific stock of tench between 2 and 3 lb, plus roach, rudd, pike and bream, including one or two whoppers. There is a prolific head of mirror carp running into double figures plus one or two exceptionally large specimens. Carp over 30 lb have been caught in seasons past.

Day tickets cost £3 from the bailiff, who calls round. The fishery is controlled by Cawston Angling Club.

Route: From Norwich, take the road to Reepham and, just before Reepham village, turn right to Haveringland and Buxton. Keep straight ahead for a distance of about one and a half miles, and the pit is then on the left-hand side of the road, hidden by a hedge of tall trees. It is not the easiest of spots to find in daylight, let alone in the dark.

Boughton Pond, *West Norfolk*
This is a shallow pond covering around

1½ acres and surrounded by grassland. It is weedy and usually nicely coloured, containing a mixed stock, with roach predominating. It is ideal for the younger angler. Fishing is free.

Route: From Norwich, take the A47, branching onto the A1122 Downham road and about five miles past Swaffham look out on the left for a road to Barton Bendish. Go through the village, following signs to Boughton. The pond is then in the middle of Boughton village, on the left, close to the road.

Breakaway Pit, *Melton, Suffolk*

This tree-lined gravel pit of around 2 acres has one island and nestles beside the River Deben, close by Wilford Bridge. Depths shelve to over 10 feet, and the stock comprises roach, rudd, specimen perch, tench and a fine head of bream with specimens to over 10 lb. There is also a good head of carp to over 20 lb.

Day tickets cost £2 from dawn until dusk, and there is also a 24-hour ticket at £4.50 that should be obtained in advance from Breakaway Tackle in Ipswich (Tel: 01473 741393) or from Rod and Gun of Woodbridge (Tel: 01394 382377).

Route: From Ipswich, take the A12 to Woodbridge, turning off at the Bentwaters roundabout. Go over the level-crossing, and the entrance to the fishery car park is then on the left, just past the Wilford Bridge public house.

Bridge Fishery Lake, *Lenwade, Norfolk*

This well-established 5-acre lake has a long spit in the middle, almost splitting it into two halves. The banks are nicely wooded and reed-lined with a choice of both shallow and deep swims in depths ranging from 6 to over 20 feet. Species include perch, roach and pike as well as a good head of tench between 3 and 5 lb. A strong head of bream in the 5 to 6 lb range is also present (fish the deeper swims) plus carp weighing into double figures.

Day tickets (for two rods) cost £5 from dawn till dusk or from dusk till dawn and are available from the pub, fishery lodge or bailiff who calls. A limited amount of yearly permits costing £60 are also available. The cost of day tickets includes adjacent fishing on a fast and shallow 600-yard stretch of the River Wensum, famous for its chub, roach and barbel (see River Wensum). For additional information, telephone the Bridge public house on 01603 872248.

Route: From Norwich, take the A1067 Fakenham Road into Lenwade and turn right immediately over the bridge spanning the River Wensum, which takes you straight into the pub car park.

Brooke Pit, *Norfolk*

A most unusually situated, steep-sided old gravel pit of around 2 acres which is very deep in places. There are secluded swims cut into the banking, affording wind-shielded fishing over lily pads for roach, perch, some sizeable crucian carp, pike and a good head of tench to over 4 lb. Livebaiting for pike is not allowed. Day tickets are available from the bailiff, who will call round. No-one is allowed under eighteen.

Route: From Norwich, take the A146 and then the B1332 Bungay road. One mile past Poringland look on the right for the Dove public house, and the pit is then at the bottom of the hill on the right, through gravel workings.

Broome Pits, *near Bungay, Suffolk*

These four irregularly shaped gravel pits vary in size from 1 to 4 acres and are generally quite deep. Almost throughout, apart from the two small pits, a depth of 10 feet or more can be found just a rod-length out. They provide excellent sport on the float for a variety of species, with roach predominating, and there is a super stock of mirror carp, the best in recent years being a 26 lb whopper. There are also crucian carp to 2 lb and bream to 8 lb. Pike grow large in these pits, the best being a 27-pounder, though there are numerous jacks to wade through.

Livebaiting is not allowed. Bungay Cherry Tree Club controls the waters and has a policy for stocking. A leaflet about the pits has been produced by the club and is available to members. Anyone may join for £20 per season through the secretary, Ian Gosling, 37 St Mary's Terrace, Bungay (Tel: 01986 892982), and the club has numerous other waters, both running and still within the area. The administrator for Broome Pits is Barney Earrye (Tel: 01986 895188), and anyone wishing to arrange matches should contact him. Day tickets cost £2 (two rods) and £1 for juniors from the bailiff at the pits, who calls round to anglers. Only club members may night fish.

Route: Take the B1332 from Norwich to the large bypass roundabout just before Bungay. Turn left, and the pits are then on the left, hidden behind hedging one mile further on.

Buckingham Pits, *Mundford, Norfolk*
There are two pits here, each of around an acre and both shelving down to 12 feet deep. They hold good stocks of tench, averaging around the 3½ lb mark, plus bream in all sizes, with eels, roach and some perch up to a pound. There is also a fair head of king carp up to the 20 lb mark.

These are Mundford Angling Club waters, and day tickets, which cost £3, must be obtained in advance from the Rod 'n' Line Tackle Shop in Thetford (Tel: 01842 764825).

Route: From Norwich, take the A47 to Swaffham, then the A1065 to Mundford. About a mile from Mundford, in Ickburgh village, turn left at white cottage, and council houses and the pits are a mile further on, one each side of the road, just before the road crosses the River Wissey.

Bure Valley Coarse Lake, *near Aylsham, Norfolk*
This oblong gravel pit of 4 acres varies in depths from 6 to over 15 feet. It nestles beside the tiny, upper reaches of the River Bure and for several years was a trout fishery (part of the Bure Valley Trout Lakes fishery) before changing over to coarse fishing in 1994. It holds roach and perch, including individual fish of specimen proportions and a stock of carp to over 25 lb.

Day tickets cost £5 from the adjacent fishery office and should be purchased in advance. For additional information, telephone 01263 587666.

Route: From Norwich, take the A140 to Aylsham and proceed into the town (ignoring bypass), turning left onto the B1354 Saxthorpe road. The entrance to the fishery is then on the right and well-signposted around four miles out of Aylsham.

Buss Creek, *Southwold, Suffolk*
Buss Creek was in fact named after the boats which, in medieval times, carried herring to Southwold, and was given to the town council to mark its charter. Now, this spring-fed, completely dammed, one-and-a-quarter-mile channel provides coarse fishing and is a tribute to members of the Southwold and District Freshwater Angling Preservation Society, who re-established it as a fishery by clearing the overgrown bed and banks. Thirty-plus swims are available on the Reydon bank only. No night fishing, one rod only. It contains both bream and tench to over 7 lb as well as rudd.

Day tickets cost £3 (£1.50 for juniors). These should be booked in advance from Purdy's Newsagents, High Street, Southwold (Tel: 01502 724250).

Route: From Southwold, take the A1095. Access is either on foot from the road bridge spanning Buss Creek or proceed to the society's car-park area, serving Reydon Pits, and enter by the footpath at Gordon Bridge (west) end.

Cawston's Pit, *near Attleborough, Norfolk*
A shallow, weedy little pit of around half an acre, this is an ideal spot for youngsters, holding small tench, eels, rudd, roach and perch. The fishing is free.

Route: From Norwich, take the A11 and, three miles beyond Attleborough, turn left at Old Buckenham crossroads. Proceed across the railway line and take the first turn on the right. The pit is then immediately on the right, close to road.

Chapel Road Lake, *Roughton, Norfolk*
This 1½-acre, long, narrow and irregularly shaped man-made lake has two small islands and is heavily reeded along the margins. Depths vary from 3 to 8 feet, and the water is always well coloured. Species include roach, rudd, perch and tench plus a most prolific head of carp of between 5 and 15 lb and the possibility of bigger fish. Fishing is from dawn till dusk, and day tickets cost £3 from the bailiff, who calls round. Night fishing is only by prior arrangement. Tel: 01263 761369.
Route: From Norwich, take the A140 Cromer Road to Roughton and turn left just past the garage onto the B1436 Felbrigg road. The entrance to the fishing is then just 200 yards along on the left, beside the Old Forge.

Chiswick Pit, *Stow, Norfolk*
This is a typical, well-coloured farm pond, averaging around 5 feet deep and pleasantly tree-lined. It holds a prolific stock of rudd, a few tench as well as common and mirror carp weighing into double figures. Fishing is from dawn until dusk only. No night fishing. Day tickets cost £2.50 and must be obtained in advance from Stow Estates Office in Stow Bardolph village (Tel: 01366 383194). Only three tickets are issued for each day. Boilies not allowed.
Route: From Norwich, take the A47, branching onto the A1122 Downham road to Stradsett. Then turn right onto the A34 towards King's Lynn. In Shouldham Thorpe, turn left and, a mile further on, turn left down a farm track. The pond is then 300 yards further on, on the left, opposite the farmhouse.

Cobbleacre Park Lakes, *Hevingham, Norfolk*
This interesting complex of three man-made gravel and clay pits offers a variety of species. In the largest, 3½-acre, lake, which is oval in shape and has two islands, depth varies from 4 to 12 feet. There is a prolific stock of ghost koi and mirror carp to over 25 lb as well as tench, big bream, crucian carp and roach.
The second lake is oblong in shape with three islands and covers around 1½-acres, the depths varying from 4 to 10 feet. Species present are crucian carp, bream, roach, rudd and tench.
The third lake is just a quarter of an acre in area, averaging around 4 feet deep and L-shaped. It holds roach, rudd, crucian carp, tench and bream. There is an anglers' car park with adjacent showers and toilets, and the bailiff will call round to anglers. Day tickets cost £5 (for two rods) or £8 for a 24-hour session. Evening tickets cost £3, and there is a season permit at £140. For additional information, telephone 01603 754305 or 407848.
Route: From Norwich, take the B1149 Holt road, passing through Horsford, and three-quarters of a mile past Shorthorn crossroads, turning right alongside the wood yard down Brick Kiln Road. The entrance to the lakes is then on the right, three-quarters of a mile past Bailey's Barn.

Common Lakes, *Lenwade, Norfolk*
Situated on Lenwade Common, these fisheries are controlled by the Great Witchingham Fuel Allotment Charity and comprise three gravel pits varying between 2 and 5 acres, plus a three-quarter-mile length of the River Wensum, famous for its roach, chub and pike fishing (see River Wensum).
The pits are stocked with a variety of species, including roach, rudd, tench, perch, bream, pike, plus mirror carp weighing into double figures and specimen crucian carp. Depths fluctuate between 5 and 15 feet, and there is an

89

Common Lakes, Lenwade – superb sport with tench, bream and carp

interesting choice of swims. For bream and pike, the first lake on the left at the bottom of the lane is recommended. For carp and crucian carp, choose the first lake on the right at the bottom of the lane. Day permits cost £3 (£1.50 senior citizens and £1 for juniors) and are available from the bailiff, who calls round. For season permits, contact B. Carvin, The Street, Lenwade (Tel: 01603 872399). For those wishing to night fish, 24-hour permits cost £7.

Route: From Norwich, take the A1067 Fakenham Road into Lenwade and then take the first left turn immediately past the village bakery and butcher's shop down common lane. This leads directly to the fishery and adjacent car park.

Costessey (No. 2 and No. 3) Pits,
Costessey, Norfolk
Owned by Anglian Water, these two pits at Costessey are known locally as the Ski Lake (water-skiing still takes place) and the Carp Lake.

No. 2 pit or Ski Lake covers some 15 acres and is pleasantly wooded around the perimeter, with depths varying between 8 and 20 feet. The water is usually well coloured, and stocks include a terrific head of roach to over the pound as well as large shoals of bream with specimens to over 8 lb. The tench average between 3 and 5 lb, but specimens to over 7 lb are taken. There are also perch, eels and a fair head of pike, including a good sprinkling of doubles plus the occasional 20-pounder. There is also a modest head of carp from 15 to over 30 lb. Level swims are provided adjacent to the car park for wheelchair anglers.

No. 3 pit, also known as the Carp Lake, covers almost 6 acres and averages over 10 feet deep with extremely secluded swims cut in around the heavily wooded perimeter. This lake is well known for specimen tench, and fish in excess of 8 lb have been taken. Other species include roach, bream, perch, eels, pike and carp to over 30 lb; the best in recent years was a mirror of 34 lb 6 oz that fell to John Dunn in 1994. A big zander is not unlikely.

Day tickets are available from all local tackle dealers, the closest being Browne's Tackle Shop in Norwich Road, Costessey. A limited amount of season permits are available from the Anglian Waters Fishing Lodge a few hundred yards away at Taverham Mills Lake. For additional information, telephone 01603 861014. (See also Taverham Mills Lake).

Route: From Norwich, take the A47 Dereham Road and, two miles from city, turn right down Longwater Lane by the Roundwell public house. At the bottom of the hill, turn left at the T-junction and, half a mile further on, take the right fork. The two pits are then situated on the right, with the main entrance gate some 400 yards further on. Alternatively, take the A1067 Fakenham Road from Norwich into Taverham and turn left at the crossroads down Sandy Lane. At the bottom of the hill, go straight ahead at the crossroads and proceed over the bridge spanning the River Wensum. The pits are then on the left, with an entrance gate 300 yards further on.

Cranworth-Woodrising Carp Lake, *Cranworth, Norfolk*

This is a 2-acre man-made lake with two islands and shaped rather like a figure of eight. Depths vary from 2 to 10 feet, and the water is always well coloured. There is a prolific stock of both common and mirror carp running into double figures as well as the odd specimen over 20 lb, with tench and crucian carp. Day tickets cost £3 (£2 for juniors) from the bailiff, who calls round to anglers. Season permits costing £30 are also available. For additional information, call Mr Bunning at Jubilee Farm, Cranworth (Tel: 01362 820702). There is a caravan and camp site nearby for anglers intending a lengthy stay.

Route: Take the B1108 Watton road from Norwich to Hingham. Just beyond the village, look out on right for the road to Shipden. Follow the Cranworth sign, and Jubilee farm is in the village on the right. The lake is then a short distance away, with a car park adjacent.

Decoy Farm Fishery, *Ormesby, Norfolk*

This is a narrow and long lake of around 2 acres with a prolific mixed stock, including roach, rudd, perch, crucian carp and bream. There is also a strong head of specimen tench to 6 lb-plus, together with carp running into double figures. This is an ideal family fishery, where youngsters easily catch small fish on the float.

Day tickets cost £3 (£1.50 for an evening ticket) and are available from the farm office or from the bailiff, who calls round.

Route: From Norwich, take the A47 Great Yarmouth road and go over Acle bridge, then turn left onto the Caister road and on to the King's Arms public house in Fleggburgh. Turn left and proceed to Rollesby. At the T-junction with the A149, turn right and, after crossing the linking bridge between Ormesby and Rollesby broads, take the first left turn, following signs for the Rare Breeds Centre which leads you directly to the fishery.

Docking Village Pond, *Norfolk*

This is a most prolific fishery of around an acre, with depths varying between 3 and 4 feet. Being an old marl pit, the water is always well coloured and holds a strong head of crucians and wild, common carp up to 8 lb. There are also roach and some tench.

Day tickets cost £2 and are only issued on the same day. Just eleven tickets are available on a first-come first-served basis from the Vegetable Shop in the High Street (Tel: 01485 518064). Fishing is only from 7.30 a.m. until 11 p.m., Monday to Saturday, with no Sunday tickets.

Route: Take the A1067 from Norwich, going through Fakenham and all the way through to Docking.

Edwards Pit, *Belton, near Great Yarmouth, Norfolk*
A tiny, shallow, weedy pond holding roach, perch and tench.
  Day tickets cost £1 from the bailiff, who calls round.
  Route: From Norwich, take the A146 to Hales and look out on the left for the B1136 to Haddiscoe. In Haddiscoe, turn left onto the A143 and, four miles further on at the dual carriageway, turn left onto the Belton and Burgh Castle road. Take the first turn on the right along Butt Lane, and the pit is then 200 yards on right, down a narrow farm track.

Felbrigg Lake, *North Norfolk*
This is a beautiful estate lake of around 4 acres, dammed at one end and fed by a brook at the other. Its depth varies from 2 to 5 feet, and during the summer months the weed can sometimes be very thick. There is a most prolific stock of tench averaging around 4 lb, plus eels, pike and plenty of rudd, including fish to over 2 lb.
  Day tickets cost £4 and must be purchased in advance from Holt Tackle and Bait in Holt (Tel: 01263 712855) or from Tatters Tackle in North Walsham (Tel: 01692 403162) – only three are issued daily. Fishing is from dawn till dusk only, and tickets are available only from 1 July to 1 November. Note that members of the Norfolk Anglers' Conservation Association enjoy full access to Felbrigg Lake.
  Route: Take the A140 Cromer Road from Norwich to Roughton and turn left onto the Felbrigg road, leading to the estate entrance gate on the left three miles further on.

Felmingham Mill Lakes, *near Aylsham, Norfolk*
These are three attractive stream-fed lakes of an acre each, varying between 3 and 10 feet in depth. Stocks include roach, perch, crucian carp, tench and mirror carp running up to 15 lb. Touring caravanners are welcomed here (twenty-five spaces), with toilet and shower blocks adjacent to the lakes.
  Day tickets cost £3 with juniors and senior citizens at £1.50. These must be obtained prior to fishing from Mr Moore at the Mill House adjacent to the water (Tel: 01263 735106). The price of the ticket includes fishing in the tiny mill stream, which holds roach, dace, pike, trout and even the odd grayling.
  Route: From Norwich, go to Aylsham on the A140 and take the B1145 to Felmingham. One mile before the village, take left turn down to the mill.

Felthorpe Lakes, *Felthorpe, Norfolk*
This man-made fun fishery comprises two small lakes, each no larger than three-quarters of an acre, containing a prolific head of ghost koi and mirror carp running into double figures plus perch and roach. The smaller lake also contains gold fish and smaller carp varieties.
  Day tickets must be purchased in advance from Mr Ellis on 01603 754408.
  Route: Take the B1149 Holt road from Norwich, passing through Horsford. Beyond the crossroads, take the next right turn past the kennels, and the entrance to the fishery is then on the right, 100 yards further on, adjacent to conifer woods.

Flixton Decoy, *Suffolk*
Flixton Lake is a long and narrow T-shaped water of around 17 acres, varying in depth between 2 and 5 feet. The bottom is soft mud, and there are weedbeds and lily pads. The water may occasionally become thick with algae in warm weather and it certainly colours up well during the winter.
  Flixton Decoy offers excellent sport on the float throughout the summer months with masses of rudd, plus some quality roach and perch to 2 lb. There is also a good head of bream to 4 lb, plus some nice tench. Fishing is by boat only, and there are five boats available to anglers. The

Fritton Lake provides tranquil fishing for roach and bream

lake opens on 16 June and closes for fishing at the end of August.

Day tickets are available, and bookings should be made in advance to the keeper, Mr Green, at South Lodge, adjacent to the lake (Tel: 01502 730568).

Route: From Norwich, take the A146 to Hales and turn left onto the B1136. On reaching Haddiscoe, continue along the A143 to St Olaves and turn right immediately over the bridge spanning the River Waveney onto the B1074. The lake is then situated on the right some 8 miles further on in the village of Flixton.

Fritton Lake, *Suffolk*

This 175-acre lake is part of the huge Fritton Country Park complex where, in addition to fishing, sports such as windsurfing, golf, boating, etc. may also be enjoyed. By far the largest lake in Suffolk, Fritton is actually thought to be a broad, which was dug for its peat during the Middle Ages. This was the conclusion of Dr J. Lambert, whose studies of the Broads during the 1950s brought scientific evidence to the subject.

Depth varies between 8 and 12 feet, and the water is usually well coloured. Bank fishing is restricted to the north-western end close to the entrance, where numerous swims have been cut in-between thick reedbeds – in all about 1,000 yards of bank fishing. Boats have access to much of the lake, except for areas marked with lines of buoys.

The boats cost £8 per day or £5 per half day. There are huge shoals of bream in Fritton, averaging around 5 to 6 lb. They are not always easy to track down but, when they are found, catches of over 100 lb are nothing out of the ordinary. Roach are widespread, with plenty over the pound, and float-fishing two rod-lengths out with either maggots or casters produces some good bags, as well as the odd bream and perch. There are also a few wily carp and a good head of pike that go to over 20 lb.

This is a really super, family-cum-fishing venue. Day tickets cost £3.50 (£2.50 juniors) from the main gate, and this includes entrance to the beautiful gardens and amusements. These are available from 10 a.m., and the park closes at 5.30 p.m. No night fishing. Fishing is from 16 June to 30 September only, seven days a week. There are also some excellent holiday cottages for rent, set in secluded parts of the estate. For more information, contact the manager on 01493 488288.

Route: Take the A146 from Norwich and turn onto the B1136 at Hales towards Haddiscoe. Continue over the bridge spanning the River Waveney at St Olaves, and Fritton Lake is then on the right a little further on.

Gimingham Lakes, *near Cromer, Norfolk*

These are three man-made, reed-lined, spring-fed lakes with a reputation for producing specimen mirror and common carp over 30 lb, plus tench, rudd, roach, perch and bream. The largest lake has two islands, varies in depth from 4 to 15 feet and covers around 3 ½ acres. The two smaller lakes are narrow and long, about 1½ acres each and vary in depth from 5 to 8 feet. Day permits cost £2 from the owner, who calls round to anglers. Season permits are also available. There are good car-parking and toilet facilities adjacent to the lakes.

Route: From Norwich, take the B1150 through Coltishall and into North Walsham. From North Walsham proceed on the Mundesley road for one mile, bearing left through the village of Trunch. Then go straight ahead into Gimingham village to the old mill and turn left, following signs for the fishery.

Golden Ponds, *near Hickling, Norfolk*

This is a fun fishery comprising two small man-made lakes of between a half to three-quarters of an acre each, where disabled anglers are well catered for. The stock includes roach, rudd and carp plus trout.

Day tickets are available from the adjacent bungalow. For additional information, telephone 01692 581016.

Route: From Norwich, take the A1151, passing through Wroxham and on to Stalham. Beyond Stalham, turn off to the left, opposite Sutton Staithe Hotel, and proceed to the T-junction. Turn right at the junction and then take the third turning on left to the next T-junction. Then turn right, and the ponds are 400 yards along on the left and well signposted, with an adjacent car park.

Great Massingham Village Pond, *Norfolk*

This is a typical village pond, shallow, coloured and containing a most prolific stock of wild carp. Fishing is free to parishioners and pupils of Great Bircham Primary School, who should apply to the local Parish Council. To all outsiders there are ten tickets issued each day costing £2. These are available between 7 a.m. and 6 p.m. from Mrs Glassett of Barrack House, adjacent to the Rose and Crown public house in the village. No night fishing or ground baiting is allowed.

Route: From Norwich, take the A1067 Fakenham Road and turn onto the B1145 at Bawdeswell. Go through Brisley and Litcham, and six miles further on, look out on right for the sign to Great Massingham. The pond is then bang in the middle of the village.

Green Pits, *Belton, near Great Yarmouth, Norfolk*

These are two irregularly shaped gravel pits of around 2 acres in all, with depths to 12 feet. They contain a good stock of roach and tench as well as pike, carp weighing into double figures and bream.

Day tickets cost £2.50 from the bailiff, who calls round.

Route: From Norwich, take the A146 to Hales and look out on the left for the B1136 to Haddiscoe. In Haddiscoe, turn left onto the A143, and four miles further on at the dual carriageway, turn left onto the Belton and Burgh Castle road. Take the first turning on the right along Butt Lane and, after one mile, look for the sign to the fishery on the left.

Gunthorpe Hall Lake, *Melton Constable, Norfolk*

This is a typical Norfolk estate lake of around 3 acres, set in deep woodland. Depths vary between 2 and 12 feet, with the deepest water around the dam end. Species include roach, crucian carp, rudd, perch, pike in plenty, tench and common carp weighing into double figures.

Day tickets cost £2.50 from the Hall, with only five issued per day by prior booking only (Tel: 01263 861373). No Sunday fishing. No night fishing – dawn until dusk only.

Route: Take the A1067 Fakenham Road from Norwich to Guist and turn right onto the B1110. Proceed to Melton Constable and turn left at the crossroads onto the B1354. Take the next right turn and go into Gunthorpe village, taking the second turn on the left (just before the church) down to the lake and Hall.

Gunton Park Lake, *Norfolk*

This is an almost square-shaped estate lake of around 12 acres, often referred to by its old name of Sawmills Lake. Depth varies between 2 and 5 feet, and the water is always well coloured, holding a most prolific head of bream in all sizes from 4 oz up to 7 lb. There is also a strong head of roach to over the pound, plus one or two hybrids. Other species include a few perch and a growing head of carp weighing into double figures. Also present are pike weighing into double figures as well as the odd much larger specimen. This is a good float water for mixed catches, with comfortable banks, and is an ideal family venue. Keepnets are not allowed, and there is no night fishing.

Day tickets cost £2.50 (£2 for juniors and senior citizens) from the bailiff, who calls round. For additional information and match bookings contact John Waite on 01263 768284.

Route: Take the A140 from Norwich to about five miles beyond Aylsham and look out on the left for the Alby Crafts Centre, then look out on the right for a signpost to Suffield. Turn right and, at the bottom of the hill, bear right, proceeding past an archway gate on the left, and take the next entrance on the left, which leads to the anglers' car park and lake.

Hall Farm Lake, *Burgh Hall, Norfolk*

This is an L-shaped man-made lake of around 2 acres. Behind the two small islands there are extensive weedbeds and patches of lilies. Stocks include roach rudd, tench, crucian carp to 1½ lb as well as a strong head of mirror carp running into double figures, with individual specimens topping 25 lb. Depths vary from 6 to over 12 feet.

Day tickets at £3 (one rod) or £5 for two rods, with junior and senior citizens at half price, are available from the bailiff, who calls round. For additional information, telephone 01493 781986.

Route: From Great Yarmouth, go over Breydon Water bridge towards Gorleston and turn right at the next roundabout. Proceed through a chicane up to the small roundabout and turn right. Carry on down the road to a T-junction and turn left. Then look for a left turn to the fishery entrance, some 300 yards further on just before the Cherry Tree Caravan Park, which is on the right.

Haveringland Lake, *Norfolk*

This wide and long, stream-fed estate lake that covers some 14 acres is for the most part quite shallow, with around 4 feet of water at the dam end. It contains roach, perch, some good tench and large shoals of

95

bream in the 5 to 7 lb class. Also present is a good stock of pike with specimens to 20 lb-plus and carp including a few whoppers.

Day permits cost £5 and must be booked over the telephone in advance from R. Hinde (Tel: 01603 871302). Season tickets costing £75 are also available, and both campers wishing to pitch their own tents and touring caravanners are welcome.

Route: From Norwich, take the B1149 Holt road and, at the end of Horsford village, turn left towards (signposted) Haveringland. Three miles further on, turn right between the two lodge houses of Haveringland estate and proceed straight ahead for half a mile to the office reception.

Heath Farm Pits, *Shouldham, Norfolk*
These are two small pits containing crucian carp, rudd, bream and tench. Fishing is from dawn until dusk only.

No night fishing. Day tickets cost £2 and must be purchased in advance from Stow Estates Office in Stow Bardolph village (Tel: 01366 383194). Only two tickets are issued for each day. Boilies not allowed.

Route: From Norwich, take the A47, branching onto the A1122 Downham Market road. In Stradsett, turn right onto the A134 and in Fodderstone Gap turn right to Shouldham. Look out for a track on the left with a sign to Stow Estates. This leads directly to the farm pits.

Henham Dairy Pond, *Suffolk*
This is a pond of an acre, controlled by Southwold and District Freshwater Angling Preservation Society. It is always well coloured, with a depth of no more than 3 feet, but there is a prolific stock of crucians as well as some mirror and hybrid carp, tench and rudd. A limited number of day tickets costing £3 (six only) are available on designated swims. These are bookable in advance from Mrs Fairs (Tel: 01502 578672). One rod only to be used. No night fishing.

Route: From Norwich, take the A146 to Beccles and then the A145 to Blythburgh.

Two miles from Brampton, turn left opposite cottages into Henham Park estate. The pond is then 200 yards along on the left.

Hevingham Lakes, *Hevingham, Norfolk*
There are three smallish man-made lakes at Hevingham, all pleasantly mature and reeded, situated quite close together. Their depth varies between 3 and 9 feet, and they are always well coloured. The carp fishing is really excellent for mirrors, leathers and commons, and there is a strong head between 3 and 10 lb, plus some doubles and fish over 20 lb. There are also crucians, roach, rudd, tench and bream to 5 lb. Anglers wishing to stay overnight may pitch their own tents for a small charge, and there are caravans to let on site for anglers. Toilet and shower facilities are available to all. Touring caravans are also welcome, and there is a holiday farmhouse to let.

Day tickets cost £3 per rod and these must be purchased in advance at the bungalow situated at the entrance from C.J. Matthewson (Tel: 01603 754368).

Route: Take the Holt road, the B1149, from Norwich, turning right at the second (ignore the first) signpost to Hevingham, some six miles out of the city. The fishery entrance is then on the left about one mile further on and well signposted.

Highfield Fishery, *Thorpe Abbots, near Diss, Norfolk*
This man-made fishery complex, which has well-coloured water dotted with patches of lilies, suits both the pleasure fisherman and the match angler alike and comprises three lakes. The smallest (ideal for youngsters) is sausage-shaped, averages between 5 and 6 feet deep and covers around three-quarters of an acre. The second lake is 1¾ acres in size, with a tree-clad island, and is most irregular in shape, with an average depth of between 6 and 7 feet. The third lake covers around 2½ acres with depths to 7 feet and has an

island at one end. All three lakes contain a varied stock of roach, rudd, perch, crucian carp, bream, tench and king carp, with specimen carp running to over 20 lb in the largest lake.

Day tickets cost £3.50 (dawn until dusk) from the bailiff, who calls round. Juniors and senior citizens are charged £2. Night fishing is only by prior arrangement. For additional information, telephone Ken Avery on 01986 874869. There is a special discount for block bookings from secretaries of angling clubs.

Route: From Harleston, take the A143 towards Scole, passing through Needham and Brockdish. One mile past Brockdish, take the right turn, following the signpost to Thorpe Abbots. The entrance to the fishery entrance is then on the left 400 yards further on and well signposted, with an adjacent car park via a dirt track road.

Hilgay Lakes, *Hilgay, Norfolk*
Of these two clay pit fisheries bordered by reeds and trees close to the River Wissey, the largest covers around 6 acres and is primarily for pleasure anglers, containing a prolific and mixed stock of tench weighing between 1 to 2 lb (with occasional specimens to over 6 lb), roach, perch, and carp weighing into high double figures.

The second covers just half an acre but holds roach, carp and even a few barbel.

Day tickets cost £3 per rod and are available from the bailiff, who calls round, or from the farm shop adjacent to the anglers' car park. Fishing is from dawn until dusk only and both boilies and ground bait are not allowed. There is a 'barbless hook only'-rule in force. Match bookings are available through Tom Dent, 19 Forester's Avenue, Hilgay, Downham Market PE38 0JW (Tel: 01366 385676).

Route: From Downham Market, take the A10 towards Ely, passing over bridges spanning the Cut Off Channel and River Wissey. The lakes and farm shop are then 200 yards on the right, past the next left bend. Parking is between the shop and lakes only.

Hingham Carp Fishery, *Hingham, Norfolk*
This shallow, well-coloured, three-quarter-acre and willow-clad pond contains roach, perch, rudd tench, crucian carp and prolific stock of mirror carp running into double figures. Day tickets must be obtained from the adjacent farmhouse prior to fishing. These cost £3 (£2 for juniors) and cover from 6 a.m. until dusk. No night fishing.

Touring caravanners and campers are welcome. For additional information, telephone Mr Semmence on 01953 850308.

Route: From Norwich, take the B1108 Watton road into Hingham and, immediately after leaving the village, take the left turn down the lane to Rectory Farm and the fishery, just visible from the road.

Holkham Park Lake, *near Wells-Next-The-Sea, Norfolk*
Holkham is a long and wide estate lake of around 15 acres. Depth varies between 4 and 12 feet, and there is a good weed growth, including patches of lilies. Fishing is allowed only at the north end of the lake (around 1,000 yards of bank) from dawn until dusk and from 16 June to 31 August only. There is a head of carp running into double figures, plenty of eels, some perch, tench and the odd large rainbow trout. Fish density for such a large water is, however, extremely low.

Day tickets cost £2.50, and there are special three-month permits at £15. These allow fishing only from Monday to Friday and are available from the estate office (Tel: 01328 710227). Anglers must park in the village car park. There is then a substantial walk to the lake.

Route: From Norwich, take the A1067 to Fakenham and then the B1105 to Wells and on to Holkham Hall, which is on the left.

Little Dunham Carp and Tench Lakes are exceptionally prolific waters

Holton Gravel Pit, *near Halesworth, Suffolk*
This 2-acre pit is pleasantly reeded around the perimeter and averages about 8 feet deep. The water is usually quite clear, and there is a stock of small crucians and tench as well as some roach, rudd and bream with some common and mirror carp – a really mixed-bag, fun fishery.

Day tickets cost £3 and must be purchased in advance from the Rod and Gun Shop in Woodbridge (Tel: 01394 382377) or from Anglian Photographics in Halesworth.

Route: Take the A146, then the B1322 from Norwich into Bungay. Then take the A144 into Halesworth and turn left onto the B1123 into Holton. The pit is then on the left in the middle of the village.

Ingham Pond, *near Bury St Edmunds, Suffolk*
This is an attractive little pond, surrounded by sunken trees, holding roach, perch and crucian carp. The fishing is free.

Route: From Bury St Edmunds, take the A134 to Thetford, and the pond is on the right, 300 yards past Ingham village crossroads.

Lakeside Fisheries, *East Bilney, Norfolk*
There are two lakes set in wooded surroundings, offering excellent sport with rudd, perch, tench, roach, bream, trout and carp to over 20 lb. Both are irregular in shape with depths to around 5 feet. The largest has two islands and covers 3½ acres. The smaller is around an acre. There are excellent car-parking, toilet and shop facilities on site, and meals are available. Day tickets cost £5 (which includes the use of two rods) from the lakeside office. Gates open at 5.30 a.m. Night fishing is by appointment. Tel: 01362 861015. The fishery is open all year round, seven days a week.

Route: From Norwich, take the A46, turning off into Dereham. Proceed through the town's one-way system and take the B1146 towards Fakenham. After three miles, turn down beside the Corner Nursery, which is on the left. After a further two and a half miles, look for a Renault garage and, 600 yards on, turn left down a lane just before a road bridge that leads to the fishery.

Letheringsett Lake, *Letheringsett, Norfolk*

This is an attractive 3-acre dammed lake with a centre island, varying in depth between 3 and 9 feet. It holds a good head of roach plus tench, crucian carp to 2 lb, perch eels and pike, and carp to 26 lb.

Fishing is from dawn till dusk only. Day tickets are only available from Monday to Friday (the Sheringham Club holds matches at weekends) and cost £3.50 from the King's Head public house in Letheringsett (Tel: 01263 712691).

Route: Take the B1149 from Norwich into Holt, turning left onto the B1156 into Letheringsett. At the first crossroads, turn right, and the lake is situated 400 yards along on the left, behind a bank of trees.

Little Dunham Carp and Tench Lakes, *Little Dunham, Norfolk*

This is a unique and extremely interesting series of five interconnected, long and narrow lakes that are actually part of an old railway line system that has been flooded and dammed. The banks are nicely overgrown and depths vary between 3 and 8 feet. The lakes are well stocked with a variety of species, including king carp weighing into double figures plus the odd much larger specimen with roach, rudd, tench and crucian carp, all of which can be taken on the float at close range. Fishing is from 6.30 a.m. to 8 p.m., and day tickets cost £3.50 from the bailiff, who calls round. A limited number of season permits are also available. No groundbait is allowed; barbless hooks only. For additional information, telephone 01760 725286.

Route: From Norwich, take the A47 King's Lynn road and, just before the service station at Necton, turn right, following the sign to Little Dunham. Proceed straight ahead for one and a half miles to Dunham Museum, on the left, and immediately opposite look on the right (just before an old railway bridge) for signs at the fishery entrance and to car parks.

Loch Neaton, *Watton, Norfolk*

This is a shallow lake covering an acre, controlled and well-maintained by the Loch Neaton Angling Club, who have re-landscaped the banks and heavily restocked with a variety of species, including roach, rudd, perch, bream and carp.

Limited day tickets are available (two per day) at £5 for adults, £2 for juniors. These must be purchased in advance from Rudling DIY, High Street, Watton (Tel: 01953 881760). There are limited membership tickets available at £15 yearly (adults) or £3 for juniors – also available to residents within a three-mile radius of Watton town centre. Handicapped and disabled anglers qualify for free membership. There are, in fact, two custom-built, concrete platforms for the disabled alongside the fishery car park. Micromesh keepnets and landing nets only are to be used, and no carp are to be retained in keepnets. Fishing is from 7 a.m. to dusk only. No night fishing.

Route: From Norwich, take the B1108 into Watton and turn right onto the A1075, then, 400 yards further on, turn left into Watton Sports Centre and follow a track down to a five-bar gate and car park.

Marsh Farm Lakes, *near Saxmundham, Suffolk*

This is a complex of three spring-fed clear-water lakes, man-made from peat marshes. The largest lake, of around 2½ acres, has an irregular shape, averages 6 feet deep and is nicely reed-lined. It contains a good stock of carp to over 20 lb.

Lake No. 2 is also irregularly shaped and around an acre in size with reed-lined banks and an overall depth of 6 feet, containing roach, rudd, perch, tench and bream.

Lake No. 3 is really a small pond, designed specifically for youngsters. The shallow water contains roach, rudd, carp and tench.

Day tickets cost £3 for the use of one rod only or £4 for two rods and must be obtained prior to fishing from the farm shop adjacent to the lakes.

Touring caravans are welcome here but space must be booked in advance. Telephone Mr Bloomfield on 01728 602168.

Route: From Ipswich, take the A12 towards Lowestoft and turn right onto the A1094 Alburgh road. One mile further on, take the left turn to Sternfield. Half a mile further, turn left again, following signposts to Marsh Farm Lakes.

Martham Pits, *Martham Ferry, Norfolk*
These super tench fisheries are adjacent to the tidal River Thurne, which provides free alternative fishing to the visiting angler. They are an interesting complex of small pits controlled by the Martham and District Angling Club, being heavily reed-fringed and usually weedy. The depth fluctuates between 4 and 10 feet, and the water is quite clear. There is a terrific head of tench in the 2½ to 4 lb range, plus one or two whoppers, with the odd bream to over 7 lb. Other species are roach, rudd, eels and pike; also carp to double figures. Angling is good during the early part of the season, especially for those fishing early or late. Day tickets (24 hours using two rods) cost £3 in advance from Molly's Sweet Shop, Black Lane, Martham (Tel: 01493 740366). A weekly ticket costing £7.50 is also available. A special senior citizens' yearly permit costs £15.

Route: Take the Yarmouth road from Norwich to Acle. Then take the A1064 and B1152 into Martham. In the village, take the left turn down Staithe Road, which leads to the swing-bridge ferry. Just before the ferry, fork right, keeping to the right of the dyke, which leads into the River Thurne, and the pits are 100 yards further on.

Middle Harling Lake, *near Thetford, Norfolk*
This three quarter-acre, oval-shaped man-made lake has a centre island and affords fishing for around twenty anglers. Stocks include roach, perch, bream, crucian carp and minor carp into double figures.

Daytickets cost £3 from the bailiff, who calls round. For additional information, telephone 01953 717909 (office hours); 01953 681437 (evenings).

Route: From Thetford, take the A11 and in Larling turn right towards Garboldisham. Proceed into East Harling and turn right down West Harling Road. One mile further on, look on the left for the Norfolk Agrochemicals building, then for a gate on the right (at a nasty bend) which says 'Keep Out'. This provides access to the fishery, with parking adjacent to the lake.

Mill Farm Lake, *near Long Stratton, Norfolk*
This is single-acre man-made lake is nicely coloured, oval in shape and with two islands. It offers fun fishing in depths varying from 2 to 8 feet for mixed catches of roach, rudd, golden rudd, bream, crucian carp and perch, plus an assortment of king and koi carp.

Day tickets cost £2.50 from the bailiff who calls round to anglers. The anglers car park is adjacent to the lake.

Route: From Norwich, take the A140 road and turn left at the crossroads of the B1135. The lake is then only a short distance along on the left and well signposted.

Narborough Trout Fisheries – Coarse Lake, *Narborough, Norfolk*
This well-stocked single-acre lake contains carp weighing into double figures, plus tench, roach. bream and chub.

Depths vary from 6 to over 10 feet with deep water close in over the marginal reeds.

Day tickets are available from the adjacent fisheries Lodge (see also Narborough Trout Lakes). These cost £3 from 9 a.m. until 4.30 p.m., £2 from 5 to 8 p.m. or £4 for an all-day ticket. For more information, telephone 01760 338005. The lakes are open from 9 a.m. to 8 p.m. only.

Route: Take the A47 Dereham Road from Norwich, following the signpost into the village of Narborough. The fishery entrance gate is then on the right and well signposted.

New Waters Farm Fishery, *Wortham, near Diss, Norfolk*

Visitors are quite likely to catch any one of a dozen or more species in this exceptionally well-stocked 3½-acre lake. Irregular in shape with three islands and depths varying from 2 to 5 feet, the water is heavily reed-lined and contains extensive beds of lilies. The stock comprises golden orfe, blue orfe, rudd, golden rudd, tench, golden tench, bream plus ghost koi and a prolific stock of king carp varieties to over 20 lb.

Day tickets cost £6 from the bailiff, who calls round. Season permits cost £70. There is an adjacent car park. For more information, telephone 01379 890391 (daytime); 01379 890420 (evenings).

Route: From Norwich, take A140 to Scole and then the A143 Bury road through Wortham. The lake, which is visible from the road, is then half a mile on on the right and well signposted.

Northfield Lakes (formerly Holman's Pits), *Southery, Norfolk*

These are two well-established, oval-shaped clay pits of around 1 and 1½ acres. Depths vary between 2 and 7 feet and species include roach, rudd, tench and bream plus carp to over 20 lb and the occasional large pike.

Day tickets cost £3 from Mrs Langley (Tel: 01366 377551 for additional information) who calls round to anglers. Fishing is dawn until dusk only. Night fishing is allowed only by prior arrangement.

Route: From Downham Market, take the A10 towards Ely for around five miles and turn left into Southery on the B1386. Entrance to the lakes is then via the second farm turning on the left past the potato store.

Peck Meadow Pond, *Rocklands, near Attleborough, Norfolk*

This extremely well-coloured pond of around three-quarters of an acre has depths varying from 3 to 5 feet and contains a prolific stock of both crucian and king carp. Mirror carp over 20 lb are taken every season. Other species include rudd, perch and the odd large eel. This is wonderful float-fishing at close range.

Day tickets cost £3 and must be booked well in advance by contacting the owner, S. Burroughs, on 01953 483366, who will provide directions.

Pentney Carp Lake, *near Narborough, Norfolk*

This is an extremely well-established, irregularly shaped pit of 10 acres with one island, varying from 10 to 18 feet deep. It is a well-stocked carp fishery with specimens to over 30 lb, amongst a strong head of fish weighing into double figures. Other species include roach, perch, pike, tench and bream.

There is a car park adjacent plus toilet and shower facilities and a tackle shop, and meals are available from the log cabin café. Fishing tickets may be booked over the phone on 0860 841245 or purchased on site from the log cabin. A day ticket costs £10 for 24 hours (which includes the use of two rods), £18 for a two-day, weekend ticket and £60 per week.

Route: Take A47 from Norwich to East Winch and look out on the right for the Carpenter's Arms public house. Directly opposite on the left is a byroad. Proceed down this by road for around two and a half miles, and the entrance gate to fishery is on the left.

Pentney Lakes Leisure Park, *near Narborough, Norfolk*
This is a massive 'five-lake' complex, totalling some 200 acres of prime coarse fishing.

Lake No. 1 is more of a narrow channel connecting the adjacent carp lakes (see Pentney Carp Lake) to this complex. It averages around 7 feet deep and comprises 2 acres of water holding a prolific head of small tench plus roach and bream to 3 lb.

No. 2, called the 'Ski Lake', covers some 76 acres where water-skiing is still allowed. It is oval-shaped with two islands and varies from 5 to 18 feet deep, containing a few carp, bream averaging 3 lb but with odd specimens to 9 lb, roach, tench and pike.

No. 3, called 'Reed Lake', is around 6 acres in area and oval in shape with depths varying from 6 to 14 feet. It holds a prolific head of bream to 10 lb, plus roach, rudd, tench and perch.

No. 4 is S-shaped and called Swan Lake. It is also around 6 acres, with depths averaging 7 feet. Stocks include roach, tench, pike, some specimen rudd, plus a prolific head of bream which average around 4 lb but run into double figures.

No. 5 is called Bird Lake and covers 84 acres. It is irregular in shape with one island, and depths vary from 5 to over 20 feet. It holds bream weighing into double figures, roach, tench and pike, including a few whoppers. To fish all these lakes, day tickets are available from the bailiff, who calls round to anglers, or from the reception cabin (Tel: 01760 338668). A dawn-until-dusk day ticket costs £4 and a 24-hour ticket is £6.

Route: As for Pentney Carp Lake.

Railway Pit, *near Attleborough, Norfolk*
A tiny, shallow, weedy pond of around a quarter of an acre, this contains small tench, roach, perch, pike and mirror carp.

The fishing is free.

Route: From Norwich, take the A11 and three miles beyond Attleborough turn left at Old Buckenham crossroads. Proceed across the railway line, and the pit is immediately on the left, surrounded by trees.

Reepham Fisheries, *Reepham, Norfolk*
This L-shaped lake of around 3 acres was once a trout fishery. Now it provides excellent fun fishing on both float and ledger for carp weighing into double figures, plus rudd, tench and crucian carp, in depths ranging from 3 to 12 feet. There is also a stock of the unusually coloured metallic carp, known as ghost koi. Keepnets are not allowed, and the carp must only be retained in the landing net for a few minutes prior to photography. Day tickets cost £4 from the owner, Mr Daws, at the office adjacent to the lake and car park. Fishing is from 6 a.m. until 10 p.m., with night fishing only by prior arrangement. For additional information, telephone 01603 870829.

Route: Take the Reepham road from Norwich, and the fishery is on the left just before Reepham.

Reydon No. 1 Pit, *Southwold, Suffolk*
This reed-fringed gravel pit of around 3 acres is over 20 feet deep in parts. Stocks include roach and rudd plus some specimen tench in the 5 to 6 lb range and a few perch. There are also carp up to 20 lb. One rod only is to be used, and there is no night fishing. Fishing is not allowed before 9 a.m., and there is no day-ticket fishing on Sundays. A limited number of day tickets are available from Purdy's Newsagents, High Street, Southwold (Tel: 01502 724250).

Day tickets cost £3 (£1.50 juniors) and must be purchased in advance. The fishery is run by the Southwold and District Freshwater Angling Preservation Society. For additional information regarding the club's other waters, contact the membership secretary, Mrs B.M. Reid of 19 Sussex Road, Lowestoft (Tel: 01502 518198).

Route: From Southwold, take the A1095 and, after going over a bridge spanning Buss Creek, look for the Lakeside Park development on the left. The estate road leads to the car park behind the pit.

Reydon No. 4 Pit, *Southwold, Suffolk*
This 2-acre man-made fishery varies between 4 and 7 feet deep and has a centre island. It was dug as part of the Buss Creek development specifically as a carp water and contains a strong head of commons and mirrors weighing into double figures.

There is no night fishing, and one rod only is permitted. No Sunday day-ticket fishing. Day tickets (only four issued each day) cost £3 (juniors £1.50) and must be obtained in advance from Purdy's Newsagents, High Street, Southwold (Tel: 01502 724250).

Route: As for Reydon No. 1 pit, then a walk from the car park.

Richardsons Pit, *Stalham, Norfolk*
This is a tiny, well-coloured pond, quite weedy and averaging about 7 feet deep. It holds some roach, eels, tench and a few carp to 8 lb.

Day tickets cost £1.50 and must be obtained in advance from Richardson's Boatyard, directly opposite on the other side of the bypass (Tel: 01692 581081).

Route: Take the A1151 from Norwich, passing through Wroxham and on to Stalham. Just through the village on the bypass, Richardson's Boatyard can be seen on the right, with the pit directly opposite on the left.

Ringland Lakes, *Ringland, Norfolk*
This is a beautifully matured complex of seven old gravel workings set adjacent to the River Wensum at the foot of the Ringland Hills. A half-mile of the Wensum is in fact included with the fishery, containing dace, chub, roach and pike. The lakes hold a variety of coarse fish with roach, bream and tench predominating. In the largest lake, called Days Water (first along the track on the left), there is also a modest stock of large carp weighing up to 30 lb, plus a good head of bream in the 4 to 6 lb bracket. Odd good perch, crucians and rudd are spread throughout the other lakes, some of which are highly overgrown, consisting of peninsulas, bays and islands all interconnected. There is also a good head of pike, including some nice doubles. These lakes are ideal for both pleasure trips and for the specialist angler.

Day tickets cost £3 (juniors, senior citizens and disabled anglers £1.50) and must be purchased in advance. No night fishing.

Season permits costing £24 (passport-type photo required) are also available and allow the holder to fish at night. These Leisure Sport tickets are available from John's Tackle Den, 16 Bridewell Alley, Norwich (Tel: 01603 614114) and Tom Boulton's Tackle Shop in Norwich (Tel: 01603 426834).

Route: From Norwich on the A47 Dereham Road and two miles from city, turn right down Longwater Lane by the Roundwell public house. At the bottom of the hill, turn left at the T-junction and half a mile further on keep on the left at the fork. One mile further, after passing close to the River Wensum, look on right for a narrow track leading to the fishery.

Rodally Pit, *Old Buckenham, Norfolk*
A tiny, half-acre, shallow pond, Rodally Pit is always well coloured. It holds rudd, tench and common carp. Fishing is free.

Route: From Norwich, take the A11 to Attleborough and then the B1077 into Old Buckenham. The pond is then bang in the centre of the village, on the left, opposite the White Horse public house.

Rushbrook Farm Lake, *Kettlebaston, Suffolk*
An extremely well-established, oblong-shaped lake of around 7 acres, with depths varying between 3 and 10 feet. This water contains a good head of quali-

ty rudd up to 2 lb, bream to 5 lb and a prolific stock of tench to 4½ lb. Also present are perch and carp weighing into mid double figures. No night fishing is allowed. Day tickets cost £5 and are only available in advance from The Tackle Box in North Street, Sudbury (Tel: 01787 312118).

Route: From Stowmarket, take the B1115 road into Hitcham and turn right, following the signs for Kettlebaston. Once in the village of Kettlebaston, turn right at the telephone box down a dirt track. This leads (after a fair drive) eventually to car parking in an open field adjacent to the lake, which is at the top of the hill.

Ruston Reaches, *East Ruston, North Walsham, Norfolk*

This is a 1½-acre man-made lake which has been most thoughtfully created with bends and islands rather like part of a river system. The banks are heavily reed-lined, and the water is always heavily coloured with a variation of depths between 4 and 10 feet.

This is a real mixed fishery with perch, rudd, roach, tench, crucian carp and bream plus a stock of both common and mirror carp weighing into mid double figures.

Day tickets cost £3 from the fishery hut when it opens at 8.30 a.m., and fishing must cease at dusk. No night fishing. Additional information is available from the owner, Mr Mantell-Sayer (Tel: 01692 536646). There is also an adjacent trout lake (see Trout Fishing – Day Ticket (Stillwaters)).

Route: From Norwich, take the A1151 road, passing through Wroxham and almost to Stalham. Then turn left (following signs for Bacton and Happisburgh) into Stepping Stone Lane. Turn left at the next T-junction and then take the first left, following winding lanes into East Ruston. The fishery entrance is then on the left via an open field (with 'Fishing' signpost) with a line of cottages on both sides.

Scoulton Mere, *near Hingham, Norfolk*

This delightful, extremely secluded estate lake covers a sprawling 20 acres which for the most part averages just 3 feet deep. Only a third of its perimeter is actually open for fishing and this is controlled by the Norfolk County Council Staff Angling Club. The water is invariably quite clear, with patches of marginal lilies, and the stock comprises rudd, roach, bream, perch, pike (including the odd whopper over 20 lb) plus a few wily old carp and a strong head of tench averaging over 4 lb. Specimens to over 7 lb have been caught in recent years.

Day permits cost £3 (£2 juniors) from the bailiff, who calls round, or from the Norfolk County Council Staff Angling Club bailiff, J. Baker, 28 New Road, Hethersett, Norwich (Tel: 01603 811003).

Route: Take the B1108 road from Norwich to just beyond the village of Hingham. Scoulton Mere is then on the right, well screened by woods, two miles along. Turn right into the lane by a sign saying 'School Farm'. The fishery entrance is a few hundred yards further.

Selbrigg Lake, *near Holt, Norfolk*

A lovely 4-acre lake which can prove rather weedy in summer, Selbrigg holds a prolific stock of roach, perch, pike and tench. There are one or two really large perch and eels here but both are difficult to track down. Day tickets cost £2 on the bank or just £1 from Mr Wright's farm close to the lake (Tel: 01263 712366).

Route: From Norwich, take the B1149 road into Holt and turn right onto the bypass. Take the first right turn about 400 yards further on and then after two miles take the first left turn. The lake is then one mile further on, on the right.

Shallow Brook Lakes, *Bridge Farm, Costessey, Norfolk*

This is a two-lake fishery, with a lake on each side of the road adjacent to the tiny River Tud, where along a short stretch of fishing is included for dace, roach and chub. The 2¼-acre carp lake is on the farm side of the road and averages 12 feet deep, containing a prolific head of common and mirror carp to over 20 lb, plus crucian carp and some good perch. The car park is adjacent to the lake, and there are facilities for wheelchair fishermen.

No. 2 lake, better known as Snipe Lake, averages around 10 feet and offers mixed fishing for roach, rudd, perch, chub, bream and tench. Day tickets cost £5 from the bailiff, who calls round. £80 season permits are also available, as are £3 half-day tickets and £2 evening tickets. For more information, contact Mrs Green on 01603 741123 or Martin Green on 01603 747667.

Route: Take the A47 Dereham Road from Norwich into New Costessey. Turn right at the traffic lights down Norwich Road and half a mile further on the lakes are on the right and the left immediately past bridge over River Tud.

Shelfhanger Pit, *Winfarthing, Norfolk*
This is a long, narrow, quite deep pit of almost an acre. It holds some perch, roach, rudd, tench and crucian carp. The fishing is free to those who enquire from the owner, V. Wingfield of Vine Farm, adjacent to the pit.

Route: From Norwich, take the A11 to Attleborough then the B1077 Diss road. Just out of Winfarthing, take the first left and then turn right. The pit is then 300 yards further on, on the right behind the farm. Ask at the farm to fish.

Snetterton Pits, *near Attleborough, Norfolk*
Formerly known as Bert Wright's Pits, the complex comprises seven pleasantly matured and quite deep gravel pits separated by spits and islands varying in size from just one to 12 acres, nestling beside the River Thet and holding a variety of species. There is a good head of both roach and rudd, including large shoals of rudd over 2 lb, plus perch of the same weight. There are also tench and bream running to a good size, plus plenty of pike. Specimens over the 20 lb mark come out each winter, mainly to deadbaits, and there is a healthy stock of 'doubles'. Other species include eels, with some mirror carp weighing into double figures. Carp have in fact been taken to over 25 lb, the 'Mallard' pit being the most heavily stocked.

Fishing is from dawn until dusk; night fishing is by special arrangement only. Day tickets available at the fishery cost £5 per day. Season permits are also available, as are special match bookings. Additional information is available from the office (Tel: 01842 764312) or at the fishery on 01953 498289.

Route: From Norwich, take the A11 to about three miles past Attleborough and, at the Snetterton motor-racing circuit crossroads, turn right and proceed into the village. Then turn left and take second turning on the right, which leads directly to the fishery.

Sovereign Lake, *Pentney, Norfolk*
This well-established, irregularly shaped old gravel working is studded with islands and varies in depth between 2 and 6 feet. During construction of the Narborough bypass it was cut in half so that it can now be seen on both sides of the A47 King's Lynn to Norwich road. Stocks include roach, bream, tench, rudd, perch, pike and carp weighing into double figures.

Day tickets cost £3 and should be purchased from John Baron at the adjacent bungalow prior to fishing. (Tel: 01760 337288 for additional information).

Route: From Norwich, take the A47 and look out for the lake on both sides of the Narborough bypass. Take the third sign on the left for Narborough, which provides access to the fishery bungalow.

Stacksford Pit, *near Old Buckenham, Norfolk*
This tiny, quarter-acre, pit is quite deep,

holding some tench, plus roach, perch and rudd. The fishing is free.

Route: Take the A11 from Norwich to Attleborough, then the B1077 into Old Buckenham. Take the Shropham road in the village, and the pit is then situated just past the second turning on the right, close to the road.

Starfield Pit, *Long Melford, Suffolk*
This is a mature 6-acre pit of a highly irregular shape, interspersed with islands and varying in depth between 2 and 10 feet with odd weed patches and holding a mixed stock, with roach predominating. There is also a head of bream in most size ranges plus tench averaging around the 2½ lb mark. The pike weigh into double figures, and there is a good stock of mirror carp to over 10 lb.

Day tickets cost £3.50 and must be obtained in advance from the secretary of the Long Melford and District Angling Association, N. Mealham, 6 Springfield Terrace, East Street, Sudbury (Tel: 01787 377139). Club membership costs £23, which in addition to the pit covers super fishing throughout the Stour valley with numerous pieces on the river from Clare down to Long Melford – renowned for its excellent dace and roach fishing.

Route: Take the A134 from Sudbury to Rodbridge Corner and turn left onto the Foxearth road. Half a mile on, carry straight ahead at a sharp left turn, passing through Liston towards the chemical factory. Keep left of the factory and go down a track on the right in Liston Garden. Starfield Pit is then at the bottom of the track on the right, adjacent to the London Angling Association pits.

Station Pit, *Bungay, Suffolk*
This tiny pit is situated near the disused railway station at Bungay Common and is ideal for youngsters. It is shallow and the fishing relatively easy. Light-float-fishing is recommended. There are plenty of

The Station Pit on Bungay Common, renowned for perch and crucian carp

small roach, dace and eels, but a surprise may be in store in the way of big perch which are known to inhabit the pit. Specimens are caught from time to time up to the 3 lb mark. There are some good crucian carp too.

Day tickets cost £2 (which also includes over 3 miles of fishing on the nearby River Waveney, which skirts Bungay Common) and are available in advance only from the adjacent Outney Meadow Caravan Park reception, which opens at 9 a.m. No night fishing is allowed.

Touring caravanners and campers are welcome at the park, who rent out boats and canoes on the river. Anglers who stay at the park can also fish a 100-yard stretch of the river frontage. For further information, telephone Mr Hancy on 01986 892338.

Station Pit is under the control of the Suffolk County Angling Association, whose members plus those of the local Cherry Tree Angling Club can fish on their club cards.

Route: From Norwich, take the A146, then the B1332 to Bungay. Turn right at the bypass roundabout towards Homersfield and proceed to the next roundabout. Then look on the right for the entrance to Bungay Common (just off the roundabout). The pit can then be clearly seen only 150 yards away, adjacent to the caravan park.

Swale Pit, *Waldringfield, Suffolk*

This is a 3-acre, irregularly shaped gravel pit varying in depth from 4 to over 15 feet. It is well-stocked with carp of all sizes from mere ounces up to double-figure specimens, plus rudd, roach, bream and tench.

Day tickets are bookable in advance at £2.50 from The Rod and Gun Shop in Church Street, Woodbridge (Tel: 01394 382377), who issue four tickets per day and from Markham's Tackle Shop in Woodbridge Road, Ipswich, who issue ten tickets per day (Tel: 01473 727841). Fishing is from Monday to Saturday only – no Sunday fishing.

Route: From Ipswich, take the A14 towards Felixstowe, turning left towards Waldringfield at the roundabout. One and a half miles further on, look on the left for Wilding & Smith's Gravel workings, where the pit is situated. Until 5.30 p.m. cars may be parked next to the pit, otherwise they must be left at the top of the lane.

Swangey Lakes, *near Attleborough, Norfolk*

These two gravel pit fisheries cover 4½ and 1½ acres. Depths vary from 2 to over 30 feet, offering a wide selection of different swims. The main stock is carp, including commons, mirrors and leathers to over 20 lb, as well as crucian carp and tench to specimen proportions. Other species include perch, rudd, roach and bream with a chance encounter of wels catfish over 20 lb.

Day tickets cost £6 (£3 juniors) and are available at the lakes from the bailiff, who calls round. A special 24-hour night-fishing ticket is also available at £10. Further enquiries may be made to M&M Enterprises (Tel: 01953 883344).

Route: From Norwich, take the A11 and on the Attleborough bypass take the turning on the right to West Carr. Half a mile along, turn left when road forks and 100 yards further on turn right. Continue over the ford across the river and then turn sharp left into the fishery entrance.

Swanton Morley Fisheries, *Norfolk*

This fishery comprises over 30 acres of gravel workings, split into two small and two large pits. Depth fluctuates between 3 and over 20 feet and can vary within just a few feet, especially around the many bars and peninsulas. There is a super stock of roach, including specimens to over 2 lb, an increasing head of bream to 8 lb and a fine head of tench between 3 and 4 lb. There are also perch, including the odd whopper, a few crucian and common carp, plus a prolific head of pike. Specimens over 25 lb are taken most winters, and there is a healthy stock of doubles

107

Swangey Lakes offer superb carp fishing

among the hordes of jacks. Deadbaits usually sort out the quality pike.

Running behind the pits and included with the fisheries is a super three-quarter mile length of the River Wensum which contains some good roach, dace, chub and pike plus the odd barbel.

No night fishing is allowed. Day tickets cost £5 (£3 juniors and senior citizens) from the bailiff, who calls round, and are from dawn till dusk only. Season permits are available at £30 (£15 for juniors and senior citizens). All these tickets are also available from Churchill's Tackle Shop in Dereham (Telephone 01362 696926 for additional information).

Route: Take the A1067 Fakenham Road from Norwich to Bawdeswell and then the B1147 to Swanton Morley. Go over the Wensum and turn sharp right. The pits are then about 400 yards along on the right.

Tannery Lake, *Worthing, Norfolk*

This attractive, secluded man-made fishery comprises a single-acre lake and an interesting reach of the tiny River Blackwater, well known for its specimen dace, roach, trout and chub. The lake is fed from the stream and averages over 10 feet deep with a stock of roach, perch and tench to 4 lb. No night fishing.

Day tickets cost £2 from the owner, who calls round to anglers. For additional information, telephone Mr Eve on 01362 668202.

Route: Take the A1067 Fakenham Road from Norwich and in Bawdeswell branch onto the B1145, going through Billingford village. Proceed over the bridge spanning the River Wensum and take the next left turn. Go over the bridge across the little River Blackwater, and the lake is immediately on the right with adjacent car parking beside a huge chestnut tree.

Taswood Lakes, *Flordon, Norfolk*

This is a collection of five well-maintained lakes which vary in size from 1 to 3½ acres plus a half-mile stretch of the adjacent River Tas, best known for its dace and roach fishing. Depths vary from around 5 feet in the four small lakes with swims to 16 feet deep in the large lake. All contain a mixture of roach, rudd, bream, tench, perch, crucian carp and pike but are best known for a prolific stock of carp, the lake record being a 30 lb 5 oz specimen caught in 1993. There are carp of all strains here, including commons to 25 lb some ghost koi and the exotic grass carp to over 16 lb.

Toilet facilities are on site, and anglers are asked to note that there is no entry to the fishery during the hours of darkness and that night fishing is by prior arrangement only. Day tickets are available from the adjacent bungalow from 7 a.m. and must be booked in advance. Also night, 24-hour and long-stay tickets are available. Contact David or Brenda Edwards on 01508 470919. Yearly membership tickets are available on application.

Route: From Norwich, take the A140 to Newton Flotman and take the right fork to Flordon. One and a half miles further on, turn left to Tasburgh. The lakes are then a further 200 yards on on the left.

Taverham Mills Lake, *Taverham, Norfolk*

Owned by Anglian Water, this beautiful, irregularly shaped, well-established former gravel working covers some 20 acres. Depths vary between 2 and 12 feet, and there are extensive beds of lilies, mostly the dwarf pond lily, over its entire surface, providing numerous float-fishing swims close in. There is a prolific stock of double-figure carp plus odd specimens to 30 lb and an even larger head of tench in the 3 to 6 lb bracket. Other species include roach, rudd, perch, pike – including the odd whopper – and a small stock of bream between 6 and 10 lb. Day tickets must be purchased prior to fishing from the lodge adjacent to the anglers' car park. There is a six-hour ticket (daylight hours only) at £4, a £6 ticket which covers fishing from an hour before dawn to an hour after dusk, and a 24-hour ticket for £8. Special angling accommodation next to the lodge is also available for both overnight and holiday purposes. Telephone 01603 861014 for additional information about the fishery, which includes a superb part of the River Wensum. A limited number of 'river only' tickets are issued each year (see River Wensum).

Route: From Norwich, take the A1067 Fakenham Road into Drayton and the left fork along Taverham Road immediately

Taverham Mills Lake – fabulous tench and carp fishing

109

past the large garage on the left. Proceed for one mile, and at the first crossroads in Taverham village the fishery entrance can be seen on the left.

Thompson Water, *near Merton, Norfolk*
This huge reed-lined lake of over 30 acres is for the most part quite shallow, between 2 and 5 feet deep although holes to 10 feet have been excavated. It holds a prolific stock of tench around the 3½ lb mark, plus a few over 5 lb and some quality roach and rudd that run to over 1½ lb.

There are also bream, common carp and the lake was stocked with mirror carp in 1984 that now weigh into double figures. A big pike is also not unlikely among the hordes of smaller fish.

Day tickets cost £3 (£5 two rods) from the bailiff, who calls round. For further information, telephone 01953 883370.

Route: From Norwich, take the B1108 into Watton and then the B1110 road into Merton and through to Thompson village. Turn down Marlpit Lane (on the right) and carry on straight down the unmade road on to Peddars Way (an old Roman road), and the lake is then on the left adjacent to the roadside.

Thorpeness Mere, *Suffolk*
This 50-acre sheet of water, dotted with numerous islands, is considered more of a boating lake than a fishery. Despite its lack of depth (the lake is just 1 to 2½ feet deep), it does contain some nice fish, including a good stock of roach to over the pound, some rudd, eels and carp weighing into high double figures.

Fishing is free but from a short 100 yard length of the northern bank only; no night fishing. The rest of the perimeter is restricted and barred to angling. There are over 100 boats to hire on the mere, which provides an ideal family-cum-fishing day out.

Route: From Norwich, take the A146 then the B1332 going through Bungay, and on to the Halesworth A144 road. Go through Halesworth on the A144 and branch onto the A12(T) going to Yoxford.

Waveney Valley Lakes – the most prolific carp waters in Norfolk

Then take the B1122 to just beyond Leiston and turn left onto the B1353, which leads directly to Thorpeness and the mere.

Turf Hole Pond, *Potter Heigham, Norfolk*

This is a pond of approximately three-quarters of an an acre with an overall depth of 4 to 8 feet. It contains a good stock of quality roach, rudd, bream and hybrids, some pike to 25 lb, tench and a small stock of carp.

No night fishing is allowed. Day tickets cost £3 (only fifteen tickets are issued per day) in advance from Red Roof Farm, Ludham Road, Potter Heigham (Tel: 01692 670604) or from the office inside the fishery gates. B&B is available at the farm.

Route: Take the A47 from Norwich to Acle, turn left onto the A1064 towards Potter Heigham. Continue over the River Thurne, past the ambulance station on the left-hand side. The farm yard can be found opposite on the right-hand side of the road at Station Road junction. Pull into the farm yard from the A149, then continue along the track for 500 yards.

Waveney Valley Lakes, *Wortwell, Norfolk*

This complex is without question the best-stocked group of carp fisheries available on day ticket in East Anglia. There are in fact eight lakes, ranging in size from 2 to 5 acres and affording a variety of swims in a well-wooded setting. Depths vary between 3 and 12 feet and the water is usually well coloured in most of the lakes with a good covering of marginal reeds.

Day tickets are available on the bank from the bailiff, who calls round. These cost £8 for 12 hours, £16 for 24 hours or £75 for a weekly ticket (all for two rods). From October onwards, there are special half-price day-ticket rates (Tel: 01986 788676 for additional information).

The shop stocks tackle, a good variety of carp baits and general holiday provisions. Anglers wishing to rent one of the luxury lakeside caravans should book well in advance, and there are five-star showers and toilet facilities on site for all visitors. Touring caravanners are also welcome, and anglers may pitch their own bivvies. No dogs are allowed.

Route: From Norwich, take the A140 road, turning left to Pulham Market. Continue along the B1134 into Harleston and then take the road into Wortwell village. The lakes are well signposted and in the centre of Wortwell on the right.

Welmore Lake, *Salters Lode, Norfolk*

This 1½-acre man-made lake averages around 7 feet deep and contains an interesting stock of specimen fish, including both bream and tench to over 5 lb and carp to 20 lb. Also present are roach, rudd and pike. This is an ideal venue for the specialist angler. Fishing is from dawn till dusk only, and day tickets at £3 must be purchased in advance from Bob Riches of 15 Sandy Lane, Denver. Tel: 01366 383291.

Route: From Downham Market, take the A1122 Wisbech road and just through the village of Salters Lode take the first left turn and go over two bridges, following the track to Welmore Lake Sluice. The lake is then well signposted, with adjacent car parking.

Weybread Fishery, *Mill Lane, Weybread, Suffolk*

Formerly 'Weybread Trout Fishery', this lovely oval-shaped lake has been extended to around 2½ acres and varies in depth from 3 to 12 feet with an island accessible by a bridge. The banks are extremely well established, with extensive beds of reed, rush and sedge. The stock of fish includes quality roach, rudd, tench, and perch to over 3 lb, and also provides fun fishing for carp that weigh into double figures. Big chub also exist here. Day tickets cost £3.50 (one rod) or £4.50 (two rods) and there is an evening ticket for £2.50, available from the owner who calls round to anglers. For additional information, telephone 01379 588141.

Route: From Norwich, take the A140 Ipswich Road, turning onto the B1134 through Pulham Market and on to Harleston. In Harleston, take the B1116 road to Weybread. In Weybread, take the first left turn past the garage. The fishery is then around 300 yards down the lane on the left, adjacent to a thatched cottage.

Weybread Gravel Pits, *near Harleston, Norfolk*

The Harleston and District Angling Club control this super complex of six pleasantly matured former gravel workings. Two are for members only (anyone can join) and four are available to all on day tickets. Depths vary considerably from 3 to over 30 feet, and the banks are easily accessible with good adjacent parking. There is a superb stock of mirror carp in the No. 1 and the middle pit with numerous doubles and specimens to over 20 lb, plus roach, perch, tench, bream pike and sizeable crucians spread throughout the complex.

The largest pit, aptly called the Ocean Pit, is an immense sheet of water of over 100 acres and is easily the largest gravel pit in Norfolk. It holds a fine head of specimen bream, quality roach in profusion plus tench, pike to over 25 lb and a small stock of wily, but large carp.

Day tickets cost £3 (per rod) and £1.50 for juniors and senior citizens (per rod). These should be purchased in advance from Waveney Angling of London Road in Harleston (Tel: 01379 854886). Weekly tickets cost £12 per rod or £5 for juniors. The Harleston and District AC offers two types of fishing: to join the club costs £12 and entitles members to fish several miles of the River Waveney, in addition to the two club pits (not available on day tickets), then, for an extra £16 per rod (£8 juniors), members have access also to the four day-ticket pits – and only members may night-fish these waters. Additional information from Nigel Poll (Tel: 01379 853571).

Route: Take the A140 from Norwich, turning left at Pulham Market onto the B1134 Harleston road. Then take the Weybread road, and after crossing the River Waveney at Shotford Bridge the pits will be seen to the right and left of the road half a mile out of Harleston.

Wickham Skeith Mere, *Suffolk*

Really more of a pond, this little water is ideal for youngsters on the family outing. The water is quite shallow and becomes fairly weedy during the summer months. Carp and jack pike are the predominant species. Fishing is free.

Route: Take the A140 road from Norwich to Stoke Ash (twenty-seven miles), turning right at the signpost to Wickham Skeith. The pond is on the village common.

Windmill Ponds, *Denver, Norfolk*

These two attractive, interconnected ponds of about half an acre apiece, offer comfortable fishing from flat banks, with depths fluctuating between 3 and 6 feet. There is a prolific stock of crucian carp, roach, rudd, bream and some mirror carp into high double figures. Fishing is from dawn until dusk only, and day tickets cost £3. These must be purchased in advance from Bob Riches, 15 Sandy Lane, Denver (Tel: 01366 383291).

Route: From King's Lynn, take the A10 to Denver and at the church follow the sign for the windmill. The ponds are then next to the windmill with adjacent car parking.

Woodlakes Holiday Park, *Stow, Norfolk*

There are over 20 acres of water at Woodlakes, comprising one large and three small lakes, all set in picturesque wooded countryside adjacent to Woodlakes Caravan and Camping Park. All the lakes are well coloured and average about 5 feet deep. They are well stocked with roach and rudd plus tench and plenty of bream in the 1 to 3 lb range, with a prolific head of carp running to 25 lb. Double-figure fish are most plentiful. For mixed bags, float-fishing along the margins with maggots or breadflake is recommended, and for the carp, high protein pastes or boilies.

This is an ideal family spot where cars can be taken down to the lakes but where the carp specialist can turn a few fish up after dark. Touring caravans are welcome, and anglers may, for a small charge, pitch their own tents. Day permits are available from the reception kiosk or, if closed, from the bailiff, who calls round. Fishing for up to six hours costs £3, up to 12 hours £6, and 24-hour tickets are £8 – all for two rods. Special weekly and season tickets are also available. Anglers who pay to camp or stay in their own caravans enjoy reduced fishing rates. There is a shop on site where flasks are filled and fresh sandwiches made to order. For additional information, telephone 01553 810414.

Also available is a fly-fishing-only lake of around 10 acres, stocked with rainbows (see Trout Fishing – Day Ticket (Stillwaters)).

Route: Take the A10(T) from King's Lynn, turning right in Stow Bardolph and proceed towards Stow Bridge. 500 yards before the bridge, carry straight ahead at a sharp left turn, and Woodlakes can be seen on the right, 200 yards further on.

STILLWATERS — MEMBERS ONLY

Alderson Lake, *Needham Market, Suffolk*
Named with deep respect after the general manager of the Gipping Angling Preservation Society (GAPS), George Alderson, who has done so much for angling in this area, the fishery comprises two gravel pits which are owned by the society. The largest, about 7 acres, is pleasantly reeded around the perimeter and has two islands. Depth varies between 6 and 16 feet, and the stock includes a good head of roach and rudd to over the pound, plus numbers of specimen tench which have been caught to 7¼ lb. Specimen pike are also taken here, and the lake has produced fish to 27 lb in recent years. The smaller lake covers about an acre and is extremely well stocked with tench, crucian carp and mirror carp, providing excellent fishing for the younger angler.

This is a members-only water of GAPS. Apply to George Alderson, 19 Clover Close, Chantry Estate, Ipswich (Tel: 01473 602828). Yearly membership costs £33 (plus a first-year entry fee) and covers a wealth of local fishing on other pits and over ten miles of the River Gipping. There are special reduced rates for juniors and senior citizens.

Route: From Ipswich, take the A14 and then the B1078 going to Needham Market. Entrance to the fishery is down the sharp left turn over the bridge spanning the River Gipping, directly opposite Bosmere Mill.

Barham Pit, *near Claydon, Suffolk*
This huge, irregularly shaped pit can be seen on the left of the track when travelling by train from Norwich to London. It covers over 20 acres with beautiful willow-clad islands and peninsulas. The depth varies between 6 and 15 feet, and the water is usually well coloured. There is a prolific stock of both roach and bream plus some good tench, carp and perch. The pike run to over 20 lb.

This is a members-only water of the Gipping Angling Preservation Society with yearly membership through George Alderson, 19 Clover Close, Chantry Estate, Ipswich (Tel: 01473 602828). Membership costs £33 plus a £10 first-year entry fee, and there are reduced rates for juniors, students and senior citizens. The society controls several other super stillwaters plus over ten miles of the River Gipping.

Route: From Ipswich, take the A14, then branch onto the Claydon road (old

Norwich Road). Turn left at Pest House Lane, which then leads directly to the pits.

Bawburgh Pit, *Bawburgh, Norfolk*
This irregularly shaped gravel pit of some 12 acres varies tremendously in depth between 3 and 18 feet, offering a variety of both shallow plateaux and deep gully swims. The stock includes a prolific head of pike to over 20 lb, bream to over 10 lb, plus roach, perch, and carp weighing into double figures. Also included is three-quarters of a mile of the River Yare, skirting the pit, which contains small numbers of specimen roach and chub.

This is a members-only water of the Yarmouth and Norfolk County Angling Association, who issue season permits costing £16 through Tom Boulton's Tackle Shop in Norwich (Tel: 01603 426834) – adults only, no juniors.

Route: From Norwich, take the A47 towards Dereham and – still within the city outskirts – turn left at the Bowthorpe roundabout. Turn right at the traffic lights and proceed around the edge of estate to a mini roundabout, taking the right turn down narrow Bawburgh Road. Entrance to the pit is then on the left several hundred yards further through the gravel company's main gate. Bawburgh Pit is on the right of the track with adjacent parking and the most westerly of a complex comprising several former gravel workings.

Billingford Pit, *Norfolk*
This boomerang-shaped little pit of around 3 acres lies in a hollow, heavily clad in undergrowth of gorse and trees all the way round. Swims have been cut into the steep banking, offering depths between 6 and 12 feet under the rod tip, though water levels do fluctuate periodically. The pit can prove rather weedy in the summer but provides excellent tench fishing with specimens to over 4 lb, along with many small roach and perch. There are also one or two large carp and a few pike. A really big perch is not unlikely.

This is a members-only water of the Dereham and District Angling Club. Membership costs £10 yearly (£4 for senior citizens, juniors and disabled anglers) from the membership secretary, D. Appleby, 6 Rump Close, Swanton Morley, Norfolk (Tel: 01362 637591). Membership cards are also available from Myhill's Tackle Shop of Church Street, Dereham (Tel: 01362 692975) and Churchill's Tackle Shop, Norwich Road, Dereham (Tel: 01362 696926).

Route: Take the A1067 from Norwich to Bawdeswell, then turn left to Billingford, taking the first left turn in the village to Swanton Morley. Proceed for about 100 yards to the first bend, and on the right is a dirt road leading to the pit.

Bircham Pit, *Bircham, Norfolk*
Also known as 'The Moor', this small, man-made lake contains roach, bream, perch, good rudd, tench, a few carp and enormous gudgeon, providing fun fishing on the float. No ground baiting is allowed, and strict rules against litter are enforced.

This is a members-only water of the Docking Angling Club and open only to local anglers, who should contact the chairman, Rob Parnell, on 01485 518315.

Route: Take the A1067 from Norwich, going through Fakenham towards Docking. Take the left fork to Great Bircham and, in the village, turn right onto the B1153 to Docking. Bircham Pit is then a short distance further on on the right, opposite Moor Farm.

Bosmere Lake, *Needham Market, Suffolk*
This 5-acre, oval mere was the subject of a study by Cambridge University a few years ago which dated its existence back 10,000 years to the Ice Age. Moving on to the turn of this century, when barges last used the adjacent River Gipping to carry coal upstream from Ipswich to all the mills, the mere was used as a turnaround, and there is still evidence of the entrance

dyke, now overgrown, from the river. When the Eastern Union Railway started up in 1849 the days of carrying goods by barge were numbered, and the old dyke silted up, leaving the mere isolated. Today, the mere varies in depth between 4 and 18 feet and is nicely wooded around the margins, with patches of lilies dotting the surface.

It holds, predominantly, bream to over 5 lb, plus roach, tench, pike and numerous eels – some very large. This is a really secluded mixed fishery with a boat available to members.

A members-only water of the Bosmere Fishing Club, season permits cost £40 from Jim Markwell, Bosmere Hall, Needham Market (Tel: 01449 721487).

Route: From Ipswich, take the A45 and then the B1078 going to Needham Market. The lake is then on the left, immediately before the road crosses the River Gipping.

Bradmoor Lakes, *Pentney, Norfolk*

These are two beautifully matured gravel pits set in the wooded outskirts of Bradmoor Plantation. Both are around 4 acres and hold a prolific stock of fish, with several species running into specimen size. The old record crucian carp of 5 lb 10½ oz was caught here by Graham Halls in 1976, and during the 1980s several bream weighing into double figures were taken. There are good numbers of roach and rudd, plus tench over 5 lb and an enormous head of mirror carp weighing into double figures. Several monsters up to 30 lb have been caught.

This is a members-only water of the Swaffham Angling Club. Membership costs £18.50 yearly (£7 for juniors, senior citizens and disabled anglers) from Kev's Tackle Shop of Norwich Road in Swaffham (Tel: 01760 720188).

Route: From Norwich, take the A47 towards King's Lynn. The lakes are then situated on the right of the Narborough bypass.

Brandon Lake, *Brandon, Suffolk*

Running adjacent to the Little Ouse, this attractive man-made lake of about 3 acres has an average depth of around 5 feet. There are extensive lily beds in the middle and species include plenty of roach, perch and small bream. There is also a decent head of quality bream to 5½ lb, as well as a stock of carp running into double figures.

This is good float water, ideally suited to young anglers.

A members-only water of Brandon Angling Club, membership cards cost £7 from the Rod 'n' Line Tackle Shop in Thetford (Tel: 01842 764825).

Route: Into Brandon via the A1066 Thetford road and then take the London road towards Lakenheath. Take the first right turn past the cinema, then 100 yards further on turn right into Remembrance Park and playing-field. The road then leads down to the lake and River Little Ouse. The river holds grayling in this area in addition to dace, roach and chub, and this fishing is also controlled by Brandon AC. Tickets are available as above.

Bures Lake, *Bures, Suffolk*

This well-matured, beautifully wooded gravel pit of 4½ acres contains a super head of specimen tench between 4 and 6 lb. In the past the lake has produced tench in excess of 8 lb, although in recent seasons fish over 7 lb have been rare. There are some bream to 9 lb, quality rudd, a few perch and a small stock of pike running into double figures. Depth varies between 4 and 6 feet, and the water is sometimes very clear with a weed growth that can be prolific one season, yet sparse the next. No night fishing.

This is a members-only water of the London Anglers Association and for clubs affiliated. There is also an associate membership for which anyone may apply, costing £25 yearly, £12.50 for juniors, senior citizens and disabled. Apply by sending a stamped, addressed envelope to the London Anglers Association, Isaac

115

Walton House, 2A Hervey Park Road, London E17 6LJ (Tel: 0181 520 7477).

Route: From Colchester, take the B1508 into the village of Bures and proceed over the bridge spanning the River Stour. Then turn right immediately past the church and proceed along the Nayland road, passing the mill, and 500 yards further on the LAA sign and entrance gate can be seen on the right, with the lake adjacent to the northern bank of the Stour.

Camelot Lake, *Wortwell, Norfolk*
This beautifully landscaped man-made fishery, which can be seen beside the A143 Wortwell bypass between Homersfield and Harleston, is an irregularly shaped former gravel working of around 2½ acres with one small island and an interesting assortment of swims affording depths of between 8 and 15 feet close in beyond the marginal shelf.

Species include roach, specimen perch and bream, eels, tench and carp to over 30 lb. Lakeside facilities include timber-framed seating, bar and barbecue, electricity points, water, etc. – in fact everything for the organised family or corporate day out. The lake may be booked for the day, or longer, by parties of up to ten anglers for private or match purposes, at prices available on request from the owner, Baroness Urquhart (Tel: 01508 482296).

Route: From Norwich, take the B1332 to Bungay and turn right at the first roundabout onto the bypass, which goes straight alongside the lake just beyond Homersfield.

Causeway Lake, *Great Blackenham, Suffolk*
This 7-acre lake is unique in that it has the River Gipping flowing in one end and out the other. Depths vary between 5 and 17 feet and the water is usually well coloured by the river. Bream are the predominant species, with good stocks of all sizes, including fish to 6 lb. Bream bags of 100 lb are nothing out of the ordinary here. There are also some tench, specimen roach and chub which filter through from the river. Perch have been taken to over 3 lb in recent years, and a good pike is always on the cards.

This is a members-only water of the Gipping Angling Preservation Society with yearly membership through George Alderson, 19 Clover Close, Chantry Estate, Ipswich (Tel: 01473 602828). Membership costs £33 plus a first-year entry fee of £10, and there are reduced rates for juniors, students and senior citizens. The society controls several other super stillwaters as well as over ten miles of the River Gipping.

Route: From Ipswich, take the old A14, going through Claydon on the B1113. Half a mile through Great Blackenham, turn right down a private road and proceed over the railway bridge. The lake is then on the other side of the River Gipping.

The Deep Hole, *Frostenden, Wrentham, Suffolk*
Though small, this old clay pit is between 14 and 20 feet deep. The water is invariably well coloured, with a stock of perch, odd chub, roach, rudd and mirror carp weighing into double figures.

This is a members-only water of the Southwold and District Freshwater Angling Preservation Society, who control fishing on five other pieces of stillwater. The subscription is an £8 joining-fee plus £16 yearly (juniors £5). Apply to the membership secretary, Mrs B.M. Reid, 19 Sussex Road, Lowestoft (Tel: 01502 518198).

Route Take the A12 from Lowestoft, going south through Wrentham, and turn right immediately before the Wangford Plough pub and dual carriageway bypass. The pit is then one mile further on, on the right, opposite the first cottage on the left.

Diss Mere, *Diss, Norfolk*
Situated right in the middle of Diss with adjacent parking and shopping facilities, this almost round mere of some 4 acres shelves down to 20 feet in places with a

variety of swims around two-thirds of the perimeter (the other one-third is private frontage), varying between 3 and 10 feet just a rod-length out. It holds a prolific head of roach, rudd and especially crucian carp which run to over 2 lb but average around 12 oz. There are also some eels, tench to 4 lb and a strong head of mirror and common carp weighing into double figures.

This is a members-only water of the Diss Angling Club with yearly tickets at £14 (£6 senior citizens and juniors) from Myhill's Garden and Tackle Shop opposite the mere (Tel: 01379 642465). A two-rod permit for night fishing is available on written application to the club secretary, Ken Oldham, 36 Church Close, Roydon, Diss, Norfolk.

Route: Take the A140 from Norwich and branch off at Scole onto the A1066 to Diss. The mere lies bang in the centre of Diss, opposite Waveney Fish Farm.

Ditchingham Pit, *Bungay, Suffolk*

This attractive 3-acre pit lies alongside the River Waveney at the back of Bungay Common and is bordered by shrubs and willows. The depth varies between 3 and 7 feet, and the water is usually well coloured. Species include a good stock of carp weighing into double figures and a good head of crucians over the pound. There are also roach, perch, big eels and some tench up to 5 lb.

This is a members-only water of the Bungay Cherry Tree Angling Club. Membership costs £20 (£10 for senior citizens, £6 juniors) from the secretary, Ian Gosling, 37 St Mary's Terrace, Bungay (Tel: 01986 892982). Membership includes a wealth of other local fishing controlled by the club.

Route: Take the B1332 from Norwich to the large roundabout just before Bungay. Go completely round the roundabout to face Norwich again and take the first lane on the left beside a bungalow. This leads to the car park and pit.

Fosters End Pits, *Blackborough End, Norfolk*

These are three tiny pits plus the main pit of around 8 acres. Depths in the big pit vary considerably from 3 to over 25 feet. It holds some hefty crucians and rudd plus both carp and pike weighing into double figures. Pike well in excess of 20 lb are taken every winter. Also present are

Diss Mere is full of crucian and other carp varieties

bream to over 10 lb and a good stock of specimen tench. No night fishing allowed.

This is a members-only water of the King's Lynn Angling Association. Membership cards cost £15 (£7 for senior citizens and £3.50 juniors) from all local tackle shops and from the secretary, M. Grief, 67 Peckover Way, South Wootton, King's Lynn PE30 3UE (Tel: 01553 671545).

Route: From Norwich, take the A47 King's Lynn road to East Winch. In the village turn left down a track just before the church and the pits are then one mile ahead on the left.

Glemsford Lake, *near Sudbury, Suffolk*

These three irregularly shaped former gravel workings have been made a triple-S site (a Site of Special Scientific Interest) by the Countryside Commission. They are well matured, nicely interspersed with islands and surrounded by deep woodlands in the Suffolk Stour valley. No night fishing is allowed.

No. 1 pit lies along the Stour's southern bank and is the largest at around 18 acres. The water is always well coloured and holds a prolific head of roach, rudd and bream to 4 lb, plus tench of a similar size. There are also pike and carp weighing into double figures.

No. 2 pit covers around 4 acres and exceptionally shallow. Though it contains roach, rudd and tench, fishing is virtually impossible due to the exceptionally heavy weed growth.

No. 3 pit is the smallest at 3 acres, with depths varying from 4 to 12 feet. It holds roach, rudd, pike and zander plus a strong head of tench to over 4 lb. Bags of up to ten tench at a sitting are commonplace.

This is a members-only water of the London Anglers Association and for clubs affiliated. There is also an associate membership, for which anyone may apply, at £25 yearly (£12.50 for juniors, senior citizens and disabled). Apply by sending a stamped, addressed envelope to the London Anglers Association, Isaac Walton House, 2A Hervey Park Road, London E17 6LJ (Tel: 0181 5207477).

Route: From Sudbury, take the A134 to Long Melford and then the A1092 to Cavendish. The lakes are then situated on the left, almost opposite the Glemsford Road, immediately after crossing the River Glen. This entrance is for No. 1 lake only. For No. 2 and No. 3 lakes, take the first left turn past the entrance to No. 1 lake and 50 yards along go over a level-crossing. The LAA gate and signpost is then immediately on the left before crossing the River Stour.

Greenmeadows, *Stowmarket, Suffolk*

This pretty, yet tiny pond of around three-quarters of an acre varies between 2 and 9 feet deep and contains roach, rudd, crucian carp and some mirror carp to 8 lb.

This is a members-only water of the Gipping Valley Angling Club, who control the fishing for Mid Suffolk District Council. Yearly, January-to-December tickets cost £12 (£7.50 to senior citizens) from David Shipp of Bosmere Tackle, 57 High Street, Needham Market (Tel: 01449 721808) and entitle members to fish a much larger lake (see Needham Lake) and two stretches of river.

Route: From Ipswich, take the A14 to Stowmarket and proceed around the ring road to the football ground. Greenmeadows pit is then directly behind the ground, beside the A14.

Iceni Lake, *Cockley Cley, near Swaffham, Norfolk*

Set in a nature conservancy area, this irregularly shaped man-made lake covers some 8 acres, has a centre island and affords depths ranging from 2 to 8 feet. It holds a strong head of tench averaging 5 lb as well as roach, rudd, perch and bream.

Iceni Lake is a members-only water of the Swaffham Angling Club. Membership costs £18.50 yearly (£7 for juniors, senior citizens and disabled anglers) from Kev's Tackle Shop of Norwich Road, Swaffham (Tel: 01760 720188).

Route: From Norwich, take the A47 into the town of Swaffham, going through the market-place and turning right onto the Stoke Ferry Road. Four miles beyond Swaffham, look on the left for the Cockley Cley Iceni village, where Iceni Lake is adjacent and well signposted.

The Irrigation Lagoon, *Beccles, Norfolk*

This is a man-made, horseshoe-shaped fishery with depths ranging between 2 and 14 feet, situated adjacent to the River Waveney, which forms the borderline between Norfolk and Suffolk. The lagoon can prove rather weedy but contains a fine stock of bream running to 6 lb, plus tench in the 2 to 3 lb bracket. Other species include roach, rudd, perch and pike weighing into double figures.

This is a members-only water of the Southwold and District Freshwater Angling Preservation Society. Subscriptions include an £8 joining fee plus £16 yearly, juniors £5. Apply to the membership secretary, Mrs B.M. Reid, 19 Sussex Road, Lowestoft (Tel: 01502 518198).

Route: From Norwich, take the A146 to just before Beccles and turn right at the large roundabout, going under the footbridge and turning right again. Then take the second right just before the public house and turn left down King's Dam, which leads to the fishery, via a dirt track at the sharp right-hand bend.

Kingfisher Fishing Club Lakes, *Lyng, Norfolk*

For over twenty years a trout fishery, this interesting complex of four well-matured gravel pits (plus a three-quarter-mile stretch of the River Wensum) changed over to coarse fishing in 1994 when the Kingfisher Fishing Club was formed by the owners. In fact, the three small lakes have always been coarse fisheries and

Kingfisher Fishing Club Lakes are renowned for big pike, carp and bream

119

contain a good stock of roach, perch, tench, bream and pike, but it is the huge 26-acre former trout water which has captured everyone's attention by producing at least two pike nudging 40 lb. A shoal of huge bream is also present, and a 14 lb monster was taken by D. Cross in 1994 plus several other specimens over 9 lb. Depths vary from 5 to 14 feet in this prolific lake which is irregularly shaped with several islands. It also contains some quality roach and tench plus a tremendous head of carp to over 20 lb.

The three-quarter-mile stretch of the Wensum (see also River Wensum in the rivers chapter) skirts the big lakes northern shoreline and contains, in addition to roach over 2 lb chub and pike, small groups of specimen bream weighing into double figures.

Contact Cyril or Paul Rogers of Walsis Farm, Lenwade, Norfolk (Tel: 01603 872333). The annual (January–December) subscription costs £100, which also entitles members to the bar and restaurant facilities at the adjacent Leisure Complex.

Route: Take the A1067 Fakenham Road from Norwich to around two miles beyond Lenwade and turn left, following the Lyng signpost. Proceed over the bridge spanning River Wensum and in the middle of the village turn right down the quarry lane at the crossroads, following the signpost to the fishery.

Lyng Pit, *Lyng, Norfolk*
This is a most attractive little pit of about 4 acres, which is wooded nearly all the way round with willow-clad peninsulas offering a variety of sheltered swims. The depth varies between 3 and 8 feet, and the water is invariably well coloured. There is a good stock of roach and bream in all sizes; though most are small there are a few up to 4 lb. The tench average around 3 lb, and there are a few pike plus a very small stock of large mirror carp. Dereham and District Angling Club, who control the fishing, have swims on only about half the lake,

along the river bank – around twenty swims in all. Included is a half-mile stretch of the adjacent River Wensum, which contains a few dace, chub, trout and one or two big roach.

Membership costs £10 yearly (£4 for senior citizens, juniors and disabled anglers) from the membership secretary, D. Appleby, 6 Rump Close, Swanton Morley, Norfolk (Tel: 01362 637591).

Membership cards are available also from Myhill's Tackle Shop of Church Street, Dereham (Tel: 01362 692975) and Churchill's Tackle Shop, Norwich Road, Dereham (Tel: 01362 696926).

Membership includes fishing on other local pits and on the River Wensum in choice locations (see River Wensum).

Route: Leave Norwich on the A1067 Fakenham Road, turning left at the Lyng signpost. At the village of Lyng, take the right arm of the crossroads (which is in fact a track), and the pit is 50 yards on the right through a gate.

Nar Valley Fisheries, *Pentney, Norfolk*
Open for the first time in June 1995, these four newly landscaped gravel pit fisheries are part of operating gravel workings which will eventually comprise a considerably larger fisheries development, covering over 200 acres and including over a mile of roach, dace and bream fishing on the delightful River Nar.

Lake No. 1 is rectangular in shape with a variation in depth between 2 and 20 feet and covers around 4 acres. Stocks include roach, rudd, bream and a prolific head of small carp. Also present are some tench in the 4 to 6 lb bracket plus specimen-sized eels. Fishing is from marked swims along the two long banks only.

Lake No. 2 is oblong-shaped and around an acre and a half with depths to 11 feet. Species present are crucian carp, roach, rudd, bream, perch and quality tench to over 4 lb.

Lake No. 3 is just half an acre and kidney-shaped with depths to 8 feet and thick beds of weed. It is an ideal water for youngsters, holding prolific stocks of perch, roach, rudd and small tench.

Lake No. 4 holds some quality bream and tench plus some double-figure carp and pike in an area of around 2 acres with depths to 12 feet. Fishing is from a limited number of marked swims only, to preserve the quality of the sport and surroundings. It is very much a specialist's lake. Barbless hooks are to be used at all times on this complex, which is only for members of Nar Valley Fisheries.

Yearly permits (no day tickets) cost £30 and are available from Middleton Aggregates office, Mill Drove, Blackborough End, King's Lynn. Contact Peter Lemon on 01553 841044 for additional information.

Route: From Norwich, take the A47 towards King's Lynn and turn left in East Winch, opposite the Carpenters' Arms public house. Continue past the gate to Pentney Coarse Lakes, which is on the left, following signs for Wimpeys and Middleton Aggregates, whose entrance gate is then on the right. Parking is adjacent to the lakes.

Needham Lake, *Needham Market, Suffolk*

This 7-acre lake is a mere stone's throw away from the railway station at Needham Market. Depths vary between 6 and 20 feet, and the banks are of an open aspect. Stocks include roach but rudd, perch, pike, bream, mirror and crucian carp predominate. This is a multi-use water with facilities for sailing, windsurfing and miniature power boats, etc. The fishery includes a half-mile beat of the adjacent River Gipping, which backs onto the lake's north bank.

This is a members-only water of the Gipping Valley Angling Club, who run the lake for Mid Suffolk District Council. Yearly (January–December) tickets cost £12 (£7.50 senior citizens) from David Shipp of Bosmere Tackle, 57 High Street, Needham Market (Tel: 01449 721808) and entitle members to fish another smaller pit (see Greenmeadows) as well as two stretches of river.

Route: From Ipswich, take the A14 and then the B1078 going to Needham Market. The lake is then on the right, sandwiched between the river and the railway line just over the river bridge.

Nunnery Lakes, *Thetford, Norfolk*

This fast-developing and extremely interesting fishery comprises six pits ranging in size from 1 to 10 acres and in depth from 2 to over 20 feet, situated beside the charming River Little Ouse on the outskirts of Thetford. Owned by the British Trust for Ornithology, who have organised a generous and continuous stocking policy for the future, these lakes offer superlative sport.

Based to a large extent on carp fishing, three of these lakes regularly produce specimen mirrors, leathers and commons over 20 lb, plus a host of double-figure fish, along with tench, rudd, roach, big perch and specimen pike. The largest carp to be taken weighed 35¼ lb and fell to the rod of G. Maulkerson in 1994.

For details of membership apply with a stamped, addressed envelope to the Nunnery Fishery, J. Davies, Bridge Farm, Caston, Norfolk NR17 1DJ.

Pedmarsh Lake, *near Sudbury, Suffolk*

Due to the enormous costs involved, estate lakes are rarely made these days. Pedmarsh Lake, however, is an exception and has been created by damming a valley to provide some 20 acres of water.

Depth varies from just 18 inches at the shallow end, which has been designated a nature reserve, to around 16 feet at the dam end.

Stocks include roach, perch, tench, bream and a strong population of carp.

This is a members-only water of the Colchester Angling Preservation Society, who issue season permits costing £30 from the secretary, M. Turner, 29 Lodge Road, Braintree (Tel: 01376 323520). This permit covers a wealth of local fishing in several stillwaters, including famous Layer Pits and several miles of the Suffolk Stour (see Suffolk Rivers). Anyone may join the club.

Route: From Sudbury, take the A131 Halstead road, following signs for Pedmarsh and turning left three miles out of Sudbury. At Pedmarsh, turn right towards White Colne. Continue for a mile, and the entrance to the lake is then via a track on the right and well signposted.

Pettistree Lake, *Wickham Market, Suffolk*
This fishery comprises two man-made irrigation reservoirs of half an acre and around 1 acre which hold a stock of rudd and carp.

These are members-only waters of the Framlingham and District Angling Club. Anyone may join for a yearly subscription of £12.50 (£6.50 juniors and senior citizens) which includes sport on several other local ponds and lakes plus a stretch of the River Deben. Apply to Saxmundham Angling Centre, rear of the Market Place, Saxmundham (Tel: 01728 603443).

Route: From Saxmundham, take the A12 to Wickham Market and then the B1438 into Pettistree. Turn right at Pettistree Three Tuns public house, then take first left at the water tower. Next take the first right turn at the signpost to Hungarian Hall, and the reservoirs are one mile further down the road on the left, beneath electricity pylons.

Railway Lake, *North Elmham, Norfolk*
This is a pretty, wooded lake of about an acre with depths varying between 2 and 11 feet. It is usually well coloured and holds tench, jumbo-sized crucian carp, roach, rudd, perch and bream to 6 lb, plus a small stock or specimen mirror carp.

Railway Lake is a members-only water of the Fakenham Angling Club. Membership is open only to those living within a ten-mile radius of Fakenham and available from Dave's Tackle Shop of Norwich Street, Fakenham (Tel: 01328 864637). There is a first-year entry fee of £3 plus £8 per season thereafter which covers sport on additional stillwater fishing plus some excellent trout and coarse fishing on the River Wensum.

Route: Take the A1067 Fakenham Road from Norwich to Bawdeswell and turn left onto the B1145. Just past Billingford village, the road goes over the River Wensum, then look out on the left for the Railway Tavern public house. Just before the pub, access to the lake is through a gate and over a cattle-grid, then across a meadow to the far left-hand corner.

Redgrave Lake, *Botesdale, Suffolk*
Redgrave is huge, a really long, wide estate lake with open banks, except for the dam end, which is heavily wooded. It is fairly shallow at the eastern end, deepening towards the dam end, which traditionally produces some good early season bags of tench averaging between 3 and 5 lb. There is a terrific stock of bream which have provided the bulk of the catches in recent years, with specimens to over 8 lb. There are numerous skimmers, of course, plus a good head of roach and perch to over the pound, eels, carp (only a few – but large), and a prolific stock of pike in all sizes. There is a good head of doubles, and fish of over 25 lb are taken each winter.

This is an excellent summer venue for truly mixed catches on the float or feeder.

Apply to Redgrave Park, Redgrave, Suffolk (Tel: 01379 898205). Annual membership (January–December) for adults costs £40, juniors £20.

Route: From Norwich, take the A140 to Scole and then the A143. Redgrave Lake can then be seen on the right-hand side of the road, a half mile outside Botesdale. Turn right on the Redgrave B1113 road and look for a concrete track on the right, bordering woodlands on the lake's dam end, which leads to a car park.

Red House Farm Moat, *near Peasenhall, Suffolk*

This is an attractive little fishery of about half an acre, holding a mixed stock of crucian carp, roach, rudd and tench to 3 lb, provides really good fun fishing in a depth of about 3 feet, where the water is usually well coloured. It has a typical farm pond environment and comfortable sport on the float.

This is a members-only water of the Framlingham and District Angling Club. Anyone may join for an annual subscription of £12.50 (£6.50 juniors and senior citizens), and this covers sport on several other local ponds plus a stretch of the River Deben. Apply to Saxmundham Angling Centre, rear of the Market Place, Saxmundham (Tel: 01728 603443).

Route: From Harleston, take the B1116 into Dennington and turn left onto the A1120. Three miles further on, halfway between Badingham and Peasenhall, look for a lane on the left (it is the only lane), which leads directly to Red House Farm, which is then on the right just round the bend.

Reydon No. 2 and 3 Pits, *Southwold, Suffolk*

No. 2 is a 1-acre pit with depths to over 20 feet and holds specimen tench, odd chub, plus rudd, bream, roach and perch. The banks are reed-fringed with just eighteen swims available along one bank only.

No. 3 pit, open for the first time in 1989, having been dug specifically for fishing, varies between 4 and 6 feet deep and is just half an acre in size. It provides easy fishing, especially for youngsters, and contains a variety of species, including roach, rudd, perch, tench and crucian carp. Both fisheries allow one rod only and no night fishing.

This is a members-only water of the Southwold and District Freshwater Angling Preservation Society. Subscriptions include an £8 joining fee plus £16 yearly, juniors £5. Apply to membership secretary, Mrs B.M. Reid, 19 Sussex Road, Lowestoft (Tel: 01502 518198).

Route: From Southwold, take the A1095 and after going over the road bridge spanning Buss Creek look for the Lakeside Park development on left. The estate road leads to the car-parking area close to No. 2 pit. Walk from the car park to No. 3 pit along the footpath.

Rushbrooke Lake, *Bury St Edmunds, Suffolk*

Covering about 3 acres with 8 feet of water at the dam and shallows at the opposite end, Rushbrooke Lake contains a good stock of quality roach, some bream and tench, plus carp to over 20 lb. No night fishing is allowed.

A members-only water of the Bury St Edmunds Angling Association, yearly membership costs £17 (£8.50 juniors and £3 senior citizens) from Tackle Up of Bury St Edmunds (Tel: 01284 755022). Membership also allows the holder to fish West Stow Country Park Lake.

Route: From Bury, take the A14 Ipswich road. Two miles out of Bury, turn right at the AA box and then second right, signposted to Wellnethan. The lake is then on the left at the bottom of the hill.

Scottow Pond, *Scottow, Norfolk*

This is a shallow, 5-acre lake holding an excellent head of tench. Scottow Pond's banks are reed-fringed and the water crystal clear. The bottom is silty and daphnia abound, which is possibly the reason why the tench average over 3½ lb. There is also a head of pike and eels, and the lake was well stocked with mirror carp in 1983.

Season permits are available at a cost £12 from Mr Townsend, 1 Work House Corner, Scottow (Tel: 01692 538671).

Route: Take the B1150 from Norwich,

passing through Coltishall, Buxton Lamas and on to Swanton Abbot. The lake is in the wood of Mr Shaw's estate at Scottow.

Shropham Pit, *Shropham, Norfolk*
This ia a large irregularly shaped pit of around 6 acres which has three, reed-clad islands and is heavily fringed with beds of lilies. Depth varies from 5 to over 10 feet, and the stock includes a good head of bream to 7 lb, as well as tench, quality crucian carp, roach, rudd, eels and pike weighing into double figures. There is also a small, wily stock of carp to over 20 lb.

This members-only water of the Wymondham and District Angling Club has permits costing £20 from the secretary, T. Binks of 25 Rosemary Road, Norwich (Tel: 01603 405341) and through Myhill's Tackle shops in Attleborough and in Dereham.

Route: Take the A11 from Norwich and at the end of the Attleborough bypass look left for the Breckland Lodge. One mile further on, turn right at the crossroads to Shropham. One and a half miles further, proceed over the bridge spanning the River Thet and turn left immediately after the carrot factory. The pit is then 300 yards on the left, down an apparent dead end.

Sparham Pool, *Lyng, Norfolk*
This extremely well-matured and heavily wooded former gravel pit is a nature reserve shared with the Norfolk Naturalists Trust. It is irregular in shape and covers around 14 acres with a variation in depth from 3 to over 15 feet. Stocks include a strong head of roach to the pound as well as perch, rudd, eels and a good head of tench averaging around 4 lb.

This is a members-only water of the Norfolk Anglers' Conservation Association (NACA), who issue just four tickets daily to members for Monday to Saturday only – no sunday fishing. These cost £3 and must be booked in advance. They are available only to NACA members through Bert Moseley, 7 Soanes Court, Lyng, Norfolk (Tel: 01603 870253). A strict keepnet ban is in force.

To join the NACA, contact Malcolm Hitchens, Woodside House, 5 The Meadows, Aylsham, Norwich NR11 6HP (Tel: 01263 732752).

Route: From Norwich, take the A1067 Fakenham Road and turn left following the Lyng signpost one mile beyond Lenwade. At the bottom of the hill, 100 yards before the bridge spanning the River Wensum, turn left along the track which leads to the NACA car park.

Stantons Farm Lake, *Little Cornard, Suffolk*
This is an oblong, man-made reservoir of some 3 acres with depths ranging from 4 to 12 feet. There is a mixed stock, including roach, rudd, bream, tench and carp running into double figures. No night fishing.

A members-only water of the Sudbury and District Angling Association, membership costs £25 (reduced rates for juniors, senior citizens and disabled) from T. Fairless, 39 Potkiln Road, Great Cornard, Sudbury (Tel: 01787 312536).

Route: From Sudbury, take the B1508 Bures road to Workhouse Green, then turn left at the telephone box, and the lake is literally at the foot of the huge television mast one mile further on on the right through the farm entrance.

Tottenhill Pit, *King's Lynn, Norfolk*
This large pit, varying in depth between 5 and 8 feet, generally has clear water with a little weed. The pit holds a good mix of roach, rudd, bream, specimen tench, crucians and some really large pike topping the 25 lb mark. No night fishing.

This members-only water is controlled by King's Lynn Angling Association which has open membership with club cards costing £15 (£7 senior citizens and £3.50 juniors) from all local tackle shops and from the secretary, M. Grief, 67 Peckover Way, South Wootton, King's Lynn PE30 3UE (Tel: 01553 671545).

Route: Take the A47 from Norwich, branching onto the A1122 Downham road. In Stradsett, turn right onto the A134 towards King's Lynn. Four miles on, turn left to Tottenhill, and the pit is then situated (rather well hidden from view) half a mile further on behind a housing estate diagonally across the common.

University Broad, *Norwich, Norfolk*
This is really pleasantly landscaped and well-matured gravel pit of about 10 acres and is the only large fishable stillwater within the city boundaries. Depths fluctuate between 4 and over 20 feet with at least 10 feet of water close in around much of the perimeter.

University Broad offers comfortable float-fishing for roach, rudd, tench and bream in the 7 to 8 lb range. There is also a good head of carp with specimens over 20 lb having been taken.

A huge koi carp of 12¼ lb was taken by Nick Waller in 1984. There are a few eels and a strong head of pike. Each winter, several fish in the 20 to 26 lb range are taken, usually on static deadbaits. There is a 'no livebaiting'-rule in force, and night fishing is open only to members of two years' standing who pay an extra £12.50 for a special night syndicate ticket.

This members-only water is controlled by the University of East Anglia. Yearly permits cost £20 (£10 for juniors and senior citizens) from Ron Ashby of the Biology Department, UEA, Norwich. Apply in writing with a stamped, addressed envelope or telephone 01603 56161, ext. 2238.

Route: Keep to the B1108 Watton road from Norwich centre and turn left onto Bluebell Road in Earlham village. The university and broad are then seen down in the Yare valley on the right.

Wensum Fisheries, *Costessey, Norfolk*
Four well-established old gravel workings beautifully set in wooded countryside in the Wensum valley, these super fisheries vary between 2 and 10 acres with depths to 14 feet. The largest, called the Back Lake, holds a prolific stock of roach and rudd with specimens to over 2 lb, as well as shoals of bream in the 4 to 6 lb range, although specimens over 9 lb have been caught in recent years. A big pike is also not unlikely. Clear Water Lake holds the best stock of tench, averaging over 4 lb, plus a few bream to 7 lb and carp to 30 lb. Rainbow Pool contains roach, bream, tench and a few carp, while the Roach Lake holds roach, tench and bream. Also included is a three-quarter-mile length of the River Wensum, containing good chub and roach. No night fishing is allowed. Members have their own keys.

Permits for this members-only water of the Norwich and District Angling Association are available from the secretary, C. Wigg, 3 Coppice Avenue, Norwich (Tel: 01603 423625).

Route: Take the A47 from Norwich and, two miles from the city, turn right by the Roundwell public house down Longwater Lane. At the T-junction, turn left and half a mile on take the right fork. The fisheries are then just 200 yards on the right, behind iron gates.

West Stow Country Park, *Bury St Edmunds, Suffolk*
This 18-acre pit is situated in a bird sanctuary with depths between 3 and 25 feet around three islands. It holds a good head of roach and perch plus bream and pike. There is also a stock of tench running to over 5 lb and some carp weighing into double figures. No night fishing is allowed.

This members-only water of the Bury St Edmunds Angling Association offers annual membership at £17 (£8.40 juniors and £2 for senior citizens) from Tackle Up of Bury St Edmunds (Tel: 01284 755022). Membership also allows the holder to fish Rushbrooke Lake.

Route From Bury, take the A1101 Mildenhall road. Just out of Lackford village, the road goes over the River Lark, and the country park is then immediately on the right.

Wickham Market Reservoirs, *Suffolk*
These two irrigation reservoirs cover around 1½ acres apiece. One is 6 feet deep and weedy. The other has depths to 14 feet. Both contain a variety of species, including roach, perch, rudd, bream and tench. No night fishing is allowed.

A members-only water of the Framlingham and District Angling Club, anyone may join for £12.50 (£6.50 juniors and senior citizens) which covers several other local ponds and stretches of the River Deben. Apply to Saxmundham Angling Centre, rear of Market Place, Saxmundham (Tel: 01728 603443).

Route: From Norwich, take the A140, turning onto the B1134 at Pulham Market to Harleston. Then take the B1116 Framlingham road on to Wickham Market. Just before the town, look on the right for the Easton road (ignore previous signs), and the reservoirs are then on the left, just 300 yards further on, visible from the road.

The Willows (formerly Tatts Pit),
Downham Market, Norfolk
This is a pleasantly coloured, tree-lined pit of an acre, holding a strong head of tench to 4 lb skimmer bream as well as some crucians and mirror carp weighing into double figures.

This is a members-only water of the Downham Market Angling Club, who issue membership cards at £10 through Rose's Tackle Shop of Bridge Street (Tel: 01366 382938).

Route: From Norwich, take the A47 Dereham Road, branching onto the A1122 to Downham Market. In the town, follow the route for Wisbech through the one-way system and look out on the left for a sub post office just before the railway station. Turn left, following the track, and the pit is just 100 yards along on the left behind trees.

Wilsmore Water, *Fakenham, Norfolk*
An irregularly shaped man-made lake of about 1½ acres, Willsmore Water averages 5 feet deep. It contains a good stock of mirror carp weighing into double figures as well as roach, perch, bream and tench.

This is a members-only water of the Fakenham Angling Club. Membership is open only to those living within a ten-mile radius of Fakenham and available from Dave's Tackle Shop of Norwich Street, Fakenham (Tel: 01328 864637). There is a first-year entry fee of £3 and £8 per season thereafter, which covers additional stillwater fishing plus some excellent trout and coarse fishing on the River Wensum.

Route: From Norwich, take the A1067 into the town of Fakenham and branch onto the old road which runs parallel to the bypass, crossing the River Wensum at what used to be Gogg's Mill. The lake access is then via Hayes Lane, off Sandy Lane.

Worthing Gravel Pit, *Worthing, Norfolk*
This is a rather windswept pit of around 8 acres, varying between 10 and 20 feet with deep water close in, in most swims. It holds a good head of roach plus a strong head of bream in the 5 to 12 lb bracket which are best contacted at night. There are also some tench, eels, odd perch to over 2 lb, carp and a good head of pike weighing into double figures. Ledgered deadbaits seem to account for the better fish. There is also a short streamy length of the River Wensum running behind the pits, holding dace, chub, barbel and roach.

This pit is a members-only water of the Dereham and District Angling Club. Membership costs £10 yearly (£4 for senior citizens, juniors and disabled anglers) from the membership secretary, D. Appleby, 6 Rump Close, Swanton Morley, Norfolk (Tel: 01362 637591). Membership cards also available from Myhill's Tackle Shop of Church Street, Dereham (Tel: 01362 692975) and Churchill's Tackle Shop, Norwich Road, Dereham (Tel: 01362 696926).

Route: Take the A1067 from Norwich to Bawdeswell then the B1145 going past Billingford village and over the River Wensum. Turn left 300 yards past the bridge and left again immediately after crossing a bridge over a small stream. The pit is then 600 yards along on the left with access through an open gateway.

STILLWATERS — CARAVANNERS ONLY

Gatton Waters, *near Sandringham, Norfolk*
This well-stocked 8-acre lake, containing a variety of species including roach, rudd, perch, tench and carp, is available to both touring caravanners and campers with day tickets from the office costing £2. Telephone 01485 600643 for more information. Fishing is from 8 a.m. until dusk only. There is a bar with food and toilet facilities on site.

Gunssons Lake, *White House Farm, Sibton, Suffolk*
A 1-acre, shallow and heavily coloured pond contains a prolific head of carp weighing into double figures plus the odd larger specimen as well as tench and bream. Day tickets cost £2.50 or £10 weekly to caravanners only on top of overnight charges. For further information, phone Mr Kitson on 01728 660260.

STILLWATERS — CAMPERS AND TOURING CARAVANNERS

Haveringland Lake, *Norfolk*
This is a 14-acre estate lake holding roach, perch, tench, bream, pike and carp. Telephone R. Hinde on 01603 871302. Day-ticket fishing costs £5 from the reception office. Both campers and touring caravanners are welcome.

Lakeside Lake, *Denver, Norfolk*
This small gravel pit fishery has two islands providing excellent fishing in around 1½ acres adjacent to parking. It holds a prolific stock of roach and rudd as well as quality tench and bream with some carp over 20 lb.
Touring caravanners only. Fishing is from dawn until dusk only.
Day tickets cost £3 in addition to charges for touring caravans. Apply to Bob Riches, 15 Sandy Lane, Denver (Tel: 01366 383291).
Route: From King's Lynn, take the A10 to Denver and at the church follow signs to the Windmill. Then proceed ahead from the Windmill following signs to Lakeside Caravan Park and fishery.

Lakeside Leisure Park, *near Saxmundham, Suffolk*
Lakes of 4 and 2 acres are the attraction here. The larger contains a prolific head of carp weighing into double figures, whilst the smaller lake is a mixed fishery with roach, bream, perch and tench. The lakes are available only to campers who pitch their own tents and to touring caravanners, for which there are some 400 spaces available.
Fishing costs £1 daily or £5 weekly on top of overnight camping or caravan charges. For additional information, telephone 01728 603344.

Little Lakeland, *Wortwell, Norfolk*
This is a half-acre lake with depths to 12 feet containing roach, perch, bream, tench and a stock of carp weighing into double figures, available to caravanners only.
Fishing is from dawn until dusk and included in the caravan charges. Contact P. Leatherbarrow on 01986 788646.

Orben Beck, *Sheringham, Norfolk*
Available only to campers, this tiny pond holds roach, tench, crucian carp, rudd, bream and eels. Depth varies from 6 to 12 feet, and the water is usually quite coloured, with patches of lilies. Orben Beck offers fun fishing on the float and is an ideal camping location for youngsters during the summer months.

Day tickets are available at a cost of only £2 from Beeston Regis site office (Tel: 01263 823614).

White House Farm, *Rendham, Saxmundham, Suffolk*
This half-acre lake is available only to touring caravanners – no camping. Species include roach, perch, crucian carp, tench and mirror carp weighing into double figures in depths ranging between 2 and 4 feet.

Caravanners at White House Farm are charged £1 per day to fish. For additional information, telephone Mr Tate on 01728 663485.

STILLWATERS – MATCH FISHING ONLY

The Ponds, *Great Melton, near Norwich, Norfolk*
These three small lakes, each of around an acre in size and each with a centre island, average between 4 to 7 feet in depth and can in total accommodate thirty-two pegs. The lakes are exceptionally well stocked with a variety of species, including roach, rudd, perch, crucian carp, chub, both common and mirror carp, as well as some ghost koi.

The ponds are used only for match fishing, and club secretaries should contact Mr Bush on 01603 811135 for bookings and all additional information.

STILLWATERS – SYNDICATE WATERS

Bridge Lakes, *Lenwade, Norfolk*
These are gravel pits, two small, one large, holding roach, rudd, bream, tench, carp and pike. There are a limited number of yearly permits available from the City of Norwich Angling Club secretary, Tom Boulton (Tel: 01603 426834). A waiting-list is in force.

Brooke Park Lakes, *Brooke, Norfolk*
These two interconnected, mature estate lakes total some 7 acres and hold prolific stocks of roach, rudd, tench, pike and carp. There are a limited number of yearly permits available from M. Holl of Hillside Farm, Brook, Norfolk (Tel: 01508 550260).

Colston Hall Lakes, *Badingham, near Framlingham, Suffolk*
These two well-stocked lakes hold a mixed stock of rudd, tench, carp, bream carp and ghost koi. Season permits are available at a cost of £70 from Gerry Powell of Fishing Management Services, 19 Sirdar Road, Ipswich, Suffolk IP1 2LD (Tel: 01473 213468).

Gayton Road Fisheries, *Norfolk*
A 1¾-acre clay pit, dug and landscaped specifically for angling, contains a stock of specimen roach, rudd, tench and carp, with depths to 12 feet. There are a limited number of season permits available by writing to Chris Newell, 12 Castle Close, King's Lynn, Norfolk PE30 3EP. A waiting-list is in force.

Gayton Road Fishery Estate Lake, *Norfolk*
A well-established small estate lake of around one acre, this is set in attractive woodlands and contains a small stock of sizeable carp, as well as bream, roach, rudd and pike. There are a limited number of season permits available by writing to Chris Newell, 12 Castle Close, King's Lynn, Norfolk PE30 3EP. A waiting-list is in force.

Gunssons Lake, *Suffolk*
A 1-acre pond, this contains a prolific stock of carp weighing into double figures as well as tench and bream. Yearly syndicate tickets cost £25 from Mr Tate of White House Farm, Sibton, Suffolk (Tel: 01728 660260).

Manor Lake, *Rocklands, near Attleborough, Norfolk*
An irregularly shaped man-made and spring-fed fishery of 2½ acres with one island and depths ranging from 4 to over 10 feet, Manor Lake holds a good head of tench to over 4 lb and mirror carp to over 30 lb, in addition to crucian carp, chub, perch and pike.
Annual permits are available from S. Burroughs (Tel: 01953 483366).

Snakes Meadow Fishery, *Stokesby, Norfolk*
This is a 1½-acre lake, well-stocked with common and mirror carp to over 20 lb, plus roach, tench and crucian carp. A limited number of season permits are obtainable at £75 from Ray Chapman (Tel: 01493 369757).

Stradsett Lake, *near King's Lynn, Norfolk*
A 20-acre, triangular and picturesque lake with an average depth of around 7 feet, this rich fishery contains a strong head of tench to over 5 lb, roach to 2 lb and pike to over 20 lb. There is also a shoal of huge bream and a handful of carp.
Interested anglers should contact Chris Newell (Tel: 01553 675546) who issues a limited number of syndicate annual permits costing £40.

STILLWATERS – HOTEL ACCOMMODATION

Gunton Hall Lake, *near Lowestoft, Suffolk*
This is an attractive, weedy lake of around 2 acres. The water averages about 5 feet deep, is invariably well coloured, and stocks include tench around the 2 lb mark, roach, rudd and mirror carp weighing into double figures. The fishing is open to hotel guests only.
Gunton Hall is a holiday centre with facilities such as golf, tennis and archery available to resident guests. For further information, telephone 01502 730288.
Matches (twenty-peg) can be arranged. Club secretaries should contact P. Gilley on the above number.
Route: From Lowestoft take the A12 towards Great Yarmouth, and Gunton Hall is on the right, before the turn off to Corton.

Lenwade House Hotel, Lake and River, *Lenwade, Norfolk*
Fishing here, set in 18 acres of woodland, is available to guests only and comprises a single-acre lake with a centre island, holding a mixed stock of coarse species, plus several hundred yards of the picturesque and winding River Wensum, which holds dace, roach, chub and pike.
Other facilities available to hotel guests include lawn tennis, crochet, squash, a gymnasium, sauna and an outdoor pool. For further information, telephone 01603 872288.
Route: From Norwich, take the A1067 Fakenham Road to Lenwade where the entrance to the hotel is on the left just before leaving the village.

Stillwaters — Holiday Cottages

Colston Hall, *near Framlingham, Suffolk*
Here one can stay in a sixteenth-century cottage and fish two lakes. The pond close to the house averages over 10 feet deep and contains bream, golden orfe, ghost koi, rudd, tench, etc. The second lake contains a good stock of mirror carp weighing into double figures in depths to 8 feet. Also bed and breakfast accommodation in a farmhouse is available. Contact John and Liz Bellefontaine, Colston Hall, Badingham, near Framlingham, Woodbridge, Suffolk IP13 8LB (Tel: 01728 638375).
Touring caravans are also welcome. Day tickets cost £6 for both lakes.

Stillwaters — Farmhouse Holiday Accommodation

Brooke Park Lakes, *Brooke, Norfolk*
Set in rolling countryside next to woodlands, these two inter-connected mature estate lakes total over 7 acres and contain a prolific stock of roach, rudd, tench, pike and carp. Contact M. Holl of Hillside Farm, Brooke, Norfolk (Tel: 01508 550260) for details.

Trout Fishing — Day Ticket (Rivers — Fly Only)

River Wensum, *Fakenham, Norfolk*
One of the prettiest, streamiest parts of the River Wensum is immediately above and below the town of Fakenham where both day ticket and even free trout fishing is available.

The upper Wensum in these parts is generally quite fast and shallow with odd pools and during the summer months very weedy. It produces well to the wet fly fished down and across during the early season when fly-fishing begins on 1 April and then to the upstream nymph and dry fly as soon as the weed comes up.

The Fakenham Angling Club controls around two miles of the river here and issues day tickets costing £3 for a two-fish limit through Dave's Tackle Shop, Norwich Street, Fakenham (Tel: 01328 862543).

The fishery is split up into several parcels above the mill, and there are regular stockings of brown trout. There are a few 'escapee rainbows' from adjacent fisheries and the odd grayling, in addition to a few dace and roach for those also wishing to try their fly outfits on coarse fish. Much of the banks is open to free fishing (see map), particularly downstream of the mill, and the polite 'enquiring angler' will no doubt enjoy free fishing along other parts of the Wensum.

Only anglers living within a ten-mile radius of Fakenham may join the Fakenham Angling Club through Dave's Tackle Shop. There is a first-year entry fee of £3, plus £8 per season thereafter, which covers all the club's holdings on the River Wensum and two local stillwater coarse fisheries.

Trout Fishing – Day Ticket (Stillwaters)

Bure Valley Trout Lakes, *near Aylsham, Norfolk*
The fishery is situated beside a delightful, overgrown stretch of the upper Bure (which anglers may also fish) and comprises one lake of about an acre and another of around 7 acres. Depths vary from 5 to over 18 feet, and the stock includes both brown and rainbow trout from 1½ lb upwards.

There are all-day, half-day and evening tickets available as well as season permits (Tel: 01263 587666 for additional information). Anglers' catches can be smoked on site for an additional charge.

The owner provides free tuition for beginners (booking advised) and clubhouse facilities with toilets and refreshments. There is also a well-stocked tackle shop with rods for hire.

Route: Take the A140 from Norwich to Aylsham, then the B1354 to Saxthorpe. The fishery is then on the right (well signposted), four miles out of Aylsham.

Cross Green Fly-Fishers, *Cockfield, near Lavenham, Suffolk*
This fishery comprises four man-made and pleasantly landscaped gravel pits, ranging in size from half an acre to 2 acres with depths to 20 feet. Two are oblong in shape, one triangular and one circular. Stock includes rainbow trout of varying sizes, from 1½ up to 6 lb.

A beginner's day ticket to fish the small lake costs £16 for a four-fish limit. A day ticket to fish the three main lakes costs £25 for a four-fish limit. Season rods are also available at £315 (comprising 15 visits split up into whole or half-day sessions, working on the basis of two fish per half day and four fish for each whole day. A half-season rod at £165 is also available. These are purchased from the Fishing

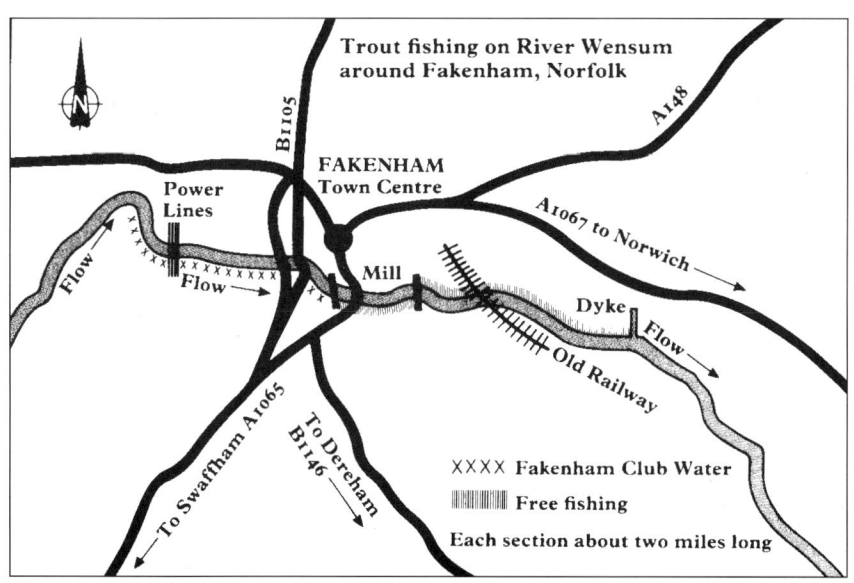

131

Office. Telephone Bob Waters on 01284 828882 for additional information. Fishing is from 9 a.m. until dusk only.

Route: From Norwich, take the A11 to the Thetford bypass and then the A134 to Bury. Proceed around Bury on the A14 ring road and join the A134 again going towards Sudbury. Turn left onto the A1141 to Lavenham and some 400 yards along on the left is the fishery entrance, which is well signposted.

East Tuddenham Fishery, *near Norwich, Norfolk*

This superb fishery comprises two spring-fed and dammed lakes. The upper lake, which flows into and feeds the lower lake, varies between 5 and 8 feet deep and covers around 3 acres, with a centre island from which anglers may fish with access via a bridge. The lower lake shelves to 12 feet at the dam end andcovers about 4 acres also with a centre island. This is a highly consistent fishery from lures in the early season to plenty of scope through the summer for the nymph and dry fly enthusiast. When the weed is up, the lakes can fish well during the last hour of daylight. The stock includes brownies to 4 lb and rainbow trout to over 6 lb.

Day tickets – available to all – cost £15 for a four-fish limit and are obtainable from East Tuddenham post office at the top of the lane, only a short drive from the lakes, or from John's Tackle Den, 16 Bridewell Alley, Norwich (Tel: 01603 614114), or from Ted Fenn (Tel: 01692 402162). The lakes open on 1 April and close 31 October, dawn till dusk. Controlled by the Norfolk and Suffolk Fly-Fishers Society, membership costs £9 from D. Armes, 100 Cozens Hardy Road, Norwich (Tel: 01603 423169). Members can take out a 'full rod' on the lakes (any day weekly) for £150 yearly or a half rod for £90 (any day once a fortnight). The club has a busy social calendar with monthly meetings, including well-known guest speakers and other functions.

Route: Follow the A47 Dereham Road from Norwich and take the Honingham/Mattishall turn off on the left through to East Tuddenham. In the village, turn right at the crossroads (through a farm), and the lakes are then on the left, 500 yards further on.

Hatchery House Trout Fishery, *Bury St Edmunds, Suffolk*

There are three lakes here, each over an acre, but only two are available to fish at any one time. The water is clear and well weeded and fishes consistently all summer through.

The fishery is well stocked with rainbow trout to over 3 lb.

Day tickets cost £12 for a four-fish limit or £7 for an evening ticket (two fish). Booking in advance is accepted by phone during office hours only: 9.30 a.m.– 4 p.m. Monday to Friday (Tel: 01284 810300).

The lakes are open from 1 April and close 1 October, sunrise to sunset.

Route: From Norwich to Thetford on the A11 and take the A134 to Bury St Edmunds. From Bury take the A14 Newmarket road and four miles out look for the Willow public house. Take the next turn on the left down Mill Lane (Barrow and Higham signpost), which leads to the fishery with lakes on either side of the road.

Larkwood Trout Fishery, *West Stow, Suffolk*

This interesting fishery with a reputation for large trout comprises two lakes of about 2½ acres apiece, with depths to 20 feet.

The lakes are stocked with both browns and rainbow trout. The largest brown trout on record here weighed 9 lb, while the biggest rainbow was 12 lb 6 oz.

Day tickets at £12 for a four-fish limit are available from the fisheries lodge. As only sixteen anglers are permitted at any one time, booking is always advisable. Telephone the manager, Ian McGregor on 01284 728612 for additional information. The fishery is open all year, 9 a.m. until dusk.

Route: From Bury St Edmunds, take the A1101 Mildenhall road, turning right by Flempton church and proceed over the River Lark to West Stow village. Then turn left onto the Icklingham road, and the fishery lies between the road and the River Lark, on the left a short distance along.

Mendham Trout Fishery, *Mendham, Suffolk.*

The fishery comprises two well-stocked lakes, each of around an acre in area, with depths varying from 5 to 7 feet. It is regularly stocked with rainbow trout in the 1½ to 6 lb range, and specimens over 10 lb have been taken.

Day tickets cost £12 for a four-fish limit or £8 for a two-fish limit. Alternatively, anglers may prefer to take up the option of a four-hour catch-and-release ticket at £5, provided they use a barbless hook. Season tickets are also available on application to J. Horrex (Tel: 01379 852328), who also organises tuition. Equipment is for hire at the fishery.

The lakes open in February and close in November, but are closed every Monday, except for Bank Holidays.

Route: Take the A140 from Norwich towards Ipswich and turn left at signposts to Pulham Market on the B1134. Proceed into Harleston and turn left onto the bypass then immediately right down Mendham Lane. Proceed over the crossroads into Mendham, and the fishery is on the left, opposite Mendham church.

Narborough Trout Fisheries, *Narborough, Norfolk*

These are a series of four pleasantly landscaped, stream-fed lakes varying between 1 and 1½ acres, with depths from 3 to 10 feet. The density of fish in each varies considerably so that – depending on individual skill – one may plan the day accordingly. There are excellent stagings and facilities for wheelchair anglers on level ground adjacent to the car park lake. Also included is a fast-flowing, narrow stretch of the River Nar several hundred yards long which flows between the lakes. There is also a nature walk for non-fishing members of the family.

There is a prolific stock of rainbows of all sizes – from 12 oz to over 10 lb. The best fish ever was caught by John Millar from Holt, who took a magnificent brace of 17½ lb and 15¾ lb one afternoon in 1988.

The gates open at 9 a.m. all year round (depending on the weather), and day tickets cost £5 from 9 a.m. until 4.30 p.m. From May until September, there is also an evening ticket costing £4 from 5 p.m. until 8 p.m. Trout caught are charged at £1.65 per pound. All fish caught must be killed, weighed in and purchased; no fish are to be returned. For additional information, telephone manager Rod Skerry on 01760 338005. Tackle is for hire from the fishing lodge, and casting tuition is available.

Route: From Norwich, take the A47 Dereham Road and follow the signs into the village of Narborough. The fishery is then on the right and well signposted.

Ruston Reaches, *East Ruston, North Walsham*

This is a most thoughtfully designed man-made fishery, built rather like a river with bends and islands, offering over 400 yards of fishable bank around 1½ acres of water. The banks are heavily reed-lined, and the water is usually extremely clear, with depths from 4 to 10 feet. The stock includes both brown and rainbow trout, which have been taken to over 6 lb.

Day tickets cost £8, for which anglers may catch any number of trout which are then charged at £1.60 per pound. Those using barbless hooks may fish on a catch-and-release basis. Tickets are purchased on arrival from the fishing hut, which opens at 8.30 a.m. (fishing is until dusk) all year round, but weekends only during the

133

winter. For additional information, telephone Mr Mantell-Sayer on 01692 536646.

There is also a coarse fishing lake close by (see Ruston Reaches, under Stillwaters – Day Ticket).

Route: From Norwich, take the A1151 through Wroxham and continuing almost to Stalham. Then turn left (following signs for Bacton and Happisburgh) into Stepping Stone Lane. Turn left at the next T-junction and then take the first left, following winding lanes into East Ruston. The fishery entrance is then on the left via an open field (with a 'Fishing' signpost), with a line of cottages on both sides.

Valley Fisheries, *Walpole, Suffolk*
This attractive 2½-acre, spring-fed, man-made lake offers depths between 3 and 12 feet. It is well established and pleasantly reeded around the perimeter and stocked with both rainbow and brown trout. Day tickets cost £20 for a five-fish limit. Also available are tickets at £12 with a three-fish limit for sessions from 8 a.m. until 2 p.m. and 2 p.m. until sunset. An evening ticket costs £9 for a two-fish limit.

Tickets must be purchased in advance from the adjacent fishery lodge. For additional information, telephone Paul or Henry Murphy on 01986 784488.

Route: From Ipswich, take the A12 (heading towards Great Yarmouth) and turn left at Yoxford onto the Peasenhall road. Just before Walpole village, look on the right for a water tower, and the fishery entrance (well signposted) is half a mile further on on the right.

Whinburgh Trout Lakes, *near Dereham, Norfolk*
This delightful fishery consists of two interconnecting man-made lakes of around 1 and 3 acres. Depths vary between 3 and 8 feet, and there is invariably a good catch during the early evening throughout the summer months.

There is a prolific stock of rainbows and brown trout between 1 and over 8 lb with rainbows predominating. The lake's record rainbow stands at 11¼ lb, caught in 1994. Day tickets cost £10 for a nine-hour catch-and-release (barbless hooks only) session or £6 for a five-hour session. Anglers wishing to purchase their catches instead of releasing them may do so at a

Valley Fisheries – superb trouting in deepest Suffolk

Whinburgh Trout Fishery, renowned for hectic action with rainbows

cost of £1.70 per pound. Smoking of trout is done on site. There is also an experienced casting instructor at the lakes. For additional information, telephone D. Potter on 01362 850201. The lakes are open all year, dawn until dusk.

Route: From Norwich, take the B1108 Watton road, forking onto the B1135 towards Dereham around ten miles from the city. Go through Garvestone and, half a mile further on at the bottom of the hill (where a stream passes beneath road), turn right just before white railings. The fishery is then at the end of the track.

Willow Lakes Trout Fishery, *Ash Farm, Chediston, Suffolk*

The fishery comprises two superb, extremely clear man-made lakes of 1½ and 2½ acres. Both are oblong in shape and shelve down to over 12 feet deep. The larger has a centre island.

The lakes are stocked with brown and rainbow trout to 3 lb and the record for the fishery is a rainbow of over 8 lb. Day tickets cost £13 for a four-fish limit or £7.50 for a two-fish limit and should be purchased prior to fishing from Ash Farm, just 400 yards from the lakes. (Tel: 01986 785392 for additional information). The fishery opens on 15 March and closes on 15 October, operating from 7 a.m. until dusk.

Route: From Halesworth, take the B1123 Harleston road and take the first right turn (about one and a half miles out of Halesworth) signposted to Chediston Green. Ash Farm is then on the right, about half a mile further on.

Woodlakes Trout Fishery, *Stow, Norfolk*

This is an irregular-shaped, deep, clear-watered lake of around 12 acres which during high summer sports a prolific weed growth. Naturally, fishing unleaded nymphs and dry flies is very much the order of the day during the summer, although lures will produce when the water is still cold at the beginning of the season.

135

The stock is rainbows to 2½ lb.
Day tickets cost £8 for a two-fish limit or £12 for a four-fish limit. These must be purchased prior to fishing from the lake kiosk. The fishery is open all year round from 7 a.m. until dusk. For additional information, telephone 01553 810414.

Route: Take the A10(T) from King's Lynn, turn right in Stow Bardolph and proceed towards Stow Bridge (over the Relief Channel). About 500 yards before the bridge, carry on straight ahead at a sharp left turn. Woodlakes can be seen on the right, just 100 yards further on.

TROUT FISHING – SYNDICATE WATERS

Norfolk Fly-Fishers Lake, *Swanton Morley, Norfolk*
This is a 20-acre gravel pit, well-stocked with rainbow trout. A waiting-list is in force. Apply to the secretary, R. Gibbons (Tel: 01362 858315).

River Lark, *near Bury St Edmunds, Suffolk*
River trouting is controlled by the Lark Angling and Preservation Society on a delightful, twisting section of this little river, switching from bank to bank and covering almost four miles from Lackford down to the A11 road bridge at Barton Mills. It is regularly stocked with browns, and a rod for the season costs £100, which covers two fish per visit.
Anyone may join the Lark Club for a £10 annual subscription which also covers good coarse fishing on the River Lark starting at Barton Mills, for roach, dace and bream. Apply to the secretary, E. West, 8 Arrowhead Drive, Lakenheath (Tel: 01842 861369).

Spring Lake Trout Fishery, *Beccles, Suffolk*
Here, there are 6 acres of lakes comprising one large spring-fed lake and a collection of long, narrow waters, all stocked with rainbows weighing between 1 and 7 lb. Apply to the secretary, B. Bingham (Tel: 01502 712201).

River Glaven, *North Norfolk*
About one mile of delightful river fishing, stocked mainly with browns plus a few rainbows. There is a waiting list in force but interested parties may contact Peter Suckling, 8 Home Farm, Letheringsett, Holt, Norfolk (Tel: 01263 712636).

SALMON AND TROUT ASSOCIATION WATERS – OPEN MEMBERSHIP

For membership apply to P. Pledger of Drishaig, Letton Green, Thetford, Norfolk IP25 7PT (Tel: 01362 820677). This costs £16 yearly. Members may then enjoy any of the following five well-stocked fisheries at varying prices.

RIVERS

River Bure, *Ingworth*
Two and a half miles stocked with browns only. Season rods cost £65 and day tickets cost £8 (for a two-fish limit) from P. Pledger (Tel: 01362 820677).

River Nar, *Narborough, West Norfolk*
This lovely little river is fairly narrow in parts, flows swiftly and is generally quite shallow. It contains both rainbow and brown trout and is particularly suitable to the upstream nymph. From the road bridge in Narborough the beat stretches

for over two miles on both banks to the waterworks at Marham.

Season rods cost £90 and day tickets cost £10 (for a two-fish limit) from D.E. Burrows (Tel: 01760 337222).

River Wensum, *Bintry Mill, Norfolk*
Delightful two and a half mile winding stretch of the upper Wensum, stocked with brown trout. Excellent upstream nymphing.

Season rods are available at £100 from A.H. Chapman (Tel: 01362 698287). Day tickets cost £10 (for a two-fish limit) from L. Temple-Richards (Tel: 01328 78217).

STILLWATERS

Lenwade, *Norfolk*
This is a 9-acre lake stocked with rainbows and browns. Season rods cost £150 and day tickets cost £12 (for a four-fish limit) from P. Pledger (Tel: 01362 820677).

Roosting Hills, *near Dereham, Norfolk*
This is a 6-acre lake stocked with rainbows and browns. Season rods cost £140 and day tickets cost £10 (for a four-fish limit) from R. Bunning (Tel: 01362 860633).

SEA FISHING

The Norfolk and Suffolk coastline offers the angler over 100 miles of fishing from Hunstanton in the north to Felixstowe in the south.

The coastline has a bonus attraction in the form of long sandy beaches with safe swimming, together with picturesque fishing villages and staithes much loved by photographers and several tiptop holiday resorts, led by Great Yarmouth, the second largest in England. For the family man who also happens to be an angler, this coastline is a haven.

Hunstanton Although on the East Coast, Hunstanton looks out across the famous Wash from a westerly aspect. Once renowned for its prolific tope fishing, the area is now relatively underfished, yet on the right day can still produce catches of tope, smooth hound, dog fish and stingrays.

The best tope on record here is a 62½ lb fish taken in 1964 by Guy Morton. As a rule, the largest tope are taken by boat-fishing offshore, but the potential for shore-caught fish still exists. Generally, the beaches produce eels and flatties, although in recent years good numbers of bass have shown when onshore winds create a good surf. The immediate area around the town also offers a plentiful bait supply, with lugworm and ragworm being the easiest to collect but razor fish and peeler crab are there for the finding.

Holme next the Sea Now a National Trust area, this offers only limited beach fishing but offshore lies Thornham Hole, a good tope and skate mark. A tope of 70 lb is said to have been taken here in 1956 but was not officially recorded.

Brancaster beach offers dabs, flounders, soles and eels to visitors, who may actually drive their cars to within a stone's throw of the sea. Around the harbour, much visited by tourists, mullet, bass and sea trout inhabit the various creeks and inlets but are rarely fished for. Those willing to put in the effort will find that the mullet can be tempted with float-fished bread-paste or the tiny harbour ragworm, and the sea trout which are commercially netted locally will sometimes strike at a spinner or worm bait.

Burnham Overy is a delightful little Norfolk fishing village full of charm and character. Close by, the village of Burnham Thorpe has the distinction of being the birthplace of Lord Nelson.

Down by Overy Staithe, which is much

137

used by holiday-makers at weekends, there is some swimming, good shrimping at low tide and lugworm-digging. Anglers may also launch their own craft from the staithe.

Flatties, bass, mullet and the occasional largish sea trout run through Burnham harbour and up the creeks with the flood tide. Local netsmen sometimes take specimen-sized sea trout in their nets but it would take considerable effort to catch these on rod and line.

Holkham is also a popular fishing venue with many coarse anglers who fish the lake by the hall (see Stillwaters – Day Ticket) as well as offering beach anglers some flatties, including soles when the tide is up. At low tide there is good bait-collecting in the form of gathering cockles and digging for lugworm.

Wells-Next-The-Sea was once famous for its smuggling activities but now its quaint narrow streets are walked by tourists. The main shipping channel runs into Wells and is used by fairly large vessels. Although subject to fairly strong tidal flows, it offers good potential for flatfish, eels, bass and sea trout. A visit at low tide would reveal the route of gullies and positions of sandbanks to locate a good spot to fish as the tide floods.

Stiffkey has the same name as the little river which flows through the town and under the A149 coast road. The river spills its water into the estuary via a sluice gate south of Blakeney Point. Sea trout and big mullet are taken periodically in the creeks and channels which fill with the flood tide. There is good lugworm-digging along the salt marshes at low tide.

Morston and Blakeney Although these towns are two miles apart, they can be classified as one entity as far as the angler is concerned. This is because boats which fish out of these spots actually share a permanent anchorage in the deep section of Blakeney harbour, known as Blakeney Pit, which is about the only deep water suitable for permanent mooring in the whole harbour. Anglers who have booked to fish offshore with local skippers are then ferried out by tender from Morston Quay.

Newcomers to the area must beware of the tremendous fall and rise of the tides, which affect entry to and exit from the harbour at Blakeney. Local fishermen will give advice to those wishing to launch their own boats – but extreme care must be taken.

The entire southern half of the harbour is good lug-digging ground, and anyone who digs for lugworm would do well to respect the future availability of this excellent bait by not taking immature worms.

Deepsea boat-fishing out from Blakeney takes place from early April until the beginning of October, the popular species sought by anglers being thornback skate, known locally as 'roker'. These average around 8 to 10 lb but specimens high into double figures are taken regularly. There is also the odd tope to 40 lb and always plenty of dabs, with some dogfish and good mackerel in season. The skipper of the boat usually supplies fresh bait in the way of sandeels and lugworms, but for much of the summer the angler may catch his own fresh bait by feathering for mackerel, one of the supreme sea baits and very good eating too. Within the limits of Blakeney harbour sea trout, which show up over much of the North Norfolk coastline, are occasionally taken.

For weather details, contact Joe Reed, Warden of Blakeney Point (Tel: 01263 740480). Boat-fishing trips can be arranged through Mike Taylor (Tel: 01263 740998). From October onwards, many of the Blakeney skippers take their boats round the coast to Great Yarmouth, where they spend the winter taking out fishing parties bent on catching cod and whiting. At the end of March they return to Blakeney and the whole yearly procedure repeats itself.

The local tackle shop is Stratton Long Marine, Blakeney (Tel: 01263 740362), which will furnish visitors with helpful advice and also arrange boat-fishing trips.

Feathering in the vicinity of the harbour mouth will produce good numbers of mackerel from July to September and in the harbour itself, dabs, flounders and eels are taken on worm baits all the year round.

Cley represents the first 'real' beach from Hunstanton, as the area between is essentially a salt marsh. A steep shingle and sand beach offers deep water close in at all stages of the tide, so it is ideal for anglers of all abilities.

A favourite local hotspot is opposite the wreck situated to the right of the gap. Here, good bass are found, and at low tide the wreck is within casting distance.

During summer, dabs, plaice, flounders, eels, as well as the odd sole and dogfish can make fishing interesting, with good catches of mackerel likely at high tide on a hot, humid evening in July and August. During December to March, codling are caught, particularly after a period of northerly winds.

Salthouse is renowned for its fine beach fishing, where good dabs, flounders and soles may be taken along with the occasional bass during the summer months. The beach consists mostly of heavy shingle and sandy areas only 50 yards out from low tide mark. Expect codling from December onwards, on both flood and ebb tides. Fresh lugworms may be obtained from several houses along the main coast road at Salthouse.

Kelling The beach here is similar to the one at Weybourne, but there are only two access points from the coast road. The first is approximately half a mile, Weybourne side, of Salthouse beach road, which goes across Salthouse Marshes. The second is about 100 yards on the Salthouse side of the police station. These lanes are extremely rough, so cars should be driven carefully.

Species to be expected are flatties during the summer months and, particularly, goodish soles at late evening on an ebbing tide. A number of codling appear from December onwards.

Weybourne has a beach of shingle which shelves steeply into deepish water. There are sandy patches some 50 yards out where soles are taken to the left of the gap, opposite the wreck which becomes visible at low tide. Tim Oswick took a superb bass of 14 lb 8 oz here on squid in 1994.

Other species to be expected are dabs, flounders, cod, whiting, eels, etc. Skate, tope, mackerel and bass are taken from boats. Really good bass are often found around the wreck. To the right of the gap under the cliffs, the bottom is rough but many cod gather over this type of ground in the winter for the rich feed it harbours, and fishing can be exceptional at times.

There is a little boat-fishing available through local skippers but this is dependent on the wind and tide conditions. Bait is available from local diggers, and signs are displayed outside their homes along the coast road. Almost the entire coast road from Weybourne to Cromer runs close to the sea, and fishing and picnic spots abound.

Some favourite fishing locations for all the previously mentioned species will be found about one and a quarter miles north of Sheringham by turning towards the coast at the bridge to Spallow Gap – a noted cod spot during the winter, which fishes best at high tide.

Sheringham is a sizeable town, with the main street running down to the beach. To the north, the beach comprises large shingle at high water, offering deep water close in, but the ebb tide soon reveals flat sand. This is interspersed with gullies, particularly where the chalky areas show, although casting into these often causes tackle losses. To the south, rougher areas of large stones and kelp can be found which offer peeler crab in late spring

139

when the weather is warm and settled.

During onshore winds in May and June the bass fishing can be excellent with eels also evident. Flatfish can be caught during most times of the year, with good fishing for codling from December through until March. The bass can be taken at high or low water but the codling prefer the high tides, especially big spring tides. Visitors can call in at the local tackle shop, Fiddy's Tackle (Tel: 01263 822098), for fresh bait and additional information.

West and East Runton These beaches offer rocky ground interspersed with sandy patches. Bass fishing can be excellent during the summer months for those willing to risk tackle losses in the rocks. The sandy patches produce flatties during the summer and cod from December onwards. Dinghies can be launched from the slope at West Runton, and offshore fishing is good for skate, doggies and occasional tope during the warmer months.

Cromer is an ideal base for the family man who happens also to be an angler, for, added to the obvious attractions, there is an excellent golf course. There is even some excellent freshwater fishing close by in the Sawmills Lake in the grounds of lovely Gunton Park, just five miles south of the town (see Stillwaters – Day Ticket).

Cromer is well known for its fine, all-year-round sea fishing. One of the best spots is usually the pier, which offers good mixed catches of flatties, eels, the occasional bass and even the odd tope during the summer. In winter, excellent codling and whiting are had from November until March. In recent years, bass have become quite prominent as they have all around the Norfolk coastline and a big one amongst numerous schoolies can turn up from almost anywhere – even the pier.

Good local baits are mussels, lugworms and squid heads. All these and expert advice may be obtained from Marine Sports of New Street (Tel: 01263 513676).

Overstrand–Trimingham The area between these villages also offers beaches mainly of flat sand interspersed with wooden groynes. Although the water is quite shallow even at high tide, the fishing can be excellent. At Overstrand there is a sewer pipe at the bottom of the main access point to the beach and in the immediate area some very fine bass weighing into double figures have been caught. The best times are around two hours before high or low tide to slack water, and both peeler crab and squid will produce. The latter probably accounts for most of the specimens taken.

The access to Trimingham is via the Sandy Gulls caravan site, where a road leads down the cliffs to the beach. There is some parking here but the area can become crowded at peak times. Bass fishing during the spring and autumn can prove exceptionally good, with prolific catches of codling from October until April, from two hours before to two hours after high water. Some lugworm can be dug during low water springs, although a 'bait pump' is sometimes more productive for individual worms.

Mundesley is another rather flat, sandy beach but some deeper gullies show up at low tide. Flatfish, eels and bass are the expected summer species with both whiting and codling appearing from October to April. Some of the finest sport here is to be had straight in front of the main access slope which leads from the car park. Best results usually come from two hours before and two hours after high water for the codling especially, but rough, low water seas will produce the bass. Lugworm can be dug from the sand banks at low tide.

Bacton is similar to Mundesley in that it tends to fish well in the summer for dabs, flounders and odd soles, etc., with whiting and codling showing up from late October onwards. However, it has a bonus in the form of really excellent offshore boat-fishing marks within Bacton Bay.

Skate, or rather thornback ray, to give its correct name, are the prime target species at Bacton, but smooth hounds, spurdogs and tope are also taken here during the summer. Boats can be launched from the slipway at Walcott. The feature of the beach and in fact all the beaches down to Winterton is their flat, sandy nature over the initial 60 yards, dropping into a wide gully with a sandbank shelving up around 200 yards out from the low water mark.

Long-range casting can therefore really pay off over the high tide mark, so the bait is placed in the gully. Paradoxically, the ebb tide can also fish well, simply because towards low water most anglers can reach the gully, and a favourite period is three hours before to around an hour after low water.

Walcott Offshore fishing is excellent here, with easy access for small boats from the slipway on the coast road. The species are identical to those at Bacton. Beach fishing is also excellent, with flatfish all year round, plus bass during the summer and codling from October to March. Because the sea comes up to the concrete wall at high tide, the three hours before and one hour after low water are most favoured.

Happisburgh The fishing is similar to that at Walcott, and along the sandy beach to the right of the gap dabs and flounders are the usual customers to worm baits. Skate come inshore during the summer months and are occasionally taken by long-casting from the beach. From September onwards one can expect whiting and then numbers of cod between October and January. Fishing is best at high water.

Lessingham and Eccles There is easy access to a long, sandy beach which fishes all the year through for dabs, with codling from October onwards. The best prospects are over the high water period.

Sea Palling–Waxham is just a five-mile drive from Hickling Broad and Horsey Mere – both excellent coarse fishing venues (see The Broads). For the sea-angler, offshore fishing in this area is excellent for thornbacks, spurdog, the occasional tope as well as flat fish, all during the summer months, with whiting and codling during the autumn and winter. Small boats can be launched via the gap in the sea wall but rollers are necessary for the haul over the beach. Shore fishing is also consistent with eels, flatties and bass during the warmer months. North or north-west winds in December and January invariably bring codling over the offshore bank into the deep gully which runs parallel to the beach. Three hours before to two hours after high water is a prime time, although low water can also produce in calm conditions. Access to the beach at Waxham is through the small lane behind Waxham church.

Horsey It will be found that this beach fishes best for two hours before and after high water. Skate were at one time plentiful from this beach and, although not as prolific nowadays, the night angler still has a chance of contacting them during periods of thundery weather. Winter fishing is also good for cod, and catches of flatties can be taken all year through.

Winterton is a continuation of Horsey's sandy beach. Good freshwater fishing is only three miles away at Martham Ferry on the tidal River Thurne. So a holidaying, all-round angler could hardly choose a better location. The beach here is quite flat and sandy with numerous small gullies. However, these are continually changing due to the strong tides, especially around the 'Point'. At the north end, the wooden groynes that have stretched down from Horsey finish, and in the spring many good bass are caught from this location. A rough sea is favourite, with two hours before and one hour after high water being the ideal times. Crab and squid both produce, with numbers of fish falling to the former but those real specimens to the latter. In winter, flatfish and codling are caught but often strong tides bring heavy weed to spoil fishing.

Hemsby–Newport–Scratby There is access to the beach at each end of these locations, with a fair depth of water quite close in. High water favours the longer caster but low water allows the average caster to reach the best spots. Tides are strong here but the last three hours of both flood and ebb usually produce well. Flatfish, eels and the occasional large bass feature in the spring to summer period, with good catches of cod taken throughout December and January. The deepest water is at Scratby, where a 32 lb cod was caught by Ivan Smith in 1981.

Caister-on-Sea has a fairly deep sand and shingle beach, where a fast tide runs at times. There are the usual flatfish from April onwards and excellent whiting and cod fishing from mid autumn to early spring, especially at night. Caister is a popular holiday resort and so the beaches become congested during high summer. The best sport is usually found during the last three hours of the ebb and over low water. A huge grey mullet of 8 lb 6 oz was taken here by John James in 1979.

Great Yarmouth is the second largest seaside resort in Britain and it seems to become busier each year, but there is generally enough space even during the holiday season for the ardent angler to catch a few fish.

The variety of fishing is split up somewhat, in as much as one may choose to fish the sandy beaches, the harbour and river, the piers, or boat-fish well offshore. The Britannia and Wellington piers and the Jetty offer fishing all year through for flat fish, eels and the occasional bass, with whiting and cod particularly prolific during the autumn and winter months – the advantage being that fishing is good at any state of the tide.

The North Beach offers deep water close in and is noted for cod during the winter, with access available from several points off Marine Parade. Strong tides and weed can make fishing difficult but the results are often well worth the effort.

Fishing from the South Beach is also excellent, particularly during the last three hours of the flood tide but responds best to long-range casting. The area in front of the Pleasure Beach is particularly productive.

Offshore during the summer months, skate, doggies, large dabs and tope are taken, but the fishing really comes into its own from autumn to spring, when huge bags of sizeable cod are regularly taken, including many fish weighing high into double figures. The biggest cod taken off

Great Yarmouth cod from South Beach

142

shore was caught by Jim Patterson in 1979 and weighed 38½ lb.

The best bait by far is fresh lugworm, and these are generally supplied by the skipper of the boat. Local tackle dealers also supply fresh bait and will furnish visitors with valuable information on local fishing and the availability of boat-fishing.

Great Yarmouth tackle dealers are: F. Pownall, Regent Road (Tel: 01493 843873) and Dave Docwra, Salisbury Road (Tel: 01493 843563). For boat-fishing trips offshore contact John Temple (Tel: 01493 858523). Additional information regarding weather and conditions offshore can be obtained from the Coastguard Station (Tel: 01493 851338).

Gorleston-on-Sea As far as the fishing is concerned, it would be as well to class Gorleston in the same league as that of Great Yarmouth. The species are the same, with excellent flattie and eel fishing within the harbours. South of the harbour the beaches fish well for whiting and codling, especially towards the wreck which is about one mile down the beach. A large car park is adjacent to the harbour.

Local advice and fresh bait may be obtained from Gorleston Tackle Centre, Pier Walk, Gorleston (Tel: 01493 662448).

A massive 34 lb cod was caught two miles offshore here in 1973 by Cyril Easy of Northampton, but much larger specimens have been taken by commercial long-liners. In recent years, bass have started to appear in larger numbers.

Boat trips can be arranged through several local skippers, including Kevin Easterbrook, *Dorina*, (Tel: 01493 665621) and Jeff Bishop, *The Ellen Bee*, (Tel: 01493 664739).

Pakefield is one of the most popular and productive venues in the area and finding a free spot on a Saturday night during October is rather frustrating. The sloping beach of shingle and sandy is easy to fish and offers a fair depth of water reasonably close in. The flood tide is best for the last three hours for all species, but the long-casters favour the last three hours of the ebb so they can clear the sandbank.

A fair bit of inshore trawling is evident, which limits summer sport, but autumn and winter sees excellent fishing for cod, whiting and dabs. The dab fishing in January is superb both in terms of quality and quantity. Lug-tipped with a small piece of sprat seems to tempt the larger flatfish.

Access is available where the boats are pulled up on the beach, and fishing is good almost anywhere. A favourite spot is at the back of the rifle range, which unfortunately requires a fair walk over rough ground.

Kessingland has much to offer the angling-addicted family man. There is good fishing from the local beach in a fair depth of water for dabs, flounders and soles in summer and cod and whiting for the keen beach angler from October onwards. Although involving a long walk, the area around the 'Point' is a particular hotspot. A massive bass of 19 lb was taken by commercial fishermen here in 1994.

Benacre was highly popular with beach anglers because the beach here shelves deeply, affording excellent winter fishing. However, access is difficult, involving a hike of over a mile from either Covehithe to the south or Kessingland to the north. The whiting arrive early, usually in late August, followed by large numbers of cod during October, including many double-figure fish.

Covehithe The sand cliffs are constantly being eroded by the sea which reaches their base at high tide making fishing impossible at this time. More of the road which provides access disappears each year so, whether you go to the left or right, it is a fair walk to reach the beach.

143

Results on the ebb tide are good, although the inshore bank tends to favour the long-casters for whiting and cod. During October through to December catches can be excellent, especially following a south-by-south-west gale. During summer, sole are caught here, especially at night on or just over the bank, using lug or ragworm bait.

Southwold Like Great Yarmouth and Lowestoft, Southwold has a harbour and offers varied sea fishing, both in summer and winter. In the harbour, likely catches are those ultra-shy grey mullet which can be so frustrating to catch and numbers of goodish bass up to the 8 lb mark. The bass generally fall to lure anglers and to those who present crab and worm baits on fairly light tackle in summer. Best locations are from the north and south harbour entrance piers, with the greatest number of bass running close to the southern pier.

The beaches offer good cod and whiting during the winter and bass as well as some soles during the summer. A hotspot for soles is usually the groynes to the north of the old pier, blown down in strong gales several years back.

Dinghy-owners may launch their own craft from the slipway close to the old pier and in the harbour, but anglers are asked to check on local tides and weather forecasts before going offshore to fish.

Local tackle dealers sell fresh bait and will give sound advice on the fishing in and around Southwold. Southwold Angling Centre, High Street, Southwold (Tel: 01502 722085).

For boat-fishing trips, particularly deepwater wrecking trips for big cod, ling and even pollack, contact David Wright, skipper of *Prospector I* (Tel: 01502 722411).

Walberswick is situated a little south of Southwold harbour, and the fishing is much the same as that of Southwold. Good bass are taken periodically in summer on spinners and artificial rubber sandeels. At low tide, lugworms and harbour ragworm may be dug from the estuary by the Bailey Bridge (the footbridge linking Southwold and Walberswick). Although shallow, the beach does offer dabs and flounders for most of the year, with codling and whiting occasionally close in during the winter.

Dunwich Once the capital of East Anglia, Dunwich offers the angler some excellent cod fishing from the local beach which is shingle and shelves quite steeply into a fair depth of water all along Dunwich Bay.

The top bait for the area is the lugworm, and it was on this bait in April 1973 that Finningham angler Derrick Dorling surprised everyone in the sea-angling world by producing from the beach here a mammoth turbot weighing 28½ lb. Derrick hooked into the fish at 2.30 in the morning after a fruitless night and put his name in the record book by landing the biggest shore-caught turbot of all time and only 2¾ lb short of the British record.

This catch, creditable though it was, should not in any sense be considered a likely future occurrence. Although turbot may occasionally be taken from East Coast beaches, they are nonetheless a great rarity. Most people have to be content with the more usual mixed catches of flatties in the form of soles, flounders, dabs and plaice, with whiting and codling from the beach from late September onwards.

Minsmere and Sizewell There are four miles of beach between Dunwich and Sizewell, known locally as Minsmere Haven. Access is through the nature reserve to the large car park at the end of the cliffs. Fishing during the summer can be particularly good for soles, with the occasional bass to add interest. Although a fairly shallow beach, winter sees good numbers of whiting and codling, and sport is good during the last three hours of both the flood and ebb tides. Behind the power-station at Sizewell the warm water outlet attracts large numbers of 'school' bass. Unfortunately, heavy netting has taken its toll, but fair numbers of fish to 3 lb can still be taken.

Aldeburgh is one of the better fishing locations on the Suffolk coast. With its steeply shelving beach of coarse shingle and deep water it offers a wide choice of fishing. The best flattie fishing is generally up towards Thorpeness, and for whiting and cod one should turn south towards the local hotspot of 'Dirty Wall'.

Access here is now limited to a mile or so from the martello tower by a fence erected by the National Trust. However, this steep beach produces superb catches virtually all year round, with a few surprise species always on the cards.

Lugworm and fish baits are usually favourite, and either flood or ebb tides can produce good sport.

Orford Ness probably represents the very best in shore fishing along the entire Norfolk and Suffolk coastline. A steep shingle beach with very deep water within in easy casting distance. The tides are exceptionally strong, so weights of at least 6 oz may be needed to hold effectively. During summer, sole, bass, eels, dogfish, etc. are caught with worm, crab and fish baits. In winter, cod and whiting abound in numbers, an there is a real chance of hooking into a cod over that 20 lb mark. Mr Ellis of Diss landed a 43 lb conger here in 1973, so you never quite know what the next bite may bring.

The beach extends for several miles but access is rather difficult. It was once possible to drive from Aldeburgh with a four-wheel drive vehicle but the National Trust fence has stopped that. A boat from Orford Quay is the usual way of reaching the narrow spit of land known as Orford Island either on your own or on an organised trip. The latter does rather dictate the fishing time, but Peter Weir runs an excellent ferrying service for anglers with his vessel *Regardless*, which offers party trips 24 hours a day, seven days a week for the greater part of the year. Telephone 01394 450637 for reservations and information.

Fishing at all points is likely to be productive, although the area by the lighthouse and wooden tower seem to produce the best cod fishing on the ebb tide.

Shingle Street beach could hardly have been better named. It shelves sharply into deep water and in the winter months becomes crowded with whiting and cod addicts. There is a lapse until around mid April when thornback ray may be taken by beach anglers. Favourite baits are cuts from fresh herring or mackerel for thornbacks and lugworm for just about everything else. Peeler crab can be killing when available.

Apart from the usual flatties and odd useful soles, good numbers of bass are found, especially around the river mouth at the north end of the beach. Crabs and worm baits on medium to light tackle are advisable here.

East Lane is really a continuation of Shingle Street beach and stretches down as far as the mouth of the River Deben, where it is backed by the cliffs at Bawdsey. The beach is stony and shelves steeply into deepish water over a snaggy seabed. The species here include dabs, soles, bass, whiting, cod and a few skate in season. The approach to this beach is from the Woodbridge to Bawdsey road, turning right at the Star Inn. Bait and local information on the area may be obtained at Woodbridge from the Rod and Gun Shop (Tel: 01394 382377).

Bawdsey is an ideal area for codling, soles and bass. Fishing in the estuary of the River Deben is good for grey mullet and bass, with the thought that one may be lucky enough to hook into a sea trout.

Anglers should beware of the consistently heavy tide rip in the river mouth.

145

Felixstowe The town sits between two important river estuaries. The Deben, with Felixstowe's ferry on its southern bank, flows in from the north, and south of the town lies spacious Harwich harbour, which drains the Suffolk Stour (see Suffolk Rivers) and the River Orwell. Angling between these estuaries from the shingle beaches is often rewarding, with excellent whiting and cod from late September onwards, especially at night.

In summer, bass are likely, and there is always the chance of a double-figure fish. The former British record bass of 18 lb 2 oz was caught here way back in 1943 by the late F.C. Borley. The best bass in recent years is the 16 lb 5 oz beauty caught by Roger Mortimer in 1986. Another British record fish was taken from Felixstowe, namely the humble lumpsucker which, at a fat 14 lb 3 oz, was landed from the beach by W.J. Burgess in 1970. Lump-suckers, along with other species such as plaice, doggies, turbot, garfish and sea trout are all taken at various times from the estuary and beaches around Felixstowe but should not be considered common catches. Neither should the 90 lb conger eel found washed up on the local beach in January 1974 by two local anglers.

The pier fishing here really comes into its own from late September onwards when good whiting and the cod arrive. There is no night fishing allowed, and a small charge is made to anglers. During the warmer months there are plaice, soles, eels and bass to be taken as well as the proverbial dabs. Best baits are small rag and lugworms.

Offshore sport is excellent from Felixstowe and highly organised. Anglers may expect really good numbers of whiting and big cod from late September until April. The two largest fish in past years were the 43 lb cod taken by T. Marsh in 1968 and one of 40 lb 2 oz by A.C. Ashong in 1973. The general run of cod though is from 3 to 10 lb. For the summer boat angler there is just about every species imaginable, with dabs, flounders, eels, plaice, skate and bass predominating, but almost anything can happen.

In recent years, specimen catches have included a huge bass of 18¼ lb to the rod of Mike Bradley in 1994.

Additional information about the area may be obtained from Castaway Tackle and Bait (Tel: 01394 278316), which is near the Ordnance Hotel in Felixstowe.

Offshore fishing trips by boat can be arranged through the shop and through Markham's Tackle of Woodbridge Road in Ipswich (Tel: 01473 727841). There are several charter-boat skippers working out of Felixstowe, including Ron Bayley (Tel: 01394 284888) and Robert Brinkley (Tel: 01394 270853). Anglers may also launch their own small craft from almost any spot along the beach.

SEA BAITS

Obtaining fresh sea bait is not always easy, especially during the cod season from October to March, when lugworms, which are considered 'the' bait by most Norfolk and Suffolk anglers, are in such great demand.

However, there are other excellent baits which may be gathered without too much difficulty, or purchased quite reasonably from commercial fishermen and fishmongers. These baits may be used all the year round and some will be found in the list below, with hints on how to obtain and use them.

Natural Baits

Cockles are small bivalve molluscs with a most distinctive 'fluted' shell of about one inch across. They make excellent baits and are found mostly in north-west Norfolk along muddy, sandy beaches, especially at low tide. Commercially packed, pickled cockles may be used as a poor alternative.

Crabs – Soft and Peelers There are several species of small crabs found close inshore which, in their soft or peeling stage as they shed their shell to grow a larger one, make really terrific baits. They are usually found in this vulnerable state hiding from predators under boulders and large stones in the rock-pools particularly at low tide. Cod, skate, doggies and bass, etc. will all avidly take a 'peeler' or 'softy'.

Hermit Crab The local name given to this small crab which has made its home from the shell of a whelk, is a 'Jack'. They can be bought cheaply from the whelk fishermen of North Norfolk. Jacks are a good all-round bait and are particularly liked by thornback skate. To extract Mr Hermit from his shell without crushing him, hold a lighted match under the shell or chip its rear end and tickle the tail. Either way, he will soon pop out.

Harbour Ragworm These small cousins of the famous king ragworm are much paler in colour, being almost white, and rather thin for their length. They are found in the mud of estuaries and may be dug quite easily at low tide. All the flatfish will accept these small worms, and so, too, will eels, bass and mullet, which are particularly fond of them.

Lugworms are the largest burrowing worms to be found along the Norfolk and Suffolk coastline, and are without question the most popular of sea baits. They are dug at low tide from parts of most mud and sand beaches, after their distinctive 'worm casts' have been located. Lug can be kept for a few days if put into a shallow tray containing moist peat, or laid on a sheet of clean, dry newspaper and put into a cooler.

Lug is the one bait that most coastal tackle dealers are likely to sell.

Mussels are bivalve molluscs and perhaps one of the most neglected sea baits. They are abundant around the piles of all piers and breakwaters, and can be gathered easily at low tide. Once the shell has been prized open with a strong-bladed knife, the mussel should be used whole and the hook inserted into the firm part of the 'foot'. Just about every swimming creature will take this bait, including, unfortunately, crabs.

Sandeels, not to be confused with the common or conger eels, are a highly popular bait with tope and skate fishermen, especially in the early part of the season. They can be netted from the estuaries or purchased from professional fishermen and are best fished whole and preferably as fresh as possible on a large, single hook.

Shrimps The lowly shrimp can at times prove a useful bait, especially when the sea is calm and it can be lightly fished on float tackle at harbour entrances or around pier stanchions, etc. Then, one may expect such species as bass, garfish and mackerel, etc. Shrimps are easily gathered by net from the pools left in the estuaries or along sandy beaches at low tide.

If you catch shrimps surplus to bait requirements, you can always eat them.

Fish Baits

Mackerel, especially if freshly caught while out bait-fishing, is the tope bait *par excellence*. It should be used whole or, for skate, cut into large slices or chunks. Mackerel will also attract other smaller species if used in strip form and, like the shrimp, is excellent eating if freshly killed and cooked.

Herring are seldom caught by anglers and must be purchased either fresh or frozen from the fishmongers. They may be cast a long distance from the beach, either whole or in slices while frozen, and for this reason they are an extremely popular bait. Thin strips of herring make a good all-round sea bait for the East Coast.

Squid Although the squid is actually a mollusc, it appears under the heading of fish bait because it may be purchased readily from the fishmongers – and the smaller the better. The tiny ones are used whole, and with their flowing tentacles make a most desirable and deadly bait for most species of sea fish. Larger squid

147

should be cut into suitable strips. Squid is an excellent cod bait and stays on the hook well when long-casting.

Sprats are also obtained from the fishmonger and, if used whole, account for some good-sized cod. They are particularly suitable for pier fishing when short casting, because then the bait stays intact and attractive. Sprats can also be mounted on spinning tackle and used effectively around harbour entrances for bass and mackerel.

Other small sea fish and even small, silver-coloured, freshwater fish like dace and roach can be effectively used as sea baits. They work especially well if used whole – and can be made more attractive if one injects pilchard or sardine oil into them. A hypodermic syringe can be purchased from tackle shops and, if armed with several different fish oils, the angler is able to turn the unlikeliest of baits into something palatable.

The Tides

Rivers

The tides on Broadland rivers ebb and flow twice in each lunar day of 24 hours 51 minutes. The flow, or rising, of the water is called the flood, and the reflux, or dropping, the ebb. When the moon is in the first and third quarter, there is a smaller high tide than usual, known as the neap-tide. On the full moon, the rise is greater and is called the spring-tide. On the Norfolk Broads and rivers the flood continues for about five hours and the ebb about seven hours.

The tide runs at from half a mile to five miles per hour, according to the distance from the sea. With a north-west wind, high tides can be expected, and in winter they often bring up the 'salts', or salt water. Occasionally, on particularly high tides, the water will be found brackish far up the Thurne, as far as Ludham on the Ant, Cantley on the Yare, and St Olaves on the Waveney.

Tides around the coast, moon stages and barometer readings can be obtained daily from the local press.

Sea

Sea-anglers should equip themselves with tide-tables, which can usually be obtained from tackle dealers and ships' stores. If none is available, however, consult one of the national daily newspapers, where High Water at London Bridge (LB) is given. From this, the approximate time of high water around these coasts may be arrived at by consulting the following table:

High water at			
Hunstanton	add	4 hr 40 min	to London Bridge time
Wells-Next-The-Sea		5 hr 1 min	
Cromer		5 hr 5 min	
Great Yarmouth	deduct	4 hr 55 min	from London Bridge time
Lowestoft		4 hr 26 min	
Southwold		3 hr 48 min	
Aldeburgh		3 hr 23 min	
Felixstowe		2 hr 18 min	
Harwich		2 hr 18 min	
Walton-On-The-Naze		2 hr 15 min	
Clacton-on-Sea		2 hr 1 min	

It is usual for Greenwich Mean Time to be quoted; in Summer Time add one hour.

British Record catfish of 49 lb 14 oz, caught by S. Poyntz

LOCAL SPECIMEN FRESHWATER FISH

1879–1995

It should be noted with the following lists that obviously not everyone's specimen catch is recorded. Indeed, many anglers do not wish their catches and locations made public, while, for instance, others catch so many large carp now that big carp are available to all. I could literally have filled the following pages with carp in excess of even that once magical 30 lb figure. However, rather than do this, I have chosen to provide the reader with a cross-section of specimen catches over a lengthy period from diverse freshwater locations within the counties of Norfolk and Suffolk. So if yours is not included and you want it to be, I shall be only too pleased to accept the information for the next edition.

Barbel

13 lb 6 oz	D. Plummer	River Wensum, Costessey	1984
13 lb 4 oz	M. Clowser	River Wensum, Costessey	1993
13 lb 1 oz	S. Blackburn	River Wensum, Taverham	1994
12 lb 12 oz	J. Wilson	River Wensum, Drayton	1984
12 lb 12 oz	S. Earp	River Wensum, Taverham	1994
12 lb 12 oz	S. Allen	River Wensum, Costessey	1992
12 lb 12 oz	T. West	River Wensum, Costessey	1983
12 lb 11 oz	A. Rawden	River Wensum, Drayton	1983
12 lb 7 oz	R. Westgate	River Wensum, Drayton	1988
12 lb 5 oz	R. Nudd	River Wensum, Drayton	1984

12 lb 4 oz	A. Clarke	River Wensum, Drayton	1980
11 lb 15 oz	C. Shortis	River Wensum, Costessey	1990
11 lb 14 oz	S. Harper	River Wensum, Costessey	1976
11 lb 12 oz	J. Grant	River Wensum, Costessey	1992
11 lb 12 oz	S. Coe	River Wensum, Drayton	1988
11 lb 9 oz	J. Bigden	River Wensum, Drayton	1988
11 lb 9 oz	D. Hobson	River Wensum, Costessey	1989
11 lb 9 oz	J. Nunn	River Wensum, Costessey	1984
11 lb 6 oz	S. Sutton	River Wensum, Drayton	1981
11 lb 6 oz	S. Leach	River Wensum, Costessey	1983
11 lb 5 oz	J. Bailey	River Wensum, Costessey	1979
11 lb 4 oz	M. Seaman	River Wensum, Drayton	1980
11 lb 4 oz	M. Page	River Wensum, Costessey	1981
11 lb 2 oz	J. Humphreys	River Wensum, Costessey	1979
11 lb 2 oz	J. Dunn	River Wensum, Costessey	1989

Most of the big Wensum barbel are repeat catches of the same known fish. Some anglers have caught the same fish on more than one occasion, including myself, so this list simply records each angler's largest.

Bream

14 lb 0 oz	D. Cross	Kingfisher Lake, Lyng	1994
13 lb 13 oz	L. Head	Norfolk Lake	1994
13 lb 12 oz	J. Wilson	Norfolk Lake	1994
13 lb 11 oz	L. Head	Norfolk Lake	1994
13 lb 10 oz	J. Wilson	Norfolk Lake	1994
13 lb 9 oz *	M. Davison	Beeston Lake	1982
13 lb 7 oz	L. Head	Norfolk Lake	1994
13 lb 6 oz	J. Wilson	Norfolk Lake	1994
12 lb 14 oz *	G. Harper	Suffolk Stour	1971
12 lb 12 oz	J. Davies	Norfolk Lake	1994
12 lb 10 oz	A. Turrell	River Hundered	1994
12 lb 4 oz	J. Harmer	Beeston Lake	1979
12 lb 3 oz	D. Cross	Kingfisher Lake, Lyng	1994
11 lb 8 oz	R.W. Ketton-Cremer	Beeston Regis	1879
11 lb 5 oz	J. Wilson	Wensum Pit	1989
11 lb 5 oz	K. Fickling	River Wensum, Ringland	1983
11 lb 4 oz	C. Turnbull	River Wensum, Lyng	1992
11 lb 3 oz	C. Turnbull	Worthing Pit	1993
11 lb 0 oz	D. Plummer	Costessey No. 3 Pit	1985
10 lb 12 oz	A.J. Emden	River Bure, Upton	1962
10 lb 8 oz	C. Barker	Horsey Mere	1994
10 lb 7 oz	P. Mason	Alderfen Broad	1990
10 lb 7 oz	S. Allen	River Wensum, Lyng	1992
10 lb 6 oz	P. Pyrke	Alderfen Broad	1990
10 lb 2 oz	J. Lambert	Wensum Pit	1983
10 lb 2 oz	J. Loan	Narborough Pits	1984

* Each of these bream held the British Record for several years.

Carp

39 lb 12 oz	P. Sexton	Norfolk Estate Lake	1993
38 lb 9 oz	C. Richardson	Norfolk Estate Lake	1992
38 lb 4 oz	G. Pezzotta	Alder Carr Lake	1994
37 lb 2 oz	A. Edmonds	Waveney Valley Lakes	1991
36 lb 12 oz	M. Simmonds	Waveney Valley Lakes	1994
35 lb 12 oz	N. Wilson	Homersfield Lake	1984
35 lb 4 oz	J. Dunn	Homersfield Lake	1982
35 lb 4 oz	G. Maulkerson	Nunnery Lakes	1994
35 lb 2 oz	C. Turnbull	Norfolk Estate Lake	1993
34 lb 12 oz	B. Ward	Geens Pit	1984
34 lb 8 oz	J. Palmer	Homersfield Lake	1981
35 lb 6 oz	J. Dunn	Costessey No. 3 Pit	1994
34 lb 2 oz	T. Houseago	Wensum Valley Pit	1994
34 lb 0 oz	C. Richardson	Norfolk Estate Lake	1992
34 lb 0 oz	J. Bailey	Geens Pit	1984
33 lb 1 oz	J. Wilson	Norfolk Estate Lake	1992
33 lb 1 oz	R. Williams	Homersfield Lake	1988
32 lb 12 oz	K. Howes	Gimmingham Lake	1984
32 lb 10 oz	P. Baker	Homersfield Lake	1984
32 lb 8 oz	K. Norton	Lenwade Lakes	1977
32 lb 8 oz	C. Turnbull	Geens Pit	1985
32 lb 0 oz	D. Weale	Waveney Valley Lakes	1976
32 lb 0 oz	T. Harrison	Waveney Valley Lakes	1974
31 lb 13 oz	S. Williams	Costessey No. 3 Pit	1993
31 lb 12 oz	P. Stacey	Waveney Valley Lakes	1974
31 lb 8 oz	K. Symes	Waveney Valley Lakes	1980
31 lb 8 oz	S. Earp	Bedingham Lake	1992
31 lb 8 oz	R. Carver	Waveney Valley Lakes	1979
31 lb 6 oz	M. Pye	River Yare	1992
31 lb 4 oz	G. Morris	Booton Clay Pit	1972
31 lb 2 oz	A. Battle	Homersfield Lake	1982
31 lb 0 oz	S. Moir	River Wensum, Norwich	1985
30 lb 8 oz	J. Dunn	Costessey No. 3 Pit	1982
30 lb 4 oz	S. Gardner	Gimmingham Lake	1984
30 lb 2 oz	J. Hall	Gimmingham Lake	1984
30 lb 2 oz	R. Bunn	Waveney Valley Lakes	1976

Carp (Koi)

12 lb 4 oz	N. Waller	University Broad	1984

Catfish (Wels)

49 lb 14 oz*	S. Poyntz	Homersfield Lake	1993
48 lb 0 oz	M. Banham	Homersfield Lake	1994
23 lb 10 oz	Local angler	Swangey Lakes	1994
22 lb 0 oz	Local angler	Swangey Lakes	1993
13 lb 8 oz	R. Williams	Lakeside Lenwade	1987

* The current British Record

Chub

8 lb 4 oz	M.J. Roberts	River Wissey	1950
8 lb 2 oz	P. Heywood	River Waveney	1993
7 lb 9 oz	S. Maddox	River Waveney	1974
7 lb 0 oz	S. Hunt	River Wensum, Drayton	1995
6 lb 14 oz	C. Smith	River Yare	1994
6 lb 8 oz	R. Holmes	River Waveney	1977
6 lb 7 oz	J. Wilson	Wensum Valley Pit	1980
6 lb 7 oz	R. Williams	River Waveney	1993
6 lb 3 oz	R. Nudd	Irrigation Reservoir	1985
6 lb 2 oz	R. Nudd	Irrigation Reservoir	1986
6 lb 2 oz	T. Houseago	Lakeside Lenwade	1994
6 lb 2 oz	C. Stevens	River Wissey	1959
6 lb 2 oz	R. Harris	River Wensum, Drayton	1965
6 lb 2 oz	M. James	River Wensum, Swanton Morley	1982
6 lb 2 oz	A. Rawden	River Waveney	1988
6 lb 1 oz	R. Nudd	Irrigation Reservoir	1987
6 lb 1 oz	C. Smith	River Yare	1994
6 lb 0 oz	M. Harvey	River Waveney	1986
6 lb 0 oz	R. Cork	Lakeside Lenwade	1988
6 lb 0 oz	G. Gifford	River Wensum, Hellesdon	1983
5 lb 15 oz	J. Wilson	River Wensum, Ringland	1978
5 lb 15 oz	C. Shortis	River Wensum, Costessey	1986
5 lb 14 oz	C. Gooch	River Wensum, Costessey	1970
5 lb 14 oz	J. Wilson	River Wensum, Drayton	1984
5 lb 14 oz	K. Fuller	River Wensum, Ringland	1976
5 lb 14 oz	K. Fuller	River Wensum, Ringland	1976
5 lb 14 oz	T. West	River Wensum, Costessey	1983
5 lb 13 oz	N. Glover	River Wensum, Hellesdon	1982
5 lb 11 oz	A. Morris	River Wensum, Drayton	1994

Crucian Carp

5 lb 10½ oz*	G. Halls	Bradmoor Lakes	1976
4 lb 7½ oz	G.T. Mills	Hevingham Lakes	1973
4 lb 0 oz	A. Huxtable	Weybread Pits	1981
3 lb 13 oz	B. Gibbs	Lake near Bury St Edmunds	1973
3 lb 8 oz	C. Shortis	Irrigation Pit	1988
3 lb 8 oz	C. Turnbull	Lenwade Common Pits	1992
3 lb 6½ oz	C. Turnbull	Lenwade Common Pits	1992
3 lb 3 oz	C. Turnbull	Lenwade Common Pits	1992
3 lb 1 oz	Joker Norton	Hevingham Lakes	1972
3 lb 1 oz	B. Neave	Lenwade Lakes	1976
2 lb 14 oz	D. Gladwell	Earsham Gravel Pit	1973

* Once the British Record

Dace

1 lb 4½ oz*	J.L. Gasson	River Ouse, Thetford	1960
1 lb 4 oz	D. Flack	River Ouse, Thetford	1987
1 lb 4 oz	B. Kettell	River Wensum, Fakenham	1969
1 lb 4 oz	T. Cleere	River Wensum, Drayton	1958

1 lb 4 oz	K. Burlingham	River Wensum, Elsing	1981
1 lb 3½ oz	W.L. Comer	River Tas	1943
1 lb 3¼ oz	W. Clarke	River Ouse, Thetford	1972
1 lb 2½ oz	A. Davison	River Tud, Easton	1971
1 lb 2 oz	J. Hendry	River Wensum	1972
1 lb 2 oz	K. Burlingham	River Wensum, Fakenham	1975
1 lb 2 oz	W. Barton	River Wensum	1966
1 lb 1½ oz	A. Davidson	River Tud, Easton	1971
1 lb 1 oz	G. Parsons	River Wensum, Fakenham	1975
1 lb 1 oz	K. Gardner	River Wensum, Swanton Morley	1982
1 lb 1 oz	K. Smith	River Tas	1955
1 lb 1 oz	J. Wilson	River Tud, Easton	1971
1 lb 1 oz	A. Emden	River Yare, Bawburgh	1963
1 lb 0½ oz	R.H. Clements	River Wensum, Drayton	1954
1 lb 0 oz	T. Cleere	River Wensum, Drayton	1956

Almost beating the entire list above by himself comes the late Bill Clarke from Barnham, near Thetford, who from 1951 to 1985 took an incredible forty-four dace of over the pound. Bill's largest weighed 1 lb 3¼ oz and all came from his local rivers, the Thet and the Little Ouse. Bill's pal Denis Flack also regularly gets amongst the big dace of the Little Ouse. In 1987 he took a staggering haul of eleven dace, mostly just over or just on the pound, with the heaviet going 1 lb 3½ oz and 1 lb 4 oz. This must surely rate as the best catch of dace ever.

Denis did it again in 1994 by taking from a stretch of the Little Ouse, some nine miles from where he took the above catch, no less than ten dace in a single haul, averaging over the pound, with the best tipping the scales at 1 lb 3 oz.

* The current British Record

Eel

8 lb 8 oz	R. Bratton	Feltwell Pit	1994
7 lb 8 oz	A.J. Dewsnap	Oulton Broad	1953
6 lb 12 oz	Unknown angler	Lake at Welney	1983
6 lb 11 oz	Dodger Green	Fritton Lake	1975
6 lb 4 oz	G. Dixon	Lenwade Lakes	1977
6 lb 2 oz	I. Trevors	Filby Broad	1983
5 lb 14 oz	J. Holliman	Waveney Pit	1981
5 lb 13 oz	N. Saunders	Weybread Pits	1993
5 lb 12 oz	N. Saunders	Suffolk Moat	1982
5 lb 9 oz	A. Gorham	Waveney Pit	1983
5 lb 9 oz	A. Huxtable	Suffolk Moat	1982
5 lb 8 oz	A. Gorham	Waveney Pit	1984
5 lb 8 oz	K. Whall	River Thurne	1954
5 lb 4 oz	R. Davis	Soulton Pond	1973
5 lb 4 oz	L. Wilson	Lakeside, Lenwade	1987
5 lb 4 oz	J. Knights	Lenwade Lakes	1973
5 lb 1 oz	K. Clarke	Costessey Pits	1970
5 lb 1 oz	T. Boulton	Weybread Pits	1974
5 lb 1 oz	N. Saunders	Suffolk Moat	1982

Perch

5 lb 15½ oz*	P. Clarke	Suffolk Stour	1949
5 lb 4¾ oz	H. Green	Stradsett Lake	1936
5 lb 2 oz	L. Gordon	River Waveney, Geldeston	1886
4 lb 12 oz	S. Baker	Oulton Broad	1962
4 lb 12 oz	A. Hodges	River Bure, Upton	1959
4 lb 9 oz	L. Proudfoot	Oulton Broad	1963
4 lb 9 oz	A.J. Emden	Oulton Broad	1961
4 lb 7½ oz	W. Mason	Oulton Broad	1965
4 lb 5 oz	A.J. Hodges	South Walsham Broad	1964
4 lb 3 oz	E. Allen	River Wensum, Swanton Morley	1964
4 lb 2½ oz	L. Proudfoot	Oulton Broad	1966
4 lb 1 oz	L. Head	Suffolk Lake	1994
4 lb 1 oz	I. Lambert	Selbrigg Pond	1984
4 lb 1 oz	K. Burlingham	River Wensum, Elsing	1963
4 lb 1 oz	N. Cooper	Decoy Broad	1937
3 lb 14 oz	L. Head	Suffolk Lake	1992
3 lb 12 oz	J. Bailey	Norfolk Pit	1987
3 lb 11 oz	L. Head	Suffolk Lake	1992
3 lb 11 oz	L. Head	Suffolk Lake	1992
3 lb 10 oz	P. Collins	Oulton Broad	1965
3 lb 8 oz	M. Curtis	River Wensum, Hellesdon	1973
3 lb 3 oz	J. Hunn	Greens Pit	1980
3 lb 2 oz	V. Bellars	Greens Pit	1978

* The British Record before it was deleted

Pike

42 lb 2 oz *	D. Amies	Thurne system	1986
42 lb 0 oz	J. Nudd	Wroxham Broad	1901
41 lb 6 oz *	N. Fickling	River Thurne, Martham	1985
40 lb 1 oz *	P. Hancock	Horsey Mere	1967
39 lb 8 oz	D. Leary	Kingfisher Lake, Lyng	1984
39 lb 8 oz	R. Miller	Kingfisher Lake, Lyng	1989
38 lb 0 oz	Angler from Bath	Somerton	1979
38 lb 0 oz	J. Watson	Horsey Mere	1988
37 lb 10 oz	P. Woodhouse	Thurne System	1984
37 lb 8 oz	A. Cottrell	Somerton	1982
37 lb 8 oz	D. Allen	Bure System	1972
37 lb 0 oz	B. Florey	Somerton	1981
36 lb 6 oz	D. Amies	Somerton	1982
36 lb 0 oz	M. Haliday	River Yare	1939
36 lb 0 oz	J. Bailey	Kingfisher Lake, Lyng	1985
36 lb 0 oz	F. Thorns	Haveringland Lake	1880
35 lb 13 oz	P. Belton	Thurne System	1983
35 lb 8 oz	A. Jackson	Heigham Sound	1948
35 lb 6 oz	R. Pownall	Somerton	1960
35 lb 0 oz	D. Pond	Thurne System	1989
35 lb 0 oz	F. Wright	Horsey Mere	1968
34 lb 12 oz	P. Belton	Thurne System	1983
34 lb 9 oz	B. Cannell	Kingfisher Lake, Lyng	1994

34 lb 8 oz	A. Goram	Hickling Broad	1994
34 lb 2 oz	D. Pye	Horsey Mere	1965
34 lb 0 oz	L. Spencer	HorseyMere	1967
33 lb 12 oz	C. Warnes	Wensum Valley Pit	1993
33 lb 8 oz	D. Pye	Candle Dyke	1964
33 lb 8 oz	P. Coull	Somerton	1982
33 lb 4 oz	C. Cracknell	Horsey Mere	1994
33 lb 0 oz	R. Nelson	Somerton	1980
33 lb 0 oz	D. Pye	Horsey Mere	1963
32 lb 13 oz	I. Leeks	Somerton	1982
32 lb 13 oz	R. Westgate	River Bure, Wroxham	1980
32 lb 12 oz	C. Clay	Wensum Valley Pit	1991
32 lb 9 oz	S. Harper	Somerton	1982
32 lb 8 oz	D. Eaves	Suffolk Stour	1950
32 lb 8 oz	D. Pye	Hickling Broad	1962
32 lb 2 oz	J. Tipple	Somerton	1982
32 lb 0 oz	D. Leary	River Bure, Horning	1975
32 lb 0 oz	N. Fickling	Decoy Broad	1982
32 lb 0 oz	E. Jermyn	River Wissey	1960
32 lb 0 oz	J. Tyree	Kingfisher Lake, Lyng	1986

* Each of these pike once held the British Record

Roach

3 lb 10 oz	J. Bailey	River Wensum	1986
3 lb 6 oz	F. Staples	Suffolk Stour	1955
3 lb 5 oz	J. Bailey	River Wensum	1987
3 lb 5 oz	J. Mitchell	Costessey Pits	1956
3 lb 5 oz	M. Hudson	River Ant	1954
3 lb 5 oz	A.W. Howard	Salhouse Broad	1963
3 lb 4¼ oz	K. Fuller	River Wensum	1984
3 lb 4 oz	W.C. Bly	River Bure, Horning	1949
3 lb 3 oz	J. Nunn	River Bure	1984
3 lb 2 oz	N. Glover	River Wensum, Swanton Morley	1984
3 lb 2 oz	G. Harwin	River Bure, Coltishall	1959
3 lb 2 oz	J. Bailey	River Wensum, Elsing	1976
3 lb 1½ oz	D. Crisp	River Wensum, North Elmham	1975
3 lb 1 oz	R. Westgate	River Wensum	1984
3 lb 0 oz	L. Nobbs	River Bure, Horstead	1960
3 lb 0 oz	G. Canham	River Wensum, North Elmham	1974
2 lb 0 oz	M. Francis	River Yare, Trowse	1958
3 lb 0 oz	J. Mitchell	Taverham Pits	1956
2 lb 15½ oz	T. Appleton	RiverWensum, Costessey	1979
2 lb 15 oz	J. Sapey	River Wensum, Lyng	1975
2 lb 15 oz	M. Bond	River Wensum, Hellesdon	1979
2 lb 15 oz	J. Tyree	River Wensum, Taverham	1988

Rudd

4 lb 8 oz *	Revd L.E. Alston	Thetford Mere	1933
3 lb 7 oz	R. Clements	River Ant, Irstead	1958
3 lb 6 oz	A. Holdcroft	River Wensum, Elsing	1973

155

3 lb 6 oz	D. Plummer	Lenwade Lakes	1981
3 lb 5½ oz	C. Turnbull	Lenwade Lakes	1981
3 lb 5½ oz	J. Watson	Lenwade Lakes	1981
3 lb 5 oz	D. Pye	Horsey Mere	1965
3 lb 4 oz	D. Pye	Hickling Broad	1964
3 lb 4 oz	A. Clarke	Lenwade Lakes	1981
3 lb 4 oz	D. Pye	Hickling Broad	1962
3 lb 3 oz	B. Cannel	Wolterton Lake	1975
3 lb 2 oz	A. Towers	Lenwade Lakes	1975
3 lb 1 oz	D. Pye	River Thurne, Martham	1964
3 lb 1oz	G. Tansley	Lenwade Lakes	1981

* The current British Record

Tench

8 lb 6 oz	D. Gould	Upton Broad	1992
8 lb 4 oz	S. Challis	Suffolk Stour	1975
8 lb 2 oz	L. Head	Bures Lake	1975
8 lb 2 oz	J. Haydon	Bures Lake	1973
8 lb 2 oz	D. Batten	Costessey No. 3 Pit	1986
8 lb 1 oz	D. Plummer	Costessey No. 3 Pit	1985
7 lb 12 oz	D. Humphries	Wolterton Lake	1988
7 lb 12 oz	N. Glover	Wolterton Lake	1983
7 lb 11 oz	C. Turnbull	Wensum Valley Pit	1994
7 lb 11 oz	S. Lake	Costessey No. 3 Pit	1994
7 lb 10½ oz	S. Harper	Wolterton Lake	1977
7 lb 9 oz	S. Williams	Costessey No. 3 Pit	1994
7 lb 9 oz	P. Pope	Taverham Mill Lake	1977
7 lb 8 oz	R. Miller	Costessey No. 3 Pit	1984
7 lb 8 oz	K. Clifford	Wolterton Lake	1978
7 lb 7 oz	C. Turnbull	Costessey No. 3 Pit	1985
7 lb 6 oz	K. Baker	Bures Lake	1973
7 lb 6 oz	B. Stocker	Bures Lake	1973
7 lb 6 oz	K. Clifford	Wolterton Lake	1977
7 lb 5 oz	S. Williams	Costessey No. 3 Pit	1994
7 lb 4 oz	C. Turnbull	Wensum Valley Pit	1994
7 lb 4 oz	K. Clifford	Wolterton Lake	1977
7 lb 3 oz	N. Glover	Wolterton Lake	1983
7 lb 2½ oz	C. Turnbull	Wolterton Lake	1981
7 lb 2 oz	M. Cross	Ormesby Broad	1977
7 lb 2 oz	A. Clarke	Lenwade Lakes	1978

Trout (B = Brown trout, R = Rainbow trout)

R 17 lb 15¾ oz	K. Johnson	Narborough Trout Fisheries	1994
R 17 lb 8½ oz	M. Webster	Narborough Trout Fisheries	1989
R 17 lb 8 oz	J. Millar	Narborough Trout Fisheries	1988
R 15 lb 12 oz	J. Millar	Narborough Trout Fisheries	1988
R 15 lb 6 oz	S. Welsh	Narborough Trout Fisheries	1994
R 13 lb 9 oz	J. Holliman	Narborough Trout Fisheries	1989
R 13 lb 7 oz	M. Turner	Narborough Trout Fisheries	1994

R 13 lb 2 oz	J. Tyree	Narborough Trout Fisheries	1989
B 12 lb 14 oz	G. Mays	River Wissey, Wissington	1959
R 12 lb 4 oz	J. Tyree	Narborough Trout Fisheries	1989
R 11 lb 1 oz	R. Horne	Whinburgh	1994
R 10 lb 12 oz	L. Tebbs	Narborough Trout Fisheries	1983
R 10 lb 5 oz	L. Desuza	Whinburgh	1994
R 10 lb 4 oz	M. Palmer	Narborough Trout Fisheries	1970
R 10 lb 4 oz	C. Skeggs	River Wissey, Wissington	1970
R 10 lb 3 oz	C. Bishop	Narborough Trout Fisheries	1984
B 9 lb 12 oz	M. Sayer	River Wensum, Lenwade	1964
R 9 lb 4 oz	R. Williams	Valley Fisheries	1994
R 9 lb 2 oz	Mr Allday	Reepham Trout Fisheries	1983
B 9 lb 0 oz	C. Horsley	River Wensum, Fakenham	1890
R 8 lb 7 oz	A. Varnava	Reepham Trout Fisheries	1982
B 8 lb 3 oz	D. Davey	River Wissey	1972
B 8 lb 2 oz	C. Clay	Lyng Trout Lake	1987
R 8 lb 0 oz	W. Bailey	Lyng Trout Lake	1983
B 7 lb 15 oz	J. Sapey	River Wensum, Lyng	1971
B 6 lb 4 oz	Joker Norton	River Wensum, Ringland	1968
B 6 lb 4 oz	D. Hewett	River Wensum, Hellesdon	1971
B 6 lb 4 oz	H.B. Waters	River Wensum, Hellesdon	1985
B 6 lb 0 oz	C. Bullard	River Wensum, Ringland	1956

Zander

18 lb 6 oz	D. Gaunt	Fenland Drain	1993
18 lb 2 oz	T. Ward	Fenland Drain	1995
18 lb 2 oz	R. Hughes	Fenland Drain	1993
18 lb 2 oz	D. Gaunt	Fenland Drain	1993
18 lb 0 oz	A. Wood	Fenland Drain	1993
17 lb 12 oz *	D. Litton	Relief Channel	1977
17 lb 8 oz	L. Brown	Fenland Drain	1992
17 lb 5 oz	D. Lavender	Middle Level	1994
17 lb 4 oz	C. Bloy	Middle Level	1994
17 lb 4 oz	W. Gaunt	Middle Level	1994
17 lb 1 oz	D. Lavender	Middle Level	1994
17 lb 1 oz	D. Gaunt	Fenland Drain	1993
16 lb 14 oz	N. Jones	Middle Level	1995
16 lb 8 oz	G. Hiatt	Middle Level	1994
16 lb 6 oz	S. Smith	Cut Off Channel	1976
16 lb 2 oz	M. Vials	Fenland Drain	1994
16 lb 0 oz	G. Arnold	Fenland Drain	1994
15 lb 13 oz	P. Woodford	Relief Channel	1994
15 lb 8 oz	G. Hiatt	Middle Level	1994
15 lb 6¼ oz	R. Young	Relief Channel	1977
15 lb 5 oz *	W. Chillingworth	Relief Channel	1971
15 lb 4 oz	T. Ward	Fenland Drain	1995
15 lb 2 oz	M. Leonard	Great Ouse	1977
15 lb 2 oz	P. Lawrence	Fenland Drain	1994
15 lb 2 oz	S. Willian	Cut Off Channel	1977

14 lb 13 oz	B. Culley	Relief Channel	1981
14 lb 11 oz	M. Barge	Fenland Drain	1977
14 lb 8 oz	T. Chalenhunowicz	Relief Channel	1977
14 lb 6 oz	K. Broughton	Relief Channel	1977
14 lb 5 oz	M. Rodwell	Old Bedford	1976
14 lb 2½ oz	G. Brown	Relief Channel	1974
14 lb 0 oz	P. Smith	Cut Off Channel	1977
13 lb 10 oz	I. Greenacre	Relief Channel	1982
13 lb 7 oz	R. Wright	River Wissey	1985
13 lb 5 oz	D. Ball	River Delph	1976
13 lb 4 oz	A. Williams	River Delph	1976
13 lb 4 oz	Dr B. Rickards	Relief Channel	1973
13 lb 4 oz	T. Hobbs	Cut Off Channel	1977
13 lb 4 oz	N. Malby	Wissey Pools	1975
13 lb 4 oz	C. Davis	Relief Channel	1977
13 lb 2 oz	H. Reynolds	Relief Channel	1973

* Both of these zander once held the British Record

Len Head with a double-figure bream from a Norfolk lake

INDEX

A
Alde, River 42
Aldeburgh 145
Aldeby Hall Farm Pits 70, 83
Alderfen Broad 68
Alderson Lake 113
Alton Water Reservoir 83
Ant, River 67
Attleborough Fish Farm Lake 84

B
Babingley, River 11
Bacton 116, 140
Barford Lakes 85
Barham Pit 94, 85, 113
Bartles Lodge Lake 85
Barton Broad 67, 69
Bawburgh Pit 114
Bawdsey 145
Beccles 68
Beccles Quay 68
Benacre 143
Billingford Pit 114
Bircham Pit 114
Bishopgate Bridge, Norwich 68
Black Bourn, River 42
Blackwater Stream 11
Blakeney 138
Blickling Lake 85
Blue Waters 86
Blyth, River 42
Boat Hire and Slipways within Tidal Broadland 67
Bodham Pond 86
Booton Clay Pit 86
Bosmere Lake 114
Boughton Pond 86
Bradmoor Lakes 115
Brancaster 137
Brandon Lake 115
Breakaway Pit 87
Bridge Broad (West) 71
Bridge Fishery Lake 87
Bridge Lakes 128
Broads, The 68
Brooke Park Lakes 128, 130
Brooke Pit 87
Broome Pits 87
Brundall 68
Brundall Bay Marina 68
Buckingham Pits 88
Bure Valley Coarse Lake 88
Bure Valley Trout Lakes 131
Bure, River 11, 68, 136
Bures Lake 115
Burgh St Peter 68
Burnham Overy 137
Burn, River 16
Buss Creek 88

C
Caister-on-Sea 142
Camelot Lake 116
Casting instructor 135
Causeway Lake 116
Cawston's Pit 88
Chapel Road Lake 89
Chet, River 16, 68
Chiswick Pit 89
Cley 139
Close Season Laws 83

Cobbleacre Park Lakes 89
Cockles 146
Colston Hall Lakes 128, 130
Common Lakes 89
Costessey (No. 2 and No. 3) Pits 90
Covehithe 143
Crabs: Hermit 147, Soft and Peelers 146
Cranworth-Woodrising Carp Lake 91
Cromer 140
Cross Green Fly-Fishers 131

D
Deben, River 43
Decoy Broad 71
Decoy Farm Fishery 91
Deep Hole, The 116
Delph, River 17
Disabled, Fishing for the 83 (Aldeby Hall Farm Pits), 85 (Barford Lakes), 94 (Golden Ponds), 99 (Loch Neaton), 103 (Ringland Lakes), 114 (Billingford Pit), 115 (Bradmoor Lakes; Bures Lake), 118 (Glemsford Lake), 120 (Lyng Pit), 124 (Stantons Farm Lake), 126 (Worthing Gravel Pit)
Diss Mere 116
Ditchingham Pit 97, 117
Docking Village Pond 91
Dove, River 44
Dunwich 144

E
East Lane 145
East Runton 140
East Tuddenham Fishery 132
Eccles 141
Edwards Pit 92
Eel's Foot Broad (see Great Ormesby Broad)

F
Felbrigg Lake 92
Felixstowe 146
Felmingham Mill Lakes 92
Felthorpe Lakes 92
Filby Broad 76
Fish Baits 147
Flixton Decoy 92
Fosters End Pits 117
Friars Quay, Norwich 68
Fritton Lake 93

G
Gatton Waters 127
Gayton Road Fisheries 128
Gayton Road Fishery Estate Lake 128
Gimingham Lakes 94
Gipping, River 44
Glaven, River 17, 136
Glemsford Lake 118
Golden Ponds 94
Gorleston-on-Sea 143
Great Massingham Village Pond 94

Great Ormesby Broad 67, 74, 76
Great Ouse Cut Off Channel 18
Great Ouse Relief Channel 19
Great Ouse, River 17
Great Yarmouth 142
Greenmeadows 118
Green Pits 94
Gunssons Lake 127, 129
Gunthorpe Hall Lake 95
Gunton Hall Lake 129
Gunton Park Lake 95

H
Hall Farm Lake 95, 127
Handicapped, fishing for the (see Disabled)
Happisburgh 141
Harbour Ragworm 147
Hatchery House Trout Fishery 132
Haveringland Lake 95, 127
Heath Farm Pits 96
Heigham Sound 72
Hemsby 142
Henham Dairy Pond 96
Herring (bait) 147
Hevingham Lakes 96
Hickling Broad 67, 72
Highfield Fishery 96
Hilgay Lakes 97
Hingham Carp Fishery 97
History of the Broads Enigma 54
Holkham 138
Holkham Park Lake 97
Holmans Pits (see Northfield Lakes)
Holme next the Sea 137
Holton Gravel Pit 98
Horning 68
Horsey 141
Horsey Mere 73
How to Fish the Broadland Waterways 61
Hundred Foot Drain 20
Hundred, River 45
Hunstanton 137

I
Iceni Lake 118
Ingham Pond 98
Irrigation Lagoon, The 119

K
Kelling 139
Kessingland 143
Kingfisher Fishing Club Lakes 119

L
Lakeside Fisheries 98
Lakeside Lake 127
Lakeside Leisure Park 127
Lark, River 46, 136
Larkwood Trout Fishery 132
Lenwade 137
Lenwade House Hotel, Lake and River 129
Lessingham 141
Letheringsett Lake 99
Lily Broad 74, 75
Little Bridge Broad (see Bridge Broad (West))

159

Little Dunham Carp and Tench Lakes 99
Little Lakeland 127
Little Ormesby Broad 74
Little Ouse, River 20
Local Specimen Freshwater Fish 149
Loch Neaton 99
Loddon Marina 68
Lugworms 147
Lyng Pit 120

M
Mackerel (bait) 147
Malthouse Broad 77
Manor Lake 129
Marsh Farm Lakes 99
Martham Ferry 68
Martham North Broad 76
Martham Pits 100
Mendham Trout Fishery 133
Middle Harling Lake 100
Middle Level Drain, The 22
Mill Farm Lake 100
Minsmere 144
Minsmere, River 46
Morston 138
Mundesley 140
Mussels 147

N
Nar, River 22, 136
Narborough Trout Fisheries 133
Narborough Trout Fisheries – Coarse Lake 100
Nar Valley Fisheries 120
Natural Baits 146
Needham Lake 121
New Bedford Drain (see Hundred Foot Drain)
Newport 142
New Waters Farm Fishery 101
Norfolk Fly-Fishers Lake 136
Norfolk Rivers 9
Northfield Lakes 101
Norwich 68
Nunnery Lakes 121

O
Old Bedford River, The 23
Orben Beck 127
Orford Ness 145
Oulton Broad 67, 77
Overstrand 140

P
Pakefield 143
Peck Meadow Pond 101
Pedmarsh Lake 121
Pentney Carp Lake 101
Pentney Lakes Leisure Park 102
Pettistree Lake 122
Ponds, The 128
Potter Heigham 68
Pulver Drain, The 23

R
Ragworm, Harbour 147
Railway Lake 122
Railway Pit 102
Ranworth Broad 77
Rattlesden River 47
Redgrave Lake 122
Red House Farm Moat 123

Reedham Ferry 68
Reepham Fisheries 102
Reydon No. 1 Pit 102
Reydon No. 2 and No. 3 Pits 123
Reydon No. 4 Pit 103
Richardsons Pit 103
Ringland Lakes 103
Rockland Broad 67, 77
Rodally Pit 103
Rollesby Broad 67, 75
Roosting Hills 137
Rushbrook Farm Lake 103
Rushbrooke Lake 123
Ruston Reaches 104, 133

S
Salhouse Broad 80
Salmon and Trout Association Waters – Open Membership 136
Salthouse 139
Sandeels 147
Scottow Pond 123
Scoulton Mere 104
Scratby 142
Sea Baits 146
Sea Fishing 137
Sea Palling 141
Selbrigg Lake 104
Shallow Brook Lakes 104
Shelfhanger Pit 105
Sheringham 139
Shingle Street 145
Shrimps 147
Shropham Pit 124
Sizewell 144
Slipways within Tidal Broadland, Boat Hire and 67
Snakes Meadow Fishery 129
Snetterton Pits 105
South Walsham Broad 80
Southwold 144
Sovereign Lake 105
Sparham Pool 124
Sportsman's Broad (see Little Ormesby Broad)
Sprats (bait) 148
Spring Lake Trout Fishery 136
Squid (bait) 147
Stacksford Pit 105
Stalham Staithe 67
Stantons Farm Lake 124
Starfield Pit 106
Station Pit 106
Stiffkey 138
Stiffkey, River 24
Stillwaters 82,
 – Campers and Touring Caravanners 127
 – Caravanners 127
 – Day Ticket 83
 – Farmhouse Holiday Accommodation 130
 – Holiday Cottages 130
 – Hotel Accommodation 129
 – Match Fishing 128
 – Members Only 113
 – Syndicate Waters 128
Stour, River 47
Stradsett Lake 129
Suffolk Rivers 42
Surlingham Broad 80
Swale Pit 107
Swan Lake (see Blue Waters)

Swangey Lakes 107
Swanton Morley Fisheries 107

T
Tannery Lake 108
Tas, River 24
Taswood Lakes 108
Tatts Pit (see Willows, The)
Taverham Mills Lake 90, 109
Thet, River 25
Thompson Water 110
Thorpeness Mere 110
Thorpe St Andrew 68
Thurne, River 26, 68
Tides, The 148
Tiffey, River 28
Tottenhill Pit 124
Trout Fishing – Day Ticket (Stillwaters) 131
Trout Fishing – Day Ticket (Rivers – Fly Only) 130
Trout Fishing – Syndicate Waters 136
Trimingham 140
Tud, River 28
Turf Hole Pond 111

U
University Broad 125

V
Valley Fisheries 134

W
Walberswick 144
Walcott 141
Wang, River 49
Waveney, River 50, 68
Waveney Valley Lakes 111
Waxham 141
Waxham Cut 67
Wayford Bridge 67
Well Creek 29
Wells-Next-The-Sea 138
Welmore Lake 111
Wensum Fisheries 125
Wensum, River 29, 68, 130, 136
West Runton 140
West Stow Country Park 125
Weybourne 139
Weybread Fishery 111
Weybread Gravel Pits 112
Wheelchair fishing (see under Disabled)
Whinburgh Trout Lakes 134
White House Farm 128
Wickham Market Reservoirs 126
Wickham Skeith Mere 112
Willow Lakes Trout Fishery 135
Willows, The 126
Wilsmore Water 126
Windmill Ponds 112
Winterton 141
Wissey, River 35
Womack Water 81
Woodlakes Holiday Park 112
Woodlakes Trout Fishery 135
Worthing Gravel Pit 126
Wroxham 68
Wroxham Broad 67, 81

Y
Yare, River 37, 68